Lost Leviathan

Lost Leviathan

F. D. OMMANNEY

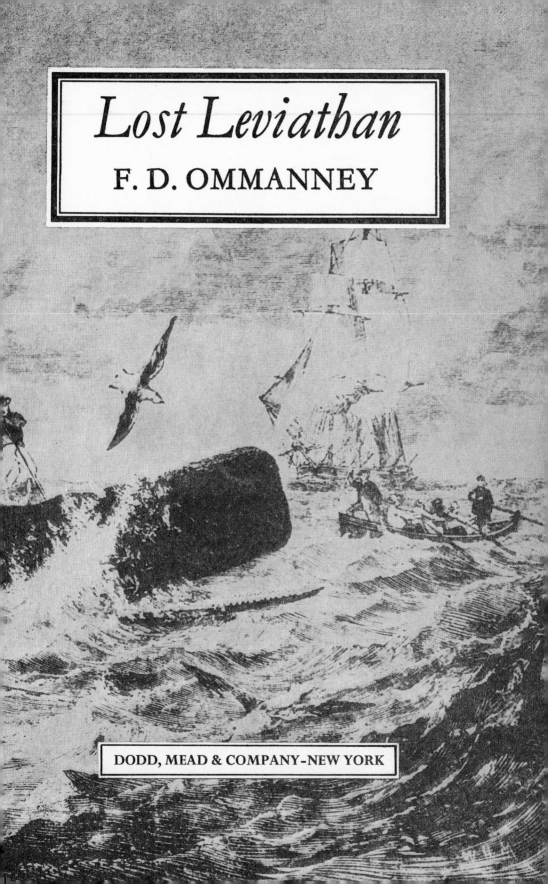

DODD, MEAD & COMPANY-NEW YORK

First published in the United States 1971

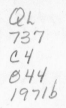

Library of Congress Catalog Card Number: 72-155066

© F. D. Ommanney 1971

Printed in Great Britain

ISBN 0-396-06253-9

Contents

CHAPTER	1	Southern Heyday	9
	2	Whales, Dolphins and Porpoises	23
	3	Produce of Whales	55
	4	History of Whaling	69
	5	At the Whaling Station	100
	6	The Rorqual	115
	7	The Chase	133
	8	Size and Age of Rorquals	158
	9	On Board a Factory Ship	174
	10	Krill	198
	11	The Sperm Whale	211
	12	Humpback and Sei Whales	232
	13	High and Dry	247
	14	How Many Whales?	255
Appendix:		Scientific Names	267
List of References			269
Index			272

Acknowledgements

I would like to thank Dr. N. A. Mackintosh, C.B.E., and his staff, Messrs. Ray Gambell and S. G. Brown, of the Whale Research Unit, National Institute of Oceanography, for their kindness and help on many occasions.

Illustrations

Between pages 64 and 65.
Humpback whaling off the coast of Western Australia. The gunner signals to the helmsman. (*Phot: Australian News and Inf. Bureau.*)
A hit. (*Phot: Australian News and Inf. Bureau.*)

A catcher arriving at Grytviken, South Georgia, with catch. Government buildings and 'Discovery' laboratory in the background. (*Phot: Author.*)
The plan in operation at Grytviken. A Blue whale being hauled up. (*Phot: Author.*)

Between pages 80 and 81.
Floating factory *Salvestria*, 1940. A whale carcass astern. (*Phot: Author.*)
The plan deck of a modern factory ship, Fl.f. *Balaena*, in operation. (*Phot: Central Press.*)

Flensing a male Humpback whale at a shore station in Western Australia. (*Phot: Australian News and Inf. Bureau.*)

Between pages 144 and 145.
Two Fin whales surfacing. In the foreground the 'slick' of a third, which has just submerged, can be seen. (*Phot: Nat. Inst. Oceanog.*)
A school of Sperm whales surfacing. In the foreground one has spouted and is about to submerge, showing the 'hump'. (*Phot: Nat. Inst. Oceanog.*)
Sperm whales submerging. The whale on the left is throwing up its tail flukes. (*Phot: Nat. Inst. Oceanog.*)

Male Sperm whale 55 ft. long at the Azores. (*Phot: Central Press.*)
Loaded whale train about to leave the jetty at Durban. (*Phot: Nat. Inst. Oceanog.*)

Between pages 160 and 161.
Flensing a Blue whale on the plan deck of a factory ship. (*Phot: Paul Popper.*)
Krill. Stomach contents of a Blue whale 72 ft. long on the deck of Fl.f. *Southern Harvester*. The flensing knife is 5 ft. long. (*Phot: Dr. R. Clarke.*)

Stranded Pilot whales, Westray, Orkney, March 1955. (*Phot: Paul Popper.*)
Stranded Pilot whales, Dunbar, Midlothian, May 1951. (*Phot: Assoc. Press.*)

The engravings on the title page and the binding case of this book are reproduced by kind permission of the Radio Times Hulton Picture Library.

CHAPTER I

Southern Heyday

'Discovery'

I was lucky to have been in the Antarctic during what may now be regarded as the heyday of southern whaling when more men were employed in the Antarctic, higher profits made and more oil produced than at any other time before or since. In October 1929 I arrived at South Georgia, a barren but beautiful island eight hundred miles east of the Falklands, in the Norwegian whaling factory ship *Antarctic*. I was a new recruit to the scientific staff of the 'Discovery' Committee of the Colonial Office which had been set up in 1923 with the object of organizing scientific research into whales and whaling in the waters of the Falkland Islands Dependencies. These, roughly speaking, were the Antarctic and Subantarctic islands and territories south of South America now known as the British Antarctic Territories. The Committee had bought Captain Scott's wooden barque, *Discovery*, now moored alongside Victoria Embankment in London, and had converted and equipped her for marine research. In 1925 she sailed for the Antarctic under the leadership of Dr. Stanley Kemp and returned in 1927. In the light of experience gained during those two years' pioneer work in the Southern Ocean the 'Discovery' Committee decided to replace her by a new, up-to-date oil-burning steamship, the *Discovery II*, which had just been completed and was being fitted out for her first voyage south when my colleague, John Wheeler, and I sailed in the *Antarctic* from Cardiff in September 1929. Our particular job was to be concerned with an aspect of whaling research quite different from but designed to run parallel with the work of the ship. It was to consist of the systematic biological examination of whale carcasses at a whaling station at South Georgia.

Dr. Kemp had assured me before we left that this work would be both laborious and odorous. Its purpose was to gather together a body of information about the biological condition of the whale population in the waters around the island, and hence about the effect of whaling on the stock of whales. It would be the sort of systematic recording which is done, largely with computers today, in all research concerned with living populations, whether fisheries, whales, wild game, birds or human beings. 'Discovery' scientists had been doing this work for some years at South Georgia before Wheeler and I arrived. Wheeler was an old hand and had been engaged on it since its beginning while I was a novice, looking upon it all as an adventure.

In 1924, while acquiring the old *Discovery* for work at sea, the Committee had established a marine biological station, with laboratory and living quarters, on a sand spit in King Edward's Cove, South Georgia, opposite the Grytviken whaling station. Here, since 1925, scientists stationed at the laboratory, of whom I was to be one, worked throughout each season on the whaling station, examining the carcasses one by one as they arrived. The whaling station was about five minutes' trip by motor-boat across the bay from the tussocky peninsula where our buildings stood with others which housed officials of the Falkland Islands Government. These were a tin-roofed customs office, a radio station and a gaol, together with quarters for government officers. Ernest Shackleton's grave faced us across the bay and a wooden cross upon a cairn of stones commemorated him at the harbour entrance. Steep dark mountains, their heads slashed with snow and their skirts clothed with tussock grass, surrounded the harbour on three sides, opening seawards to form a huge bay with glaciers. Wheeler and I worked at the whaling station daily from the time of our arrival in October 1929 until whaling ceased for the season in April 1930 when the station closed down for the winter.

The new research ship, the Royal Research Ship *Discovery II*, to give her full title, reached South Georgia in January 1930, looking very smart in her new black paint and yellow funnel. In April I left South Georgia aboard her for Cape Town.

It was believed from circumstantial evidence that during the southern winter the Antarctic whalebone whales move northwards on a breeding migration along the coasts of South America, South Africa, Australia and New Zealand. During the winter of 1926 John Wheeler and Neil Mackintosh had examined the carcasses of whales at Saldanha Bay on the coast of Cape Province, north of Cape Town. In order to supplement their work it was decided that Alec Laurie and I should work during the winter of 1930 on the east coast of South Africa, at Durban, Natal. We travelled from Cape Town to Durban in the *Windsor Castle*, a four-funneller, long ago defunct. On leaving Cape Town I sent a note by the Purser's Office to the Captain asking if I might be informed of any whales observed from the bridge during the three days' trip. To my chagrin I received no reply. The presumptuousness of youth! Laurie and I worked at one of the two stations on the Bluff at Durban from June to September and then returned in the *Discovery II*, after her refit in Cape Town, for the summer whaling season of 1930–31 in South Georgia. In May 1931 we left for home, again in *Discovery II*.

Peak Whaling Years

My first spell of two years in the south thus covered the southern summers 1929–30 and 1930–31. These may be looked upon as the peak years for whaling in the Antarctic from several points of view, from that of the total amount of whale oil produced ($2\frac{1}{2}$ and $3\frac{1}{2}$ million barrels respectively at six barrels to a ton), from that of the profits of the whaling companies (dividends 30 to 50 per cent) and from that of the total number of men employed (about 11,000). But from the point of view of the total number of whales killed these two years were far below the maximum. In 1937–38 the slaughter reached the terrible total of nearly 55,000 whales, compared with 38,000 in 1929–30 and 43,000 in 1930–31. This was a toll never exceeded even in post-war years.

Blue and Fin Whales

In 1929–30 and 1930–31 the catches of the whaling stations at South Georgia, and of the growing fleet of factory ships, consisted almost entirely of the two greatest of the whalebone whales, the Blue and the Fin whale or Finback. A few other species were also taken but they were unimportant. The Blue whale made up about 60 per cent of the catches at South Georgia and about 75 per cent of the catches in the Antarctic as a whole. The remainder was mainly made up of the smaller, though valuable, Fin whale which yields about half the quantity of top grade oil as a Blue of the same length. It was because of the very high proportion of Blue whales in the catches that these years were the peak years for oil production though not for the total number of whales killed.

Pelagic Whaling

In the early thirties the change-over was in full swing from whaling by means of shore-based stations to pelagic whaling by means of factory ships with all the equipment for rendering down carcasses on board. There were five whaling stations in South Georgia in 1929. Formerly there had been six but before I arrived one of them had been closed down and absorbed by one of the others. They operated from October to mid-April, each with five catching boats (whale catchers) which hunted within a hundred miles of the island. There was another station at Deception Island in the South Shetlands, about 1,400 miles to the south-west, but it operated a rather shorter season because Deception Island, in 60° South, is icebound for much of the year. Each South Georgia station took between 500 and 800 whales a season, giving about 200,000 barrels of oil. The station at Deception Island, in spite of its shorter hunting time, took about 500 whales a season because the catchers could hunt throughout the twenty-four hours of summer daylight, but at the end of the 1930–31 season this station closed down for good.

The great advantage which factory ships have over whaling stations on shore is that they are mobile and can, with their attendant catchers, follow the whale herds as they move about the ocean and along the edge of the pack ice. Stations on shore are static and can only take such whales as pass within the cruising range of their catchers. They are thus limited both in time and distance, especially at South Georgia where the whales are on passage to the southward. The cruising range of the South Georgia catchers was not much more than one day's steaming from the island and already in the early thirties the first sign of a coming decline in the available stock of whales was visible to those who could read it, a steadily increasing proportion of young whales in the catches.

The change from shore-based to pelagic whaling began in the early years of the present century and was set in motion by reports, which exploring ships brought back, of great numbers of whales to the south and south-east of South Georgia along the pack ice edge.

In those early days all factory ships were converted, usually ex-British, merchantmen. The Norwegian whaling companies bought them cheap, put in oil tanks, pressure boilers, steam saws, winches and tackle and sent them down to the Antarctic to catch whales. They were expensive to equip and to run but their mobility made up for this expense in increased catches. In many cases not much thought was given to the comfort of the crew and in a few even the stability of the ship seemed to be doubtful. Some of these old ships were very cranky, listing heavily and rolling horribly in a seaway. The living accommodation was all mixed up with the factory equipment so that the crew lived in an atmosphere of stench, blood and grease. None of the early ships had a slipway in the stern and the carcasses were stripped in the water alongside the ship. The men had to work over the side, walking about in spiked boots on the whale carcasses themselves. Calm water was needed for this, so that most factory ships tied up to the shore in some sheltered harbour in South Georgia or the South Shetlands. Deception Island, that grim crater whose black shores are warm and steaming, was a favourite anchorage. Here, during the mid-summer months when the harbour is free of ice, as many as thirty factory ships used to anchor during the early years in order to process the whales their catchers brought in. It was an incredibly wasteful business in those days. Only the blubber was used and the '*skrotts*', as the stripped carcasses were called, were cast adrift in the harbour. They floated ashore to rot on the beaches and to this day Deception Harbour, and many of the bays and inlets of South Georgia, are edged with ramparts of bleached bones, skulls, jaws, backbones and ribs, memorials to that uncontrolled slaughter. They bear witness to the greed and folly of mankind. At the shore whaling stations, too, similar profligate waste at first prevailed until the Government intervened to stop it.

South Georgia and the South Shetlands are British territory and were incorporated, together with other islands and neighbouring Antarctic lands, under letters patent, dated 1908, as the Dependencies of the Falkland Islands. The legality of this was somewhat doubtful but nobody contested it and the whole sector of the Antarctic south of South America is now renamed British Antarctic Territories. The Norwegian whaling companies leased the land on which their stations stood from the Falkland Islands Government and carried on whaling under licence. About this time the Government became anxious about the effect of whaling on the stock of whales and the wasteful manner in which it was being done and so regulations were drawn up and attached to the issue of licences. They stipulated that the whole of the carcass must be used and not only just the blubber, and no whale obviously running with a calf might be killed. At the same time the number of catcher boats attached to each station was limited to five. Later (1917) the Government levied a tax per barrel of whale oil processed or landed anywhere in the Dependencies, and that meant anywhere in the South American sector of the Antarctic. This was intended to provide a fund for scientific research into the natural history of the whales for, as long ago as World War I, the Government was far sighted enough to realize that regulations for the control of whaling would have to be based on a knowledge of the whales' natural history if they were to be effective. At that time such knowledge was almost entirely lacking and it was from this fund that the work of the 'Discovery' Committee (later called 'Discovery' Investigations) was financed.

The whalers resented this impost though they saw the sense of the regulations, but the result was an enormous increase in the numbers of floating factories in the Antarctic. They now became wholly pelagic and worked in the open sea along the pack ice edge, no longer in the shelter of bays and harbours, though usually taking shelter in leads among the pack ice. Thus they were outside territorial limits and free of all imposts whatever for they could transfer their oil direct into tankers without landing it ashore. From the middle of the twenties onwards factory ships were equipped with slipways in the stern (sometimes in the bows) up which the carcasses could be hauled on deck to be cut up. The factory ship *Lancing* in 1925 was the first to be thus equipped. She had a slipway in the bows and seemed to swallow her whales whole. Later, in the early thirties, factory ships were specially built for the job and the merely converted merchantmen became fewer and fewer. The *Vikingen* and *Terje Viken* were the first two specially built factory ships to arrive in the Antarctic and I remember the sensation they made when they anchored off the South Georgia whaling station. They were giants, between twenty and twenty-five thousand gross tons, with twin funnels over the stern, one on each side of the long slipway which sloped up to a huge deck space the full length of the ship. The factory and the living quarters were quite separate from one another and the crew's accommodation was luxurious by the standards of the time. The men even had shower baths.

These giants began arriving on the whaling grounds in 1930–31 and the whaling spread far out along the pack ice to the eastwards of South Georgia. In that year there were thirty-eight factory ships working in the Antarctic, but most of them were not large enough to be entirely independent of land bases, so that they had to transfer their cargoes of whale oil at South Georgia for subsequent shipment to Europe in tankers. That meant that they had to call at the island for customs clearance at the beginning of the whaling season in October or November. Many returned in the middle of the season in order to transfer their oil while others made the transfer direct into tankers at the ice edge. At the end of the season in March or April many of the factories called again at South Georgia for homeward customs clearance and perhaps for another transfer of oil. Most of these ships were, like the shore stations, owned, managed and manned by Norwegians though there were several British companies. These, too, largely employed Norwegians but some had Scots engineers and Shetland seamen. Some were well found ships, like the *Antarctic* in which I travelled south. She was converted from one of the ships of the New Zealand Shipping Company and in her the Manager and his staff, the Captain and his officers, the whaling gunners, Wheeler and I, lived in princely style. We ate delicious Norwegian tinned fish and drank *Aquavit* and champagne. At noon every day in the Manager's cabin there were cocktails and caviar sandwiches. The cabin accommodation was first class. But many fascinating old crocks still arrived at South Georgia in those years, dropped anchor in Grytviken Harbour as though with relief and called loudly to the whaling station for help. One saw the Captain hurrying ashore in his motor-boat to see the Manager of the station almost before the hook was in the water, and wondered what could be the matter and how the old girl would get through the season. But they always did and turned up again when the winter's snow began to fall, their stolid Norwegian crews looking forward to spending their hard-earned wages at home. And spend them they did in rollicking fashion, joining the old ship again broke next year, or another old crock if they couldn't get a job in something better. It was said that more ships passed through the customs at South Georgia in 1930–31 than entered the port of Liverpool in a comparable period.

From the early thirties onwards the story of whaling in the Antarctic followed a sadly familiar pattern. Along the ice edge a mass slaughter of whalebone whales took place and increased until the decline of the whaling industry in 1963 with the prohibition of the capture of Blue and Humpback whales. Initial success, high hopes and vast profits produced an ugly rush to cash in on the slaughter. Profligate waste was followed by a melancholy decline. Much the same has often been seen in fisheries and there have been the same cries of alarm when the supply of fish began to run out, fishermen, like whalers, blaming everything and everyone but themselves.

In 1930–31 42,874 whales were taken and the total oil production was 3,686,976 tons (International Whaling Statistics, 3, 1932). After World War II the average Antarctic catch of Blue and Fin whales for the four seasons 1957–61 amounted to 27,843 whales (Mackintosh, N. A., 1965). In addition there was an average of 5,140 Sperm whales as against 62 for the whole Antarctic in 1928–29. The mean oil production in the four seasons was 2,213,382 barrels (364,497 tons). In 1966–1967, the latest year for which figures are available, total oil production was down to 100,111 tons extracted from 15,260 whalebone whales and 4,968 Sperm (International Whaling Statistics, 1960).

Already in 1931 Sir Sidney Harmer had written 'It does not need much foresight to believe that the culminating point of the industry must be reached within a very few years, if indeed it has not already arrived.'

Control of Whaling—Pre-war

In the Antarctic the only difference from previous experience was the fact that during the thirties adequate research upon which regulations for control might be based had been begun by both the British, with the 'Discovery' Investigations, and by distinguished Norwegian scientists. As a result conscientious attempts were made to regulate the hunting by international agreement. Some agreement was reached but not enough to save the industry.

In 1937 an International Whaling Convention was signed and within its framework regulations were agreed upon by the governments concerned. Limits were fixed to the duration of the whaling season and to the sizes of the whales killed. The rules forbidding the taking of cows accompanied by calves and insisting on the use of the whole carcass, originally introduced by the Falkland Islands Government, were confirmed. There were also other regulations.

Not all the whaling companies obeyed these regulations and some whaling nations did not sign the convention. The Japanese, for instance, newly arrived on the Antarctic scene, carried on without regard to regulations or restrictions of any sort.

In order to watch over these regulations and ensure that they were properly observed the governments concerned agreed to appoint observers or inspectors, one to each factory ship to be appointed by the government under whose flag the ship sailed. This, in fact, meant either the Norwegian or British Government. These gentlemen were to be known as 'whaling inspectors' and the British ones were mostly ex-naval officers.

In 1937 I returned to London after three trips to the Antarctic and when war broke out in 1939 I was still on the 'Discovery' staff, working at the Natural History Museum, South Kensington.

During these days, when the sky seemed about to fall, we were lectured once a week by a member of the museum staff on first aid and what to do if there were a gas attack. In the event of war, we had been told, we scientists would be allotted jobs according to our qualifications, which would undoubtedly be of great value to the national effort. One day some enormously complicated and elaborate forms arrived in which we had to describe our qualifications and experience in minute detail with dates. 'At last!' we thought as we laboriously filled them in, and waited. Nothing happened. Some weeks later Dr. Neil Mackintosh, Director of 'Discovery' Investigations, asked me if I would be willing to go south for the 1939–40 season as a whaling inspector on board a factory ship, one of the three British ones leaving for the whaling grounds that year. It seemed better than sitting around in the Natural History Museum waiting for a summons that never came. Even the lectures on what to do in a gas attack had come to an end. So I spent the six months of the 'phoney war' at the Antarctic ice edge, as far from the scene of the apparently stillborn conflict as it was possible to get. I returned to England in April 1940 when things were starting to come alive and warm up.

After that first season of the war there was no whaling in the Antarctic until 1943 when one Norwegian factory sailed from England. She was the only vessel whaling in the Antarctic in that or the following season. The war reached the Antarctic in the southern summer of 1940–41, the one after mine. Most of the factories became tankers and, since they were slow, casualties among them were heavy. All the British ones were lost in due course, including the one I sailed in, but not until after I had left her.

Control of Whaling—Post-war

In 1945 the world shortage of oils and fats amounted to about one million tons and it was urgently necessary for whaling to start up again immediately. Nine factory ships, Norwegian and British, went south and one station reopened in South Georgia.

In 1944 it had been agreed among the English-speaking nations and Norway to bring back the whaling convention of 1937. A new scheme for the limitation of the catch was introduced, based on a standard unit of oil production rather than on the actual numbers of whales killed.

2

This unit is still in use and is known as the Blue Whale Unit. It assumes that from the standpoint of oil production one Blue whale is equivalent to two Fin whales, two and a half Humpback and six Sei whales, and so from the numbers of these four species of whales killed the oil production of any factory or station or of the whole fleet can be estimated. A quota of Blue whale units was fixed for each season and whaling stopped as soon as that quota had been obtained. The catch figures are collated by the *Norsk Hvalfangstforbund* (Norwegian Whaling Union) in Sandefjord, Norway, which gives the signal to stop when the limit has been reached. At first the quota for the whole whaling fleet was fixed at 16,000 Blue Whale Units but it has been progressively reduced throughout the post-war years down to the sad total for 1970–71 of 2,700 units. These quotas had the effect of automatically limiting the length of the whaling season which was confined to the months of January, February and March.

In 1946 a permanent body was established under the auspices of the United Nations called the International Whaling Commission. Most of the whaling nations were represented on it though not at first the Russians or the Japanese. It confirmed the fairly stringent regulations already in force and introduced some others.

Yet even with these restrictions and with this control during the fifties some twenty to twenty-five factories killed between twenty-five and thirty thousand whales a year. The restrictions brought about inevitably an increase in what is known in fishery parlance as 'fishing intensity'. Perhaps in this case we ought to call it 'catching power'. It is something which comes about when a fishery, or any animal population which is being exploited, begins to decline through over exploitation. As the quarry becomes scarcer or harder to find competition becomes keener among the hunters. Their resources, ingenuity and killing power increase. Attempts to regulate the catches merely increase the ingenuity with which the regulations are circumvented. On the whaling grounds factories became larger and more efficient. Catchers were more numerous and more powerful, and faster, so that the whale was no longer stalked as before but run down until it was spent, like a stag with the hounds after it. Thus exhausted it presented an easy target. Asdic was introduced for tracking whales and holding on to them even in thick weather. Aircraft and helicopters were tried for spotting, but not with much success since they were apt to fly off and never come back. Corvettes, veterans of the Battle of the Atlantic, were used for collecting dead whales after they had been marked with radio buoys. They towed the carcasses back to the factory so that the catchers could keep on hunting. Sometimes, too, they were used for chasing whales to exhaustion, the catchers being called up by radio telephone to fire the shot when the whale was obviously at its last gasp.

During the fifties and early sixties the numbers of factory ships in the Antarctic never equalled the numbers in pre-war years, but they were all modern specially built ships of twenty thousand tons and more, attended by as many as ten or fifteen catchers. The Russians arrived on the whaling grounds in strength and one of their ships, the *Sovietskaya Ukraina* (36,000 tons), is the largest factory ship in the world. The Japanese returned to the Antarctic with several up-to-date factories and took over under lease two stations at South Georgia, one of them being the Grytviken station where Wheeler and I worked more than thirty years before. In 1965 they used this station only but since then there have been no whaling stations operating at all in South Georgia. Soon after the war the Dutch arrived on the scene with a large, specially built factory ship, the *Willem Barendsz* (26,830 tons), but she ceased whaling in 1964. Meanwhile the Norwegians, who formerly had almost a monopoly of southern whaling, and the British have disappeared from the whaling grounds. The last Norwegian factory ship, the *Kosmos*, went south for the last time in 1967–8 and the last British factory, the *Southern Venturer*, was taken over by the Japanese in 1957.

Decline

Throughout the fifties and sixties the proportion of Blue whales in Antarctic catches declined steadily. In 1930–31 they made up 80 per cent of the total catch. In 1950–51 they amounted to only 25 per cent and in 1961–62 only 5 per cent. At South Georgia, where over a thousand Blue whales were taken in 1930–31, only four were taken in 1960–61. As Blue whales diminished Fin whales increased in importance until 1960–61, with a rising proportion of young ones, a dangerous sign. Meanwhile other species, formerly rarely taken in the Antarctic, the Sperm and the Sei, were increasing in the catches (Fig. 1), though it was not certain whether they had become more plentiful or the whalers were merely taking them in the absence of anything better. After 1960–61 the Fin whale catches began to fall away and Sei whales became the dominant whalebone whales in the Antarctic catch, but in 1965–66 they, too, began to decrease rapidly (Fig. 1a). Yet in spite of these ominous signs the nations on the International Whaling Commission failed to agree to limit their catches.

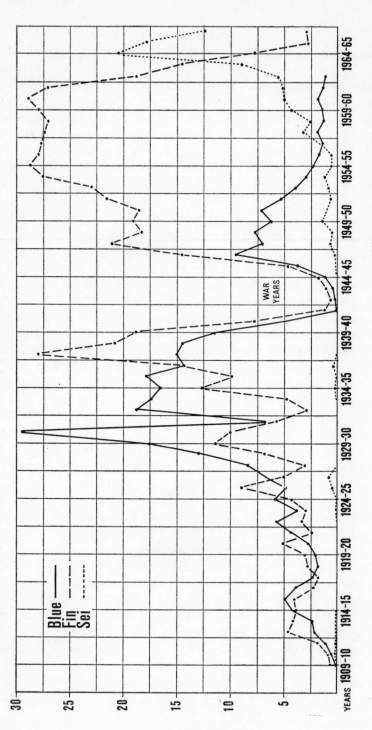

YEARLY ANTARCTIC CATCHES OF BLUE, FIN AND SEI WHALES

Blue ———
Fin – – –
Sei ······

WAR YEARS

YEARS 1909-10 1914-15 1919-20 1924-25 1929-30 1934-35 1939-40 1944-45 1949-50 1954-55 1959-60 1964-65

30 25 20 15 10 5

Fig. 1(a) From Gambell, R., *Dis. Rep.* 35.

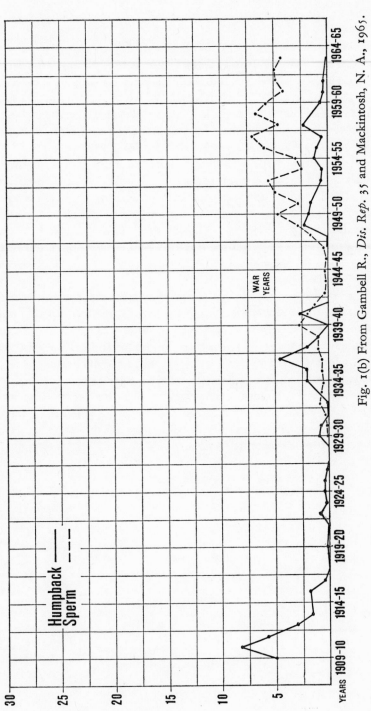

YEARLY ANTARCTIC CATCHES OF HUMPBACK AND SPERM WHALES

Humpback ———
Sperm – – –

WAR YEARS

Fig. 1(b) From Gambell R., *Dis. Rep.* 35 and Mackintosh, N. A., 1965.

Antarctic whaling is practically finished. In 1969–70 there was one Norwegian but no British factory ship at the ice edge and only three Japanese and three Russian factories were seeking what whales they could find, mainly for their meat, which is now a more important commodity than whale oil. It seems improbable that the industry will recover during the lifetime of any adult person now living and the busy harbours of South Georgia are silenced for ever.

The centre of the whaling industry has now shifted to the North Pacific where the whaling nations are Russia, Japan, Canada and the U.S.A. There are both land stations and factory ships at work and the catches have increased rapidly in recent years, but now here too they are beginning to fall off. Already there is a hot debate about the allocation of catches but the signs are that the lessons of the Antarctic have been learnt and for the year 1969 an agreement to limit catches was reached.

If the years 1929–30 and 1930–31 were a heyday for Norwegian whalers, they were something of the sort for me too. I was young and fit and newly released from what I thought was a dull life in London. Wide horizons seemed to open out before me and I rejoiced in having a job which seemed to be worth doing and took me out under the open sky. But no one working on the whaling stations in those days, except apparently the whalers themselves, could help wondering how the slaughter could possibly continue indefinitely, nor fail to be moved to astonishment, awe and pity at the sight of the gigantic, harmless creatures which were its victims.

CHAPTER 2

Whales, Dolphins and Porpoises

Fish or Mammal?

Although dolphins figure largely in Greek legends and myths, and Aristotle knew them to be warm blooded and to breathe air, yet the Ancients believed that they were fish, and to this day a kind of atavistic suspicion lingers that whales, dolphins and porpoises must really be fish. Any whale found stranded on a beach in the United Kingdom is known to the authorities as a 'fish royal' and becomes the property of the crown under an act dating from the reign of Edward II, soon to be repealed, which ruled that 'the King shall have the wreck of the sea, whales and great sturgeons'. During World War II attempts were made to popularize whale meat from the Antarctic, but the Ministry of Food directed it all to the fishmongers' shops where housewives, disconcerted by its red colour, would not buy it.

The persistence of the belief that whales are fish is perhaps due to their entirely aquatic habit and to their streamlined, fish-like shape. We now know that all Cetacea, from the common porpoise to the giant whalebone whales of the Antarctic, are in fact just as much mammals as dogs and cats, cattle, horses and pigs, and man himself. Their structure and physiology place them squarely in the class Mammalia, four-legged animals with a distinct neck of seven vertebrae, a backbone prolonged into a tail hidden beneath the skin only in man, and the body completely divided by a muscular wall, the diaphragm, which separates a forward chamber containing the heart and lungs from a rear one containing the stomach, liver, kidneys and other viscera. The heart has four chambers and the skull forms a solid box. Only the lower jaw, and a small chain of bones called the hyoid arch at the base of the tongue, are movable parts of the skull.

Like all mammals whales are warm blooded, breathe air into lungs, bear their young in a womb and suckle them with milk from mammary glands. These lie at the base of the abdomen (the inguinal position) like those of the domestic cow. Yet their wholly aquatic life has imposed a streamlined, fish-like shape on them and has affected their structure and organization in many ways. One immediately notices the loss of the hind limbs. All that remains of the hip girdle of mammals is a curved bone on either side deep in the muscles of the flank. It is quite free from the backbone and not more than a foot long in even the largest whale. Sometimes a small splint about an inch long is attached to it which represents the hind limb. This is the thigh bone and in Right whales there is another minute bone sometimes present which is the shin bone. The fore-limb, on the other hand, has become an oar-like flipper within which the fore-arm bones and four or five digits may be seen. All are bound together by skin and gristle into a solid, paddle-like flipper.

The acquisition of the fish-like shape has brought about a compression and flattening of the skull so that the nostril or nostrils (there may be only one) are pushed to the top of the head. Here they are sunk beneath the general level of the surface of the skull and all external protuberances are done away with. For instance, the aperture of the ear is a small hole, no greater in diameter than a pencil, at the side of the head with no trace of any external ear. The eye, too, is flush with the side of the head, just above the angle of the jaw, with neither eyelashes nor eyelids. The skin is quite smooth except for a few vestigial hairs on the head and upper jaw of whalebone whales and on the snouts of some dolphins. In the Sperm whale hairs are present in the unborn young but disappear before birth. In the cold watery world which whales inhabit a hairy coat would be useless as an insulator and a hindrance to movement. The whale's body is insulated by a thick layer of fat, the blubber, beneath the skin, ensheathing the body completely from head to tail.

In the fish-like shape of whales we see a classic example of what is known as 'convergent evolution', of a similar adaptation to the same conditions of life reached from widely different directions in different races. In this case the viscous, resistant, aquatic medium has imposed a similar smooth, fusiform shape upon many different animals, fishes, whales, seals, diving birds, squids and cuttlefish. The swiftest inhabitants of the aquatic world are the most perfectly streamlined. For example, the Tuna fish, which is said to be capable of speeds of 35 knots, has scales so minute that its skin is quite smooth. Its eye is flush with the surface of the head. The snout is roundly pointed and the body finely tapered to a powerful tail. The fins can be withdrawn into slits and the fore-fins fold back into recesses in the sides. This, too, is the shape of submarines and, to a certain extent, of underwater projectiles. It is the shape of aircraft and of motor-cars built to travel at speeds great enough to meet with air resistance equivalent to or exceeding that of water at lower speeds.

Swimming

Aquatic animals propel themselves through the water in various ways all of which, in fact, reduce themselves to the method of the paddle, the propeller or the jet. The jet method is used least but cuttlefish, squids and octopuses can dart backwards for short distances by squirting out a jet of water from the mantle cavity through a fleshy funnel. Diving birds such as auks and cormorants paddle with their feet and penguins with their powerful flipper-like wings. Fish and whales use the tail as a propeller. In fish it is triangular, crescentic or blade-like (eels) and vertically flattened. It beats from side to side, displacing water within the curve of the body out and back first on one side and then on the other so as to drive the body forwards. In whales the flat tail flukes are horizontal and beat up and down. They are built entirely of tendon and gristle, with no bones or any extensions of the skeleton such as we see in the tails of fish. They are well faired, as are the fore-flippers, like the wings of an aircraft, a stout, smooth, rounded leading edge tapering finely to the trailing edge which is curved like a bow with a notch on the central axis of the body.

The upward thrust of the whale's tail flukes provides the forward drive, displacing water upwards and backwards. It has been suggested that the motion of the flukes has a rotary component but ciné films of dolphins in tanks do not confirm this though they do show that the flukes have some independence of movement vertically. The tail region of the body moves up and down about a centre near the vent while the flukes make a similar movement about a second centre in the neck of the tail, so that the effect is that of a sculling oar.

Like the side fins of fishes the flippers have a stabilizing and probably braking action but do not help to drive the body forward. The back fin, when present, is also a stabilizer. It is larger in whales that swim fast than in those that swim slowly, and indeed these may lack a back fin altogether. Unlike many bony fishes, but like sharks, whales cannot reverse and, with such comparatively small brakes, it must be difficult for them to stop.

Something that has long puzzled scientists in connection with the swimming powers of whales is known as 'Gray's paradox'. Dolphins can swim at speeds of 20 to 25 knots while the great whalebone whales can reach speeds of 15 knots. But the paradox is that experiments, conducted by Sir John Gray at Cambridge with rigid models, have shown that at these speeds the resistance of the water would be so great that the animal would need to develop as much as seven times the horse-power which it is known, from measurements, to be capable of. In order to overcome the water resistance it would need muscles ten times more powerful than those of any other mammal. Yet this, it is believed, would be impossible because of the great heat which such high powered muscles would develop, and because the blood system could not supply the necessary oxygen.

The answer is thought to lie in the type of flow of water along the skin surface and in the reduction of what is known as 'drag', the amount of resistance which the surface of a moving body offers to the flow of water past it.

Ciné films have been taken of fish-shaped models towed through water rendered cloudy by a suspension of fine particles. They show that the particles in contact with the surface of the model form whorls and eddies which exercise a pull on the surface. This is called 'turbulent flow'. By using flexible models these eddies and whorls can be reduced and even got rid of altogether so that a condition known as 'laminar flow' results. In this the particles slide smoothly over one another longitudinally without any pull against the surface of the model. It is believed that the skin of dolphins, and possibly of the great whales also, is adapted so as to produce this condition of laminar flow as the animal swims. American observers, watching dolphins swimming in tanks, have noticed that when the animal swims rapidly under water certain folds and ripples appear on the surface of the skin at right-angles to the direction of motion, mostly on the lower and lateral parts of the body. They appear temporarily and last for only a few seconds, and it has been suggested that they enable the skin surface to adjust itself to inequalities of pressure resulting from water resistance or drag. It may be, too, that the peculiar structure of the outer skin also plays a part in reducing drag (Kramer, M. O., 1960). The skin of a dolphin, like that of all vertebrate animals, has a soft outer layer, the epidermis, and a hard inner one, the dermis. In most whales the epidermis is a very thin layer and the dermis is a much thicker layer of connective tissue underneath it. In the dolphins which the Americans had watched in the tanks, the

Bottle-nosed dolphin, the outer epidermis is made up of innumerable fine ducts at right-angles to the skin surface filled with a spongy material. It is thought that this layer may be able to accommodate itself to minute oscillations of the water, microscopic eddies and whorls, caused by turbulent flow.

No such structure has been found in the skin of the great whales but on the lower surface of the body the skin is very flexible and the blubber is thin with loose connective tissue underneath it. It could therefore easily form folds and ripples, like those seen in the dolphin, when the whales swim rapidly under the water.

Another feature of the skin of whales is the fact that the two layers, dermis and epidermis, are closely dove-tailed together by means of small papillae, minute protuberances, which are believed to counteract the sheering stresses set up by motion through the water. They are arranged along ridges of the dermis which somewhat resemble those we can see on our own skin, for instance in our finger prints and on the palms of our hands. These, too, serve to counteract stresses in grasping. On the whale's skin they are arranged in patterns, just as they are on our own, and it has been suggested (Purves, P. E., 1963) that this pattern may correspond to the flow lines of water past the whale's body. The ridges tend to run obliquely from the lower side of the thorax up on to the back in the tail region. From this it has been argued that whalebone whales do not swim horizontally nose first but with head slightly raised and chest meeting the water first, as it were breasting the water, the flow past the body being, relatively, upwards and backwards. In this connection it has been noted that the whale's body is streamlined, or faired, on the back but not underneath except in the tail region where it is faired both above and below.

Order Cetacea

Whales, porpoises and dolphins belong to the mammalian order Cetacea (Greek, *ketos*—a whale). The word 'whale' itself, similar in all northern European languages (Norwegian *hval*, German and Dutch *wal*), is closely related to the word 'wheel' and refers to the manner in which the animal's back seems to be turning over or revolving in the water. The Cetacea stand, in relation to other orders of mammals, near the even-toed or cloven-hoofed Ungulates (cattle, sheep, goats, pigs and camels—as opposed to the odd-toed, single-hoofed Ungulates such as the horse). The resemblances to the even-toed Ungulates are highly technical, but we may note the small number of young, usually one at a time, the position of the mammary glands and the shape of the penis. Internally there is the structure of the genital organs, the arrangement of the placental membranes before birth, the form of the stomach (not unlike that of the domestic cow) and the chemical structure of the body proteins.

All the Cetacea breathe air and at each exhalation blow out a stream of water vapour called the 'spout', for which reason the nostrils or single nostril on top of the head are referred to as 'blowholes'. In the great whales the spout is a most impressive sight, like the exhaust of a great engine pounding up from the deep. It may be a fine, narrow upstanding jet, as in the great whalebone whales, or it may be quite small and inconspicuous, as in many porpoises and dolphins. In all Cetacea a layer of blubber sheaths the body from head to tail and all the tissues, muscles, bones and viscera are impregnated with oil which helps to insulate them in their cold watery world. Over the flukes and flippers the blubber layer is thin and fibrous and it is thin over the skull and belly, but over the flanks and back it may be as much as a foot thick in whalebone whales. In a large fat animal in good condition after months of feeding in southern seas the blubber layer may be as much as two feet thick on the flanks.

Ancestors

Some hundred million years ago the whales' forbears lost contact with the land and took to their present entirely aquatic life. The great Antarctic whales, indeed, pursue their food, mate and bear their young many hundreds of miles from any land.

The fossil record gives us almost no help in deciding how and where the change from land to sea took place. Fossil creatures of archaic form, yet undoubtedly whales, appear quite suddenly in the record with no antecedents, the oldest remains being about fifty-five million years old. Possibly the lack of any record prior to this is due to the fact that the change from land to water took place in sandy or swampy estuaries where no fossils could be formed. Having left the land the whales' ancestors probably continued their evolution in the open sea where, again, no fossils could be formed.

The earliest fossil whales known had teeth in their jaws which resembled those of an extinct race of early Carnivores. (Carnivores, as their name implies, are the flesh-eating mammals—dogs, cats, bears, seals, walruses.) Both the Carnivores and the even-toed Ungulates (cattle, etc.) can be traced back to an ancestor common to both but long ago extinct which was something like our modern Insectivores (hedgehogs, moles, shrews). If we find it difficult to imagine a small creature like a shrew as the progenitor, no matter how remote, of the colossal whalebone whales of the Antarctic, we must remember that mere size is no clue to descent. Most races began as small creatures at the outset and only reached great size as they approached the end. We know that the whalebone whales were comparatively recently much smaller than they are now, while the most successful and numerous Cetacea, dolphins and porpoises, are quite small.

In 1845 a certain Dr. Albert Koch dug up some enormous vertebrae and added some others and a skull. He mounted them into a skeleton which he exhibited in New York and in Europe as the first sea serpent, 114 feet long. He called it *Hydrarchos*, the water chief. Richard Owen pointed out that it was really made up of two separate animals and was, in fact, the remains of an early whale. As he reconstructed it the creature was still 55 feet long and had a long, sinuous tail with which it must have been able to swim quickly with a whip-like action. It was a snake-shaped animal with variegated teeth and a skull resembling that of a dog in shape. The fore-limb was a flipper with five fingers in the hand and with an elbow. There were traces of a thigh bone.

Since the discovery of these early serpent-shaped whales many other remains have been found in various parts of the world, especially in Egypt and on the Gulf Coast of the U.S.A. Some of them were shaped like sea serpents and others were like modern porpoises, swimming swiftly with up and down strokes of a flattened tail. Yet none of these can be looked upon as the ancestors of any whales now living.

We can only imagine what the small creature was like which waded out into the waters of the steadily advancing shallow sea typical of the Cretaceous period about a hundred million years ago during which the chalk deposits were laid down.

This ancestral animal was part insectivore and part carnivore. It had a five-fingered foot and hand and an elongated skull like a dog with teeth differentiated into incisors, canines, pre-molars and molars, as are the teeth of carnivores today. It has been suggested that the skin may have been partly, or even wholly, covered with small plates of bone because these are found in a number of fossil whales. It probably lived in estuaries where there were gently sloping beaches of sand or mud. It may have fed on crustaceans or small fish and took to wading after them farther and farther out into the shallows. In time it took to swimming after them more and more quickly, using its tail for propulsion and its fore-limbs as stabilizers. In the course of time its five fingers became bound together into a flipper while its hind limbs, probably held back motionless against the body and taking no part in swimming, slowly atrophied and disappeared, the tail becoming widened out to form flukes. Some of these animals swam with whip-like movements of the tail, but it was from those which swam by means of vertical strokes of the tail that the modern whales came in the fullness of time. Other small animals, part insectivore and part early carnivore, living under different, perhaps drier conditions, took to running after terrestrial prey and became the ancestors of modern Carnivores. Others again became vegetable feeders and gave descent to the Ungulates.

Sub-orders—Whalebone and Toothed Whales

The modern order Cetacea is divided into two sub-orders which do not seem to be very closely related to one another. One (Mystacoceti, from the Greek *mystax*, a moustache, *ketos*, a whale) comprises those whales which have no teeth in their mouths but have instead whalebone plates, or baleen as it is called. The other (Odontoceti, from the Greek *odontos*, teeth) comprises whales which have teeth in their mouths either in both jaws or in the lower jaw only. In the first sub-order are the great whalebone whales which have been hunted for centuries in the Arctic regions and, since the beginning of the present century, in the Antarctic. Those in the second include the Sperm whale which has been hunted all over the world since the beginning of the eighteenth century but whose pursuit and capture by mankind was probably taking place many centuries before the Christian era. It also includes the Killer whale or Grampus and many other smaller whales, and those we speak of as porpoises and dolphins.

The whalebone or baleen whales (Mystacoceti) are filter feeders. Like a great many different kinds of aquatic animals, both vertebrate and invertebrate, they do not feed by means of a mouth armed with teeth but strain out of the water large quantities of minute food too small to be pursued, caught and devoured with teeth. Among invertebrates many crustacea, all bivalve molluscs and sea squirts feed in this manner. Among vertebrates many shoaling fishes, such as herrings and sardines, and the enormous basking shark feed by straining multitudes of small drifting animals and plants out of the water by means of comb-like processes on the gill clefts. Baleen whales filter their planktonic food out of the water by means of a series of triangular flexible plates, made of a horny substance we call whalebone or baleen, hanging down from the upper jaw. These are placed one behind the other with only an inch or so between them and their inner edges are frayed out so as to form a mat of coarse hairs over the roof of the mouth. On this the small animals and fishes on which the whale feeds become entangled. The whale then closes its mouth and, by means of its fleshy tongue, forces the water out between the whalebone plates and over the rampart of the lower jaw. With the mouth closed it then sweeps the food back into the throat, perhaps by means of the tongue, though just how this is done is not certain.

The toothed whales (Odontoceti) are all flesh eaters except one small vegetarian dolphin that lives in the Cameroon River, West Africa. Some, such as the Sperm whale, feed on squids while others, such as dolphins and porpoises, feed mainly on fish. The Grampus or Killer whale devours penguins, seals, fish or the flesh of other whales.

The two sub-orders of Cetacea are divided into the following families:

Sub-order—Mystacoceti (Baleen whales)
Fam. Balaenidae	Right whales
Fam. Balaenopteridae	Rorquals
Fam. Eschrichtiidae	Grey whales

Sub-order—Odontoceti (Toothed whales)
Fam. Physeteridae	Sperm whales
Fam. Ziphiidae	Bottle-nosed and Beaked whales
Fam. Delphinidae	
Sub-fam. Delphininae	Dolphins and porpoises, including the Killer whales and the Pilot whale
Sub-fam. Delphinapterinae	The Narwhal and the White whale or Beluga
Fam. Platanistidae	River and lake dolphins

Fam. Balaenidae—Right whales

This family comprises those baleen whales which the old-time whalers called Right whales because they were the right kind of whales to go for, as opposed to the Rorquals and the Sperm whale which were the wrong kind to go for. The great virtues of Right whales, from the whalers' point of view, were that they are slow and easy to kill and that their carcasses float instead of sinking like those of other baleen whales.

There are three species of Right whales, the Greenland Right whale or Bowhead (Fig. 2a), the Biscay or Black Right whale (Fig. 2b), known to the Dutch as the *Nordkaper*, and the Pygmy Right whale. The first two are the commercially important ones and both have in the past been hunted to the verge of extinction, like the Blue and Humpback today. For some years they have been protected whales, their capture forbidden by international agreement, the Greenland Right whale since the beginning of the century and the Biscay Right whale since 1929. Both are now believed to be showing signs of recovery and becoming more plentiful.

Fig. 2(a) Greenland Right Whale

The Greenland Right whale is found only in the Arctic and seldom far from the edge of the pack ice, especially in the Baffin Sea and off the coast of Greenland, but the Biscay Right whale used to be hunted in all the waters of the world, especially in temperate latitudes, but now it is rarely seen. The Black or Southern Right whale of the southern hemisphere was at one time thought to be different species from the Biscay one but the two are now known to be the same.

Right whales are grotesque in appearance. Their heads are relatively enormous and the barrel of the body tapers away rapidly to a pair of broad flukes. They have no grooves or pleats under the thorax and no back fin and the seven vertebrae of the neck are joined up together in one solid piece. In the Greenland whale the peduncle or stalk of the tail is very slender and the skull is narrow, the upper jaws arched into an almost semicircular bow, hence the name Bowhead. There are about 300 long, flexible baleen plates on each side, their tips resting in a deep channel between the high rampart of the lower jaw and the tongue. The plates are believed to bend when the whale shuts its mouth. (Fig. 2a).

The Greenland whale (Fig. 2a) runs to a length of about 60 feet and its colour is black with a white or yellowish patch on the chin, while the stalk of the tail may be grey. It is a timid creature, very slow and ungainly, wallowing along at about four knots and often less, an easy prey for open-boat whalers who had no difficulty in getting close up to it.

In the Arctic both kinds of Right whales feed on swarms of small crustaceans and also of Pteropods or sea butterflies (pelagic molluscs). They are said to use their lower jaws like a scuttle or scoop as they swim through the swarms with their mouths open.

Herman Melville in *Moby Dick* describes Right whales feeding on 'vast meadows of brit'—the name usually given to swarms of the Copepod *Calanus* on which herrings feed. He describes them as making 'a strange grassy cutting sound; and leaving behind them endless swaths of blue upon the yellow sea'.

Fig. 2(b) Biscay or Black Right Whale

The Biscay Right whale (Fig. 2b) reaches about the same length as the Greenland whale but is stockier in shape and does not have such a high arched head. The head and back are continuous in a straight line except for a slight protuberance that marks the position of the blow-holes, and the stalk of the tail is stouter than that of Greenland whales. It is uniformly black all over and bears on its snout a patch of rough-ened, thickened skin, called the 'bonnet', which is always crawling with whale lice (actually not lice but a parasitic Amphipod crustacean, *Cyamus*). Other similar patches are scattered along the lower and upper jaws but what their function is nobody knows. The baleen plates are not so long or flexible as those of the Greenland whale but the lower jaw is deeper and roundly arched.

I myself have never seen a Greenland whale and only once a Biscay Right. This was in 1931 when it was believed that the Southern Right whale was a different species from the Biscay one. One day a catcher brought a Southern Right whale into Grytviken harbour. The gunner was rather shame-faced about it because the Right whale had only lately been made a protected species. He explained that he had shot it in a fog. Perhaps as a kind of peace offering to the authorities the manager of the whaling station presented us with the skull which was in due course lashed to the fo'c'sle head of the *Discovery II* and taken to England as a present for the Natural History Museum. In the tropics it oozed and sweated grease on to the deck and I, with a proprietary air, spent a lot of time scraping it. The crew in the fo'c'sle underneath complained that it stank, but we laughed light-heartedly and told them they must be imagining it.

The Pygmy Right whale is a small rare relation of the two big ones, never exceeding 20 feet in length. Like the others it has the seven vertebrae of the neck fused together, long flexible whalebone plates and no grooves under the thorax, but it differs from them in having a small sickle-shaped back fin. Its skull is narrow and highly arched but rather less so than that of the Greenland whale. Very little is known about it and only a few stranded specimens have ever been seen.

Fam. Balaenopteridae—Rorquals

The baleen whales known as 'Rorquals' have up to a hundred parallel, longitudinal pleats and grooves in the skin of the under surface of the body running from the chin to the hinder part of the thorax or even as far as the navel. These are about $2\frac{1}{2}$ inches wide with deep grooves of about the same width between them, except in the Humpback whale in which the grooves are wider. The name 'Rorqual', given to all these whales on account of these pleats, is derived from the Norwegian *ror hval*—tube whale. It is not known what the function of the pleats may be. Lillie, the biologist on Scott's *Terra Nova* Expedition, thought that they must give greater elasticity to the skin under the mouth so as to enable the whale to engulf enormous quantities of its small food, or else to take into the mouth huge volumes of water. But this does not really account for the grooves running as far back as the navel so it has been suggested that they might perhaps provide elasticity during deep dives. Yet the Sperm whale, which is believed to dive deeper than the Rorquals, does not have any grooves, or only poorly developed ones. Another theory is that the grooves have something to do with the speed at which Rorquals swim. Most Rorquals can swim at speeds around 10 to 12 knots, and more in short sprints, whereas all the whales which lack grooves are slow swimmers. It is possible that the grooves and the ridges between them may act like bilge keels on a ship's bottom and have a stabilizing function.

The Rorpuals have a fine stream-lined shape, a flattened triangular head with two blowholes side by side on top of it, and a roundly pointed snout. The mouth is relatively huge and the baleen plates are triangular in shape but shorter, broader and less flexible than those of Right whales. The lower jaws are slender, a couple of curved rods. To this day they can be seen in the Faroes, Shetlands and Norway forming the entrance of many a retired whaleman's home. The eye, like that of Right whales, is low down near the angle of the jaw. The body is rotund and fusiform with the flanks flattened in the vertical plane.

In the middle line of the back of Rorquals, about two-thirds of the distance from the snout to the flukes, is a sickle-shaped back fin. Like the flukes it contains no bones, as do the back fins of fishes, but is built entirely of skin and fibrous tissue. Its shape varies in different species and since it is the only distinctive part of the whale ever visible above the surface at sea its size and shape enable whalers to identify the species.

The Rorquals are the most important whales commercially and, since the middle of the nineteenth century, the most hunted, nearly to the verge of extinction first in the Arctic and subsequently in the Antarctic. Before the invention of the harpoon gun mounted on a fast catcher they were much too swift to be approached by whalers in open boats.

The Blue Whale

There are six species of Rorqual but they are not all commercially valuable. The largest and most important, giving the biggest yield of first quality oil, is the Blue whale or Sibbald's Rorqual (Fig. 3a), named after Sir Robert Sibbald, an Edinburgh doctor in the late seventeenth century who founded the Botanical Gardens in that city and described what was probably a stranded Blue whale.

Fig. 3(a) Blue Whale

The Blue whale is a most majestic animal, the largest living creature on earth. A full grown cow may reach a length of nearly a hundred feet, about that of a three-car electric train, and in the middle of the body the height is about 20 feet, roughly that of a train. It is a dark slate-blue all over except for the undersides of the flippers which are white. The shade of blue varies a good deal and young whales tend to be paler then old ones. The body is flecked with white marblings which are mostly confineb to the undersides but sometimes extend up on to the flanks and back. The head is very flat and short, less than a third of the total length of the body, while the snout is obtusely rounded rather than pointed. The stout, stiff baleen plates are velvet black. The crescentic back fin about two-thirds along the length of the body is small, low and inconspicuous.

Blue whales tend to travel in small groups of up to half a dozen, usually spoken of as 'schools', which is the same word as 'shoals'. The young ones, however, are often solitary. The Blue whale frequents the edge of the pack ice during the summer and may penetrate into the ice itself.

Since 1961 Japanese and Russian scientists claim to have established the existence of a smaller kind of Blue whale, the Pygmy Blue whale, which is found in warmer Subantarctic waters of the Indian Ocean. In 1964 two Russians described this as a sub-species characterized by a smaller length at puberty and a relatively shorter tail region than in the Blue whale (Zemsky, V. A. and Boronin, V.A., 1964).

The Fin Whale

Next in size, and once second, then first in commercial importance, is the Fin whale, Finback or Common Rorqual (Fig. 3b). The cow may reach a length of 82 feet, though not often, and 75 feet is a fairly good average. It is a slimmer, more lithe and elegant whale than the Blue with a fine, pointed snout and a sickle-shaped back fin, about a foot high in a large cow. It is dark grey in colour, though when fresh it looks nearly black, on the back and sides. The throat, chest and belly are creamy white with white under the flippers and flukes. On the chin, snout and lower jaw there is a curious lop-sided distribution of the grey and white, dark on the left side but light on the right, while in the mouth the right side is dark and the left light. The baleen plates, longer and more flexible than those of the Blue, are all bluish-grey except for about the front third of them on the right-hand side which are creamy white. The reason for this strange asymmetry is not known and one can only speculate. It occurs in only one other species of whale, Bryde's whale, to be mentioned shortly, but then only occasionally and not as a general rule. It has been suggested that it may result from the Fin whale's habit of swimming on its side from time to time. All aquatic animals tend to develop dark coloration uppermost and pale tints underneath so as to be obscured to some extent both from above and below. A fish called the Nile perch swims the right way up when young and is dark above and light below like other fish, but when it grows older a maladjustment of the swim bladder causes it to turn over on its back and spend the rest of its life swimming belly upwards. It then reverses its colour pattern and becomes dark on the belly and pale on the back. That Fin whales do frequently swim on their sides is quite well known—the Norwegians call it 'boltering'. Dolphins racing alongside the bows of a ship and darting in and out of the slip-stream, 'riding the bow wave', can be seen repeatedly to turn on their sides. Bottle-nosed dolphins in the New York aquarium can be seen swimming round and round their tank on their sides. Many whales seem to find it easier to swim like this, particularly when diving or turning, so that the tail in effect strikes laterally like that of a fish.

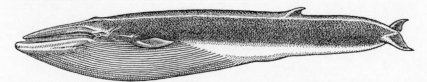

Fig. 3(b) Fin Whale

Fin whales are more gregarious than Blues and often travel in large schools. Many observers have seen hundreds of Fin whales together within a small area but I personally have never seen more than about twenty spouting together in various directions. They do not, of course, all spout simultaneously but one after the other at random, like exclamation marks against the grey sky. A dozen together is quite a common sight. Fin whales do not frequent the edge of the pack ice so much as Blues but are found more plentifully in rather warmer water some fifty miles or more away from the ice. It has been said that one of the reasons why Fin whales predominated more and more in the catches after World War II, while Blue whales became scarce, is that modern whaling expeditions are so expensive that firms hesitate to risk their ships near the ice and content themselves with the smaller, lower-yielding Fins rather than venture in pursuit of Blues near the ice edge. This, I think, is merely a refusal to admit to having killed the goose that lays the golden eggs.

The Sei Whale

Towards the end of the season at South Georgia a third kind of Rorqual used to appear in the catches. This was the Sei whale or

Rudolphi's Rorqual (Fig. 3c), named after Karl Asmund Rudolphi, Professor of Anatomy at Berlin University at the beginning of the nineteenth century, who founded the Berlin zoological museum and first described the Sei whale. It is called the Sei whale because off the coast of Norway it makes its appearance at the same time of year as the *seje* or coalfish. Sometimes it is called the Pollack whale for a similar reason. It reaches a length of about 60 feet and has a slender shape, stouter amidships than the Fin but slimmer than the Blue, with the rear part of the body finely flattened in the vertical plane. The profile of the head is a little less flat, rather more Roman, than that of other Rorquals while the back fin is more sickle-shaped and still larger than that of the Fin whale. An immediately distinctive character is that the ventral grooves, unlike those of the Blue and Fin, do not extend as far back as the navel but stop quite a long way short of it, about half-way between the tip of the flipper, when laid flat against the body, and the navel itself.

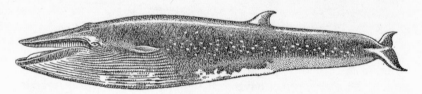

Fig. 3(c) Sei Whale

The colour of the Sei whale is bluish-black shading into grey along the sides and underneath, quite symmetrical about the head, jaws and shoulders. A conspicuous oval pale area, shading into grey on the sides, throat and belly, occupies the chest. This and the dark undersides of the flukes and flippers at once distinguish the Sei from the Fin whale, but even more distinctive are the baleen plates. They are mostly black, though there may be a few white ones here and there, but the hairs formed by the inner edges of the plates are soft and fine as a fleece, almost like silk. These enable the Sei whale to strain very small animals out of the water and off the coast of Norway the Sei whale feeds on swarms of 'brit' or herring food. Off the coasts of Japan and Korea, where the Sei whale is regularly hunted, it is known as the sardine whale (*Iwashi kujaira*) because it feeds on small shoaling fishes.

There were always long faces at South Georgia when the Sei whales appeared in February for it was taken to mean that no more of the bigger Rorquals would be caught that season, or fewer anyway. This was usually true because they had by then passed the island on their way southward and the Seis were believed to be following in their wake from the coast of South America.

The Piked Whale

When the *Discovery II* visited the Bay of Whales in January 1936 we had an opportunity to see the smallest of all the Rorquals, called the Piked whale or Lesser Rorqual (Fig. 3d). It is also known to the Norwegians as the Minke whale after a whaling gunner named Meincke who accidentally shot one in mistake for a Blue and thus achieved a rather dubious immortality. It certainly was quite a mistake for the Minke is a pygmy, not more than 30 ft. in length. It might almost be regarded as a pygmy Fin whale, and indeed it is remarkable how all the great whales seem to have diminutive cousins.

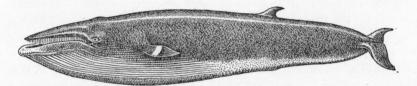

Fig. 3(d) Minke or Piked Whale

Although so small the Piked whale is rather more robust in build than either the Fin or the Sei. Its distinctive characters are the yellowish baleen plates and the white band across the middle of the flipper. The flipper and the back fin are comparatively large and the ventral pleats reach to the navel. The colours are blue-grey on the back but white underneath.

The Piked whale occurs all over the world in high latitudes and off the coast of Europe in August and September. It is seen as far north as Spitsbergen and in the Antarctic penetrates farther south than any other whale, often close up to the coast of the continent. In the Bay of Whales we saw dozens of them gambolling among the ice floes and blowing near the icing-sugar face of the barrier. It was the presence of large numbers of these frolicsome little whales that prompted Shackleton in 1908 to give the name Bay of Whales to this indentation of the barrier face.

In general this is an inshore whale and seems to shun the open sea. It often jumps right out of the water and has a way of standing vertically in ice holes, as Captain Scott described, with only the blowholes and snout showing. These small pools in the ice are sometimes breathing holes which the whales have made themselves, and which they try their dest to keep open by bumping up against the ice floes from below. It is delieved that many of them perish during the Antarctic winter because, in spite of their efforts, their breathing holes freeze over.

Piked whales have been hunted commercially off the coast of Norway and were used as food by the Norwegians during World War II. In the peak year of their fishery, 1949, nearly 4,000 were killed. In the Antarctic they are considered too small for the whalers to bother about—as yet.

The Bryde's Whale

This is a Rorqual that is rarely seen and was not recognized as a separate species until 1913. It is a subtropical whale found mainly off the coast of South Africa but it has been reported from the West Indies. It was named after Consul Johan Bryde (pronounced 'breeder') who in 1909 erected the first whaling station at Durban and, in the following year, a second at Saldanha Bay, Cape Province. It was thought to be a Sei until a Norwegian (Ø. Olsen, 1913) described it and named it. It is intermediate in size between the Sei and the Piked whale, reaching a length of about 42 feet, but is much more lithe and slender than any other Rorqual, with narrow pointed flippers. The colour is bluish-black on the back and white underneath except under the throat and chin which are blue-grey. The baleen plates are comparatively short and broad with coarse bristles. In the forepart of the mouth for about two feet they are mostly white with some grey stripes, but at the rear of the mouth they become black with grey stripes. As might be expected from the breadth and coarseness of the baleen plates this whale eats coarse food, mostly the large shoals of sardine-like fishes which abound off subtropical coasts, especially off southern Africa. Little is known about this rather rare whale, and I myself have never seen one.

The Humpback Whale

The Humpback whale (Fig. 3e) was once among the most important of commercial whales but is today almost on the verge of extinction through over-exploitation and is protected by international agreement. It is such an odd-looking animal and so different from other Rorquals that many writers do not class it as a Rorqual at all, but since this word is not in any sense a scientific term but merely a convenient collective name for all whalebone whales with ventral pleats I shall continue to call the Humpback a Rorqual. Its pleats are much fewer in number and broader than those of other Rorquals for while the Blue whale has eighty to a hundred the Humpback never has more than twenty and they are five to eight inches wide, running from the chin to the navel. It is an ungainly creature in appearance, very knobbly and barrel-shaped. It got its name because when diving it presents its short stout back fin in such a way as to give an impression of a hump. It is not actually any more humpbacked than any other whale but, as Captain Scammon has said, 'decidedly ugly' with a broad rounded snout, rotund body and long knobbly flippers about a third of the length of the body. The Norwegians call it the *knølhval*, the knobbly whale. There are knobs and bumps on the head and jaws and on the underneath of the flippers. A row of them runs along the top of the head

Fig. 3(e) Humpback Whale

from the blowholes to the snout and another series along the upper jaw, on the chin and lower jaw. They mark the positions where coarse, sparse hairs grow, one or two stout bristles sprouting from each one. The hinder margins of the tail flukes are wavy and not smooth like those of other Rorquals.

The Humpback reaches a length of about 50 feet and its colours are black and white. The back is always uniformly black, the flippers always and the flukes usually white underneath. There is a great deal of variation in the amount and pattern of the white underneath the body with more white in younger than in older animals, which show a lot more black below as well as above. The baleen plates are dark grey with bristles of the same colour, but an occasional white plate may be seen.

This is also to a certain extent a coastal whale. In tropical and subtropical waters it frequents the coasts of all the southern lands, swimming along slowly in large schools. Like the Piked whale it is playful, even skittish, and often gambols, rolling over in the water, lifting its long, flexible flippers in a flurry of foam, bringing them down with resounding smacks on the surface. Whenever it dives it lifts its tail flukes out of the water and seems to descend vertically into the depths. Sometimes it leaps bodily into the air and lands back on the water with a report that can be heard for miles and a whirlpool of foam. From the flight deck of an aircraft carrier off Brisbane in July 1945 we watched dozens of Humpbacks disporting themselves in a sea of purest blue, their white underparts gleaming as they leapt and thrashed around. Many of them were close in to the shore, for Humpbacks can often be seen rubbing themselves against rocks perhaps in order to rid themselves of the extraordinary number of external parasites which infest them, especially in warm waters. These probably irritate and itch, so that the whale loves to rub itself against rocks.

Like all Rorquals except Bryde's whale the Humpback is found in the months of the southern summer in Antarctic waters. In the winter months it is taken mostly close to the coasts of the southern continents.

It is believed that all the Rorquals roam the open ocean in the tropics and subtropics during the winter months, travelling almost as far north as the Equator. In the northern hemisphere they frequent waters off Norway, Spitsbergen, Iceland and Greenland during the summer months, moving down the coasts of Europe and America in the winter as far south as Portugal and the Azores and the coast of Virginia. In the tropics and subtropics they mate and bear their young but do not feed until they return to the polar regions in the spring.

Although the Rorquals approach tropical waters in all oceans yet the northern and southern populations do not mingle so far as is known. In fact they are permanently out of phase for when the southern population is in the tropics the northern one is in the Arctic and vice versa. This separation of two seemingly identical populations into two isolated sections at opposite poles of the earth is a common state of affairs among marine animals, spoken of as 'bipolarity'. It arises from the division of a single unified population into two sections in the not very distant geological past, which have not yet had time to evolve into distinct divergent types.

Fam. Eschrichtiidae—Grey Whales

One more whalebone whale, belonging to a separate family, must be mentioned. This is the Californian Grey whale (Fig. 4) or, as the Japanese call it, the Devil Fish (*Koku kujaira*). In many respects it may be looked upon as intermediate between the Rorquals and the Right whales. It is rather small, reaching a length of about 45 feet, and its back is slightly humped, with no back fin but with a series of about ten low bumps or undulations along the rear third of the middle line of the back. The tail flukes are thick and heavy, less deeply notched in the middle line and not faired to the trailing edge—the tail is altogether a more spade-like affair than that of Rorquals. The flippers are large and rounded and the outlines of four fingers can be seen in them. The head is small and the baleen plates are thick and heavy. There are no ventral pleats but one, very occasionally two, grooves on each side in the throat region. The colour, as the name indicates, is grey but there are numerous white flecks on the back and above and below the flippers. Bands of white or lighter grey separate the second, third and fourth fingers.

Fig. 4 Californian Grey Whale

This is another coastal whale, frequenting the American and Asian coasts of the Pacific Ocean. Fossils found when the Zuyder Zee was drained in 1937 show that it occurred fairly lately, geologically speaking, in the Atlantic Ocean off the coast of Europe, but certainly not in historical times. It makes regular seasonal migrations from the Arctic (Bering Sea) to subtropical waters, appearing off the coasts of Oregon and California in winter (November to May) when the cows enter the shallow coastal lagoons in order to give birth to their young. At this time, too, it appears off the coasts of Japan and Korea. Like the Humpback it is a playful creature and loves to roll and disport itself in the surf, often leaping right out of the water. It often lies motionless, basking in the shallows, especially in the huge fields of ribbon weed which clothe the Californian coastal lagoons. Like the Humpback it is heavily infested with external parasites and wears a 'bonnet' like the Biscay Right whale, crawling with 'whale lice'. It often rubs itself against rocks in order to scratch or rid itself of these unwelcome passengers. It is believed to feed in Arctic waters on bottom-living crustacea, though how it does so is not known. Since it was always hunted off the coast of California or Japan during the winter months when it does not feed, little is known about its feeding habits.

During the nineteenth century the Californian Grey was hunted a great deal, first by coastal American Indians, using dories and spears, and later by Yankee Sperm whalers, who came in from the Pacific using small boats with lances and a type of gun that fired a bomb lance. Later, as the Grey whales became scarcer and more shy, the Yankees used small sailing boats and chased them southwards on the prevailing northerly winds. A fearful ruthlessness characterized this hunting by the Yankees who used to kill the calves in the lagoons in order that the bereaved mothers, who would not desert their calves, should fall an easy prey. Captain Scammon estimated that 11,000 Grey whales were killed between 1846 and 1875 and they were practically exterminated by 1895, when they were protected by law. Roy Chapman Andrews found a fishery over a hundred years old for Grey whales still flourishing in Japan in 1912. In the U.S.A. the Grey whale is still protected but is now believed to be increasing in numbers. Scammon (1874) estimated that in 1853–56 there were about 30,000 Grey whales off the coast of California but during the winter season of 1959–60 a count by the U.S. Fish and Wildlife Service showed that somewhat over 6,000 Grey whales passed Point Loma, San Diego, during the season (Rice, D. W., 1961).

This completes the list of whalebone or baleen whales. The toothed whales are far more varied and numerous and most of them are of small size, such as the dolphins and porpoises. Only one toothed whale, the Sperm whale, is of importance in modern Antarctic whaling, but many of the smaller ones, such as the Bottle-nosed whale, the Narwhal, the Beluga and the Pilot whale or Blackfish, as well as the common porpoise, have in the past been commercially hunted in northern waters, and some to a certain extent still are.

The toothed whales are flesh eaters, except one small fresh-water dolphin in West Africa. They have teeth in both jaws or only in the lower and feed on squids, fish or crustacea. A few are more catholic in their diet and include diving birds. The Killer whale extends the list to include seals and the flesh of other whales.

Fam. Physeteridae—Sperm Whales

By far the most important of the toothed whales, and the only one now hunted commercially on a large scale, is the Sperm whale or

Cachalot (Fig. 5a), the latter a word of Basque origin. In appearance it is one of the strangest creatures in the world. Its body is roughly cylindrical, tapering away sharply behind to the tail flukes. The forward third of the tapering cylinder is made up of the head, which is shaped like a boiler the sides of which have been hammered in so as to make a shallow longitudinal depression along each side below the middle line. The depression becomes shallower towards the rear and fuses with the rotundity of the boiler behind the angle of the mouth where the head becomes the body. The head is rounded in front but when looked at from in front it is pear-shaped because of the lateral depressions. The greatest diameter of the body is just behind the head on top of which near the fore end is a single S-shaped blowhole, off centre to the left of the middle line, a curious asymmetry which extends to the bones of

Fig. 5 (a) Sperm Whale or Cachalot

the skull itself. Underneath the head are the narrow lower jaws, two apposed rods, each bearing twenty or thirty conical teeth made of tooth substance (dentine) but without enamel covering. They fit neatly into sockets in the upper jaw which bears no teeth, although rudiments of them can be felt with the finger inside each of the sockets. In many Sperm whales these do not break through the skin. The lower jaw of the mouth is, in fact, a single toothed bar formed by the two apposed mandibles which diverge backwards to form a Y where they join the base of the skull. The upper jaws form a longitudinal slot which receives the toothed bar. This slit-like mouth is well beneath the head and does not extend as far forward as the rounded boss which forms the forehead jutting forward a foot or two in front of the mouth. Above the angle of the mouth, in the smooth cliff of the side of the body, is the cunning little eye, quite independent of its fellow, as is that of the Rorqual, with its own individual lateral view of the world. There is no back fin but a series of six to eight low bumps, diminishing in size backwards, along the middle line of the back in its hinder third. The foremost and largest of these was called the 'hump' by the old Sperm whalers. The flippers, small and spade-shaped, are carried low down on the side of the body a little above and behind the angle of the mouth. The tail flukes are faired to their hinder margins.

The skin of the Sperm whale is smooth and there are a number of grooves and wrinkles which vary a good deal. There are always two grooves diverging backwards beneath the throat but no parallel pleasts. The colour is dark slate-grey shading to silvery or white underneath. The roof of the mouth and the insides of the lower jaws are white. Old bull whales have a lot of white about them with a white rosette on the rounded boss of the forehead. They often have a wrinkled, corrugated look like a baked apple.

The full-grown bull Sperm whale is about twice as large as the full-grown cow and may reach a length of about 60 feet. In this size difference between the sexes the Sperm and several other toothed whales are the opposite of baleen whales in which the full-grown cow is always larger than the bull.

The name 'Sperm' whale refers to the waxy substance called 'spermaceti' which the whale carries in a reservoir in its head. The word means 'sperm or seed of the whale' (*spermon*, seed, *ketos*, whale) because the old-time whalers thought it was the whale's seminal fluid. It is a waxy substance used in the past for making church candles, largely for use in Roman Catholic churches. Its function is to increase the buoyancy of the head.

The principal feeding and breeding grounds of the Sperm whale are in tropical and subtropical seas and it forms a high proportion of the catches at the whaling stations at Durban, where we saw it in 1930, and in Japan and Chile, and of the catches of factory ships all over the North Pacific. In the Arctic and Antarctic almost all the Sperm whales taken are large bulls. The diet is mainly squid, many of them of enormous size.

The Sperm whale, too, has a small relation, the Pygmy Sperm whale, which does not exceed 13 feet, in length but is known only from specimens stranded in different places all over the world. It is of no commercial importance. It resembles its large cousin in having a single S-shaped blowhole to the left of the middle line, a spermaceti reservoir in the head and teeth only in the lower jaw, but its shape is different. The head is smaller in proportion to the rest of the body and is more rotund, sloped and not boiler-shaped. The mouth is recognizable as such and is not a mere rod fitting into a slot.

Fam. Ziphiidae—Bottle-nosed and Beaked Whales

These are small whales 15 to 30 feet in length and in some respects they resemble the Sperm. They have teeth in the lower jaw only but they do not all break through. In the Bottle-nosed whale the head is rounded in front to form a bulging knee-like forehead (hence the whale's name) which carries a spermaceti reservoir in the bull but not in the cow. Beneath the forehead a tapering beak projects forward. A single crescentic blowhole is centrally placed with the concavity of the crescent facing forward. Beneath the throat two deep grooves meet to form a V. The colour is dark grey and black on top but lighter grey to white underneath.

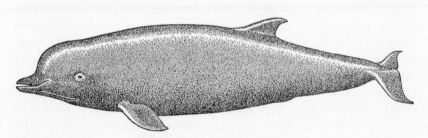

Fig. 5(b) Bottle-nosed Whale

The Bottle-nosed whale (Fig. 5b) was hunted in the Arctic in the middle of the nineteenth century when Right whales were becoming scarce and the harpoon gun had not yet been invented. In the southern hemisphere there is a Bottle-nosed whale which is a different species from the northern one and has never been hunted commercially.

The food consists of squids, often, it would seem, enormous numbers of them for thousands of their horny beaks have been found in one stomach. However, it would be a mistake to suppose that these have all been gobbled at one sitting, so to speak, for squid beaks are made of chitin and are highly indigestible. Indeed it is possible that the stomach never gets rid of them at all and they may represent a lifetime's accumulation.

Cuvier's Beaked whale (named after Baron Cuvier, the great French zoologist of the nineteenth century) or Goose-beaked whale runs to a length of about 25 feet and has no knee-like forehead but a short blunt beak. The bull has a pair of teeth at the tip of the lower jaw only, but in the cow they do not break through. The colours are dark above and light below but some specimens have been described as light on the head, shoulders and back but dark elsewhere. This, too, is a whale known only from world-wide strandings and is of no commercial importance.

Fam. Delphinidae—Porpoises and Dolphins

This family embraces all those toothed whales, both large and small, but mostly small, which we speak of as porpoises and dolphins. It is often asked what exactly is the difference between a porpoise and a dolphin, and this is a difficult question to answer because the two words are not valid scientific terms and are very imprecisely used. For instance, the beautiful green and gold deep-sea fish known as the Dorado is also called the dolphin or dolphin fish. In America what we call the Bottle-nosed dolphin (not the Bottle-nosed whale) is called the Common Porpoise while what we call by that name is quite a different animal. In general, when speaking only of the smaller members of this family, we may say that porpoises have a rounded head without a beak, a triangular back fin and spade-shaped teeth, while dolphins have a beak, a sickle-shaped back fin and pointed teeth. From this rough division, however, we must exclude the larger members of the family which usually rank as whales, as befitting their size. These are the Killer whale or Grampus, the Narwhal, the White whale and the Pilot whale or Blackfish. They are all really enormous dolphins which tend to mix the characters mentioned above.

The Killer Whale or Grampus

This (Fig. 5c), the largest member of the family, has a blunt head without a beak merging evenly with the powerful, streamlined body. The flippers are rounded in shape and the back fin triangular. The colours are black above and white below sharply demarcated from one another. A lens of white is islanded in the black above the eye and there is a rather more diffuse white saddle behind the back fin. On each flank an oval peninsula of white runs upwards from the vent on to the side. The full-grown bull, like that of the Sperm, is about twice the size of the cow and may reach a length of 30 feet. In old bulls a great increase takes place in the size of the flippers which may grow (Fraser, F. C., 1937) from one-ninth to one-fifth of the total length of the body. At the same time the height of the back fin increases also and may reach 6 feet. This great black sail is an extraordinary sight at sea as it slices through the waves. It often cannot support its own weight, for it contains no skeleton, so that its apex flops over sideways.

There are about a dozen smooth conical teeth in both jaws, flattened in a plane at right angles to the line of the jaw and spaced alternately in the upper and lower jaws, not opposite one another, so that they interlock and form a highly efficient, in fact deadly, trap-like seizing and cutting mechanism.

The name Grampus is said to derive from the French *grapois*, a contraction of *grand poisson* or *crassus piscis*, a fat fish. It is the most formidable of the dolphins, a savage and ruthless beast of prey which roams

Fig. 5(c) Killer Whale or Grampus

the oceans all over the world but is commonest in colder waters. It attacks whales, seals, birds and fish, usually hunting in packs, like wolves, as many as twenty or thirty together. It seizes baleen whales behind the back fin and bites pieces out of the flesh, and whales with wounds in this region are quite often seen on the whaling stations. Killers often go for the carcasses while they are being towed alongside the catchers back to the whaling station, tearing lumps out of the tongue as it lolls from the open mouth. There are many stories of their voracity and of the way they attack with apparent co-ordination and intelligence, but most of these stories, I think, can be taken with a grain of salt. One hears of tactics and of signals between members of the herd, but it must be remembered that even at close quarters in calm weather the behaviour of whales at sea is difficult to observe. Little can be seen but black shapes momentarily glimpsed and flurries of foam. Often the water is too opaque for more than dim shadows to be seen beneath the surface. At any considerable distance or in rough weather it becomes really impossible to see what is going on, but it is always easy to imagine and invent stories. Killers are certainly voracious feeders and devour seals and penguins in great numbers. There are records of as many as fourteen seals, or the remains of them, in the stomach of one whale, but there is no evidence of the time it took the whale to devour them and bones may take a very long time to digest. Many tales, too, have been told by Antarctic explorers about the ferocity of Killers. Ponting, on Scott's *Terra Nova* Expedition, related how they appeared in the small spaces among ice floes and, thrusting their heads vertically out of the water, glared balefully around in search of prey. They then bumped underneath the floes as though trying to dislodge the men on them. Certainly Killers are aggressive hunters and I would not care to be in the water anywhere near them, yet I do not think their aggressiveness extends to human beings not in the water. That they do appear in small spaces among ice floes and thrust their snouts above the surface is very probable. I have seen Piked whales and seals do this many times. They are not looking for prey but coming up to breathe, and Killers no doubt do the same. That they bump the floes with their back is also probable but is almost certainly either accidental or an attempt to enlarge the breathing hole in the ice.

Other Small Whales

There are several other members of this family which are large enough to be called whales, as distinct from the much smaller dolphins and porpoises.

The False Killer is related to the true Killer but is smaller and black all over. It is better known from specimens stranded on beaches than from those caught at sea. It congregates in vast herds of hundreds of individuals which are apt to get stranded in a mass on some sloping shore. The Pilot, Caa'ing Whale or Blackfish, a round-headed dolphin running to about 25–28 feet, is slaughtered in great numbers in the Faroes by being herded and driven into narrow fjords. On the Scottish coast this is called 'caa'ing', a word which does not refer, as some think it does, to the noise which the animal makes when it blows.

The above, although called whales on account of their size, are really large dolphins and are northern forms though the Pilot whale has relations in the South Atlantic, Pacific and Indian Oceans. We saw them often enough around the Falkland Islands leaping through the water in large schools.

Porpoises and Dolphins

The true porpoises and dolphins are too numerous for detailed mention. The common black and white porpoise of our seas is well known and is a pest of our inshore fisheries. It can be seen off our south coast resorts any summer's day, its black fins turning through the water as though attached to wheels beneath the surface. The head is rounded and the back fin triangular.

The common dolphin has a well-defined beak and a sickle-shaped back fin. It is black on the back and white underneath but between the two colours is a lateral strip of mixed bands of grey, white and yellow. It is larger than the common porpoise, reaching a length of eight feet, whereas the porpoise never exceeds six feet. It, too, feeds on fishes but prefers the smaller shoaling fishes such as pilchards, herring and sardines which it devours in masses. Perhaps on account of its liking for sardines it tends to frequent rather warmer waters than the porpoise but is by no means restricted to them.

In the United States what we call the Bottle-nosed dolphin (as distinct from the Bottle-nosed whale) is called the Common Porpoise. It is a large dolphin which may reach 12 feet in length with a short but pronounced beak. The back is black, grey or brown and the belly white. It is the commonest dolphin on the eastern American seaboard and during the nineteenth century was caught off the long sandy beaches of North Carolina by means of heavy seine nets 2,000 yards in length with a boat at either end. It is the dolphin which has been kept for some years at the Marineland Seaquarium, Florida, and in the New York Aquarium and studied in great detail. It has been found to be remarkably amenable to teaching and training, easily learns games and tricks and shows signs of considerable intelligence. It emits various sounds which are believed to be capable of interpretation as a kind of language.

In the Southern Ocean the commonest dolphins we saw belonged to the species known as Commerson's dolphin which is not more than about 5 feet long. It does not have a very pronounced beak and has a somewhat rounded back fin. The head is black and so is the tail behind the back fin which is included in the rear black area. Between the two black portions the body is pure white. There is an oval of white in the black under the chin and another of black in the white around the vent. We often saw these piebald shapes, especially near the Falkland Islands and the Magellan Straits, playing in the ship's bow wave. They would suddenly appear in groups of half a dozen or more, keeping up with the ship travelling at 12 knots and effortlessly overtaking her. Every now and then one or two would dart away in a wide circle and return. As they knifed through the foam of the bow wave they often turned on their sides and sometimes leapt clear of the water altogether. Then suddenly they would vanish as though bored with the game. This usually happened at the moment when I arrived on the fo'c'sle head with my camera.

Since the time of the ancient Greeks dolphins have been believed to be beneficial animals, except perhaps by fishermen, with a special affection for mankind. The Greeks believed that they carried away the spirits of the dead. One Greek story relates how the poet Arion, who had grown rich on the proceeds of his poetry and music-making, was travelling by ship to Corinth when the sailors planned to murder him for his money. He begged them to let him play a last tune and his music drew dolphins to the ship one of which bore him ashore on its back, rescuing him. Aristotle stated that dolphins have a special affection for little boys and the boy who rode on a dolphin's back was immortalized by Rafael in a statue now in the Hermitage Museum, Leningrad. Dolphins are depicted often in Greek sculpture and painting. From the time of Pliny to our day they have been reputed to help fishermen by driving fish into their nets but none of these stories, I think, would really bear close examination and most fishermen in these days regard dolphins as a pest. There are many instances, too, of dolphins supposedly piloting ships into port. Some of the dolphins which were supposed to do this became so familiar to sailors that they earned names for themselves. The most famous of these was Pelorus Jack, a dolphin or, perhaps, a Pilot whale which for thirty-two years up to 1914 used to meet ships in the Pelorus Channel, in the South Island of New Zealand, and escort them up narrow Marlborough Sound. During the last ten years of his life Pelorus Jack was a national institution, protected by law, and anyone who shot at or tried to harm him was liable for a fine of up to £100. I do not think these stories either would stand up to close examination. Even in the best authenticated case, Pelorus Jack, there was no real evidence that it was the same dolphin every time and in fact Jack was only playing in the bow wave and not escorting the ship at all. Dolphins riding the bow wave of ships entering ports the world over are a common sight.

All the foregoing members, great and small, of the dolphin and porpoise family (Delphinidae) have the seven neck vertebrae fused together in a solid block, except the Pilot or Caa'ing whale which has six fused and one at the rear independent. For this reason they are all classed together in a sub-family, Delphininae. There remain two other members of the family which have all the neck vertebrae separate and for this reason these are placed together in another sub-family, Delphinapterinae. They are the Narwhal and the Beluga or White whale, both of which are small whales or large dolphins whichever one pleases.

Both of these are found only in northern waters near the ice edge. The Narwhal runs to a length of 12 to 16 feet and has a rounded head and no back fin. It is bluish-grey in colour. It has only a single pair of teeth on each side of the upper jaw. These remain embedded in the gum in the cow but in the bull one of them, usually though not always the left one, grows forward as a long pointed, spirally sculptured tusk. Sometimes it is the right tooth that forms the tusk and in rare cases there are two tusks, both with right-handed spiralling. Like the teeth of Sperm whales the tusk is built of tooth substance (dentine) but has no enamel. It may grow to a length of 8 feet and have a circumference at the base of six or seven inches. In the early nineteenth century the Narwhal was hunted along the northern ice edge, especially in Baffin Bay, for the ivory of its tusks and the high grade oil which its blubber yields.

The tusk of the Narwhal probably gave origin to that mythical heraldic beast, the Unicorn. In the sixteenth century the Basque whalers brought back Narwhal tusks from their Arctic voyages and some were imported into England. Nobody knew where they came from or connected them with the sea in any way, certainly not with whales, so that a four-footed animal like a horse was invented to fit them.

The Narwhal feeds on squids, fish or crustaceans and has no teeth other than the pair which form the tusk or tusks. This itself does not appear to have any particular use though uses have been invented for it, giving it an offensive or defensive function. More probably it is just a secondary sexual character having no particular function.

The Beluga or White whale is found mainly in the Hudson Bay and Davis Strait area and in the Gulf of St. Lawrence. It grows to a length of about 14 feet and is not unlike the Narwhal but is snow white when young, gradually turning yellow as it ages. It has no tusk but about ten teeth on each side in both upper and lower jaws. It feeds on quite large fish, squids and crustaceans.

The Beluga is a very gregarious whale and moves about in large

herds. It is the first whale reputed to make noises, it was said, audible
from the deck of a whaling ship. Because of its yellow colour and the
squealing sounds it was said to make it was known to British Arctic
whalers as the 'sea canary'. It was at one time hunted, and to some
extent still is, for its hide, which makes excellent leather and bootlaces.

Fam. Platanistidae—River Dolphins

This is a family of small dolphins which live in tropical rivers and
lakes. The Susu or Ganges dolphin, the Boutu or Amazon dolphin
and the La Plata dolphin are examples. They all have long slender
beaks with about thirty teeth in the upper and lower jaws, though the
La Plata dolphin has 50 to 60 in each jaw. The Susu is quite blind and
its eyes are greatly reduced while the Boutu also has very small eyes
and feeble eyesight. They all feed on mud-living fishes or fresh-water
shrimps, nosing about in the mud for them with their long snouts.
The Susu feeds at night and in captivity refuses food in the daytime.
One member of the family, the Cross River dolphin of the Cameroons,
is the only Cetacean which is entirely vegetarian. It feeds on mangrove
leaves, water weeds and grasses.

CHAPTER 3

Produce of Whales

Whale Oil

Whale oil, or 'train' oil as it used to be called, from the Dutch *traan*, a tear or drop, and nothing to do with railways, is the oil of baleen whales as distinct from that of Sperm whales. It is a true fat, that is to say it consists chiefly of the glycerides of saturated and unsaturated fatty acids. The oil of Sperm and Bottle-nosed whales, on the other hand, is a liquid wax.

The saturated acids in whale oil are myristic, palmitic and stearic acids and some others, while oleic acid is one of the principal unsaturated ones. An unsaturated acid does not hold the full number of hydrogen atoms that it is capable of holding at saturation.

Every tissue of the whalebone whale's body is impregnated with oil identical with and derived from that which its food contains, but some of the tissues contain more than others. The blubber yields the largest amount and the highest quality, between 50 and 80 per cent by weight. The bones yield 40–60 per cent and the meat 6–7 per cent (Brandt, K., 1940). There are four qualities or grades of whale oil on the market. The finest is Grade 1, a clear, pale straw-coloured liquid with a specific gravity at room temperature (15°C.) of 0·92, water being 1·0. It is, therefore, slightly lighter and less dense than fresh distilled water. Grade 2 is amber in colour, Grade 3 pale brown and Grade 4 darker brown still. The yellow colour, darkening to brown in the poorer grades, is due to the presence of free or unsaturated fatty acids. In Grade 1 they amount to only about 1 per cent but Grade 4 may contain as much as 60 per cent. They give the oil a most unpleasant fishy smell and taste which inceases as the colour darkens.

Different tissues give different grades of oil. In Rorquals Grade 1 comes from the blubber and Grade 2 from a second boiling of the blubber. Grade 3 comes from a third blubber boiling or from the meat and bones. Grade 4 comes from blood, viscera and scraps. Until the early years of this century the whalers took only the blubber in order to get only the higher grades of oil and cast the stripped carcass adrift. In 1911 the Falkland Islands Government introduced regulations compelling the use of the whole carcass and they have been in force ever since. Thirty years ago these regulations necessitated the use of separate boilers for the blubber, meat, bones and for the viscera and blood, and the different grades of oil that came from them had to be stored in separate tanks. Then a regulation was introduced which required all carcasses to be used within a limited time after capture because old, decomposing carcasses give a low grade oil. When I was in South Georgia, during the middle of the season when whales were plentiful, the whaling harbours were full of carcasses rotting at their moorings, blown up like balloons by the gases of decomposition, because the stations could not deal with them quickly enough. Modern factories are much more efficient and by using absolutely fresh carcasses can produce Grade 1 oil from all parts of the body. The blubber oil now has about 0·2 per cent free fatty acids and that from the rest of the carcass about 0·6 per cent. Very little of the lower grades is produced.

The oil is extracted from the tissues in large boilers. The blubber is boiled in free steam, the boilers having open tops, and the steam is blown through the contents, but the bones and meat are boiled for about 12 hours under a steam pressure of 60–70 lb. per sq. inch. This is done in what are really big autoclaves with screw tops, called Kvaerner boilers. Those used for the meat and the viscera have an arrangement of shelves inside them which prevents the massive contents packing down so that the steam cannot penetrate through it.

In the days of the Dutch and British Greenland whalers during the seventeenth and eighteenth centuries, whale or 'train' oil was used as an illuminant and in the manufacture of soap and cosmetics. As an illuminant it was supplanted by Sperm oil in the eighteenth century until this in turn was replaced by oils derived from petroleum. Its use in the manufacture of soap and cosmetics has continued to the present day and it has now an additional use in the manufacture of margarine.

The Greenland whalers, after extracting the oil by boiling in large open 'try' pots either on board ship or ashore, stored it in wooden barrels of about 40 gallons capacity for transport. This was a most uneconomical method because barrels cannot be packed tight so that they often burst or leaked or became foul, adding to the general stink and squalor of a whale ship below decks. Today, whether aboard ship or at land stations, the oil is stored in big tanks, steam heated to prevent the oil from solidifying. Factory ships may go south with the tanks full of fuel oil and return with some of them full of whale oil. Yet, as a kind of hangover from the past, the 40-gallon barrel remains to this day as a unit for measuring quantities of whale oil, six barrels making a ton.

A Blue whale yields an average of 70–80 barrels, say 11–14 tons (Mackintosh and Wheeler, 1929), though a yield of 305 barrels (50 tons) has been recorded from a Blue at Walvis Bay (Risting, S., 1928). The average yield of a Fin whale is 30–50 barrels, say 5–8 tons. After World War II the average yield per whale increased, perhaps owing to the increased efficiency of factories. Slijper (1962) quotes a yield of between 116 and 135 barrels per Blue whale unit.

As may be expected whales vary greatly in yield according to species, size and general condition, which again depend on the time and place of capture. In spite of the general formula for a Blue whale unit, 1 Blue = 2 Fin = $2\frac{1}{2}$ Humpbacks = 6 Sei, it must be obvious that a large Fin will yield more than a small Blue, and any small whale less than any big one. After a summer feeding in the Southern Ocean Rorquals are fat, with white, thick blubber, but when they first arrive in the south in the spring, after months of fasting in tropical waters, the blubber is poor and thin and has a brittle consistency which the whalers call 'newspaper'. Cows are fat when pregnant and during the early weeks of nursing but towards weaning they grow thinner and thinner as they use up their resources in the production of milk. Whales taken in the neighbourhood of the ice, where rich feeding grounds are, tend to be in better condition than those taken farther north where food is less abundant.

In tropical waters new arrivals in the early part of the winter season are fatter than whales taken later after some months in warm waters. Cows in advanced pregnancy, due to give birth on their way south, are exceptions to this.

The oil yield per whale differs slightly in various regions of the Antarctic. It is lower, indicating that Blue and Fin whales are thinner, in the sector south of South Africa than in that west of the Greenwich meridian (0° long.). It is lower still in the mid-Indian Ocean sector.

The same sort of result is obtained when the yield per whale is expressed in percentages of body weight. During the seasons 1947–51 it was found that the average yield per whale, without distinction of species, was 22·7 per cent of the body weight for the Antarctic generally but decreased from 24·6 per cent in the South Atlantic to 22·8 per cent in the Indian Ocean and still further to 21·5 per cent south of New Zealand (Ash, C. E., 1955).

This eastward falling off of the oil yield may be due to the diminution of the amounts of available food from west to east. The vast feeding grounds of the South Atlantic thin out and retreat southwards in the Indian Ocean sector where towards the end of summer they are found close against the coast of the Antarctic continent.

Another means of measuring the relative fatness of whales is known as the 'iodine number' (Lund, J., 1950–51). This expresses the amount of iodine (grams) which a fixed quantity of oil (100 grams) will absorb. It measures the degree of non-saturation of the oil and has a relative significance, for the oil of fat whales contains more unsaturated acids than that of thin ones and so has a higher iodine number. In Grade 1 oil the iodine number varies between 105 and 135 but it decreases slightly from west to east. It is highest in oil from whales taken around South Georgia (123–128) and lowest in those from the Ross Sea (about 102). East of the Greenwich meridian to the mid-Indian Ocean (40° E. long.) the number is 118 and east of that to the Australian sector about 114. The numbers seem to be always the same for whales taken in these areas of the Antarctic and it has been argued from this that the different regions have their own separate whale populations which tend to return to them season after season.

In order that whale oil may be made into an edible fat for human consumption it has to go through a process of refinement and hydrogenation. Refinement consists in separating off solid impurities by means of powerful centrifuges on board the factory ship or at the whaling station. Hydrogenation is done at the plant where the oil is made into soap or margarine. The process consists in blowing hydrogen through the oil under pressure in the presence of a substance, known as a 'catalyst', which promotes chemical reaction but itself remains unchanged at the end of it. Hydrogenation saturates the unsaturated acids by adding the required quota of hydrogen atoms to them, thus removing the dark colour and the fishy taste and smell. This happens at an 'iodine number' of about 50. When 30–40 per cent of the unsaturated acids have been saturated the oil is suitable for the manufacture of soap, and glycerine is produced as a by-product of this. Tallow is the other basic fat from which glycerine is made and it yields about the same quantity as whale oil. Glycerine is the raw material of high-explosive (nitro-glycerin) and was a major incentive for the Germans and Japanese to go whaling in the years before the war, though the British had been similarly interested for a good deal longer. Another use for it is the curing of cigarette tobacco.

Hydrogenation hardens the oil into an edible fat with a melting point temperature between 40° and 44° C. (Brandt, K. 1940). If hardened to a lesser degree so that the melting point temperature is lower the fishy taste and smell are apt to reappear. Margarine, however, must melt in the mouth at temperatures between 30° and 32° C. In 1930 a great step forward was made when a method was found of permanently removing the fishy taste and smell from oil hardened to a melting point of only 28°–30° C. which meant that margarine could be made almost entirely of whale oil and rendered almost tasteless. This discovery greatly increased the demand for whale oil for making margarine and today it comprises 16·7 per cent of the total fats used for this purpose (Sweeney, H., 1963). Other fats may be used for margarine, derived from various vegetable and fish oils, of which the chief are coconut oil and palm, cotton-seed, pea-nut and fish (sardine) oil. The prices of these to a large degree control the price of whale oil and vice versa.

When suitably hardened whale oil makes a frying fat as good as coconut oil and is used in many commercial kitchen fats and oils.

In Europe the manufacture of margarine is the main commercial use of whale oil but in the U.S.A. it is used more in the manufacture of soap.

Whale oil has other uses. For instance, in the textile industry it is applied to wool for combing, for 'batching' flax and for preparing vegetable fibres for spinning and weaving. In the tanning industry it is used in the making of 'chamois' leather. It is applied to shoes, boots, harness and other leather goods for water-proofing and preserving and is used as a drying oil in the manufacture of oil paints. It is also used in the manufacture of oil-cloth and linoleum.

Crude whale oil mixed with petroleum oils is used as a lubricant for machinery parts and bearings where rotation does not involve the generation of great heat (Brandt, K., 1940) and also for burning in stoves for heating or as a motor fuel, though for these purposes its price is often too high. It contains a certain amount of vitamin A, lack of which in the human system may cause blindness and skin eruptions, and the livers of Blue and Sperm whales are fairly rich in this vitamin, but the oil contains no vitamin D (anti-rachitic) so that it is not at all comparable with fish liver oils such as halibut, cod or shark. These remain the principal commercial sources of vitamins A and D, particularly the former.

The price of whale oil in the open market varies greatly and depends to a large extent on the availability of the vegetable and fish oils which compete with it. During the last fifty years the price has fluctuated between £8 10s. and £175 per ton (Mackintosh, N. A., 1965) and is at present (Oct. 1970) £114 per ton. In 1930 it slumped disastrously from about £35 a ton to about £10 and scared all the whaling companies into an agreement to restrict whaling.

Sperm Oil and Spermaceti

Sperm oil, from the blubber, bones and tissues of the Sperm whale, is not a fat but a liquid wax. In a reservoir in its head, known as the 'case', the Sperm whale carries another liquid wax, spermaceti, which congeals and solidifies in contact with air at temperatures between 38° and 47° C. It then looks like a thin kind of candle grease and solidifies almost instantly as it gushes out from the longitudinal cut which the whalers make along the top of the head, or 'junk piece' as it used to be called. It is neutral and almost tasteless. At one time, thirty years ago, it was stored separately from Sperm oil but nowadays the two products are mixed together. A big (60 feet) Sperm whale yields 4–6 tons of Sperm oil and about a ton of spermaceti (Beale, T., 1839).

Sperm oil was used in the eighteenth and early nineteenth centuries as an oil for lamps, replacing 'train' oil as the northern Right whales became scarce. Spermaceti, mixed with potash, was used for making church candles. Both products burn with a clear white smokeless flame. In 1859 mineral (petroleum) oils were discovered and used for heating and lighting so that the use of Sperm oil for this purpose came to an end, though American railroads continued to use it as an oil for signal lamps until the end of World War I (Brandt, K., 1940). Sperm oil, however, still has many uses. It is the best lubricant for fine machinery such as clocks and watches and for 'breaking in' new or reconditioned internal combustion engines. Shortly before World War II a German firm invented a method of making soap from it by a sulphonation process (Brandt, K., 1940). Spermaceti still makes the best candles and is also used in face creams and other cosmetics.

Fertilizer

After the meat and bones of Rorquals, as well as the blood, viscera and stomach contents, have been boiled under steam pressure for the necessary time (about 12 hours) the steam is turned off and the clamped covers at the top and bottom of the boilers are opened. The residues of the tissues, from which the oil has been extracted, are then scraped out with long shovels and loaded into trucks for transport to the driers. These are large, slowly rotating cylinders through which hot air is blown so as to dry out the residues into a fine grey powder. This is made up into bone meal or meat meal and used for fertilizer (guano) or cattle cake. The carcass of a full-grown Blue whale yields 25 per cent of its weight as dried residue (Brandt, K., 1940) of which 80 per cent can be turned into digestible protein, either as fertilizer or cattle food.

Whalebone

Until the end of the nineteenth century it was less the oil than the whalebone which was the product sought after by the whalers. It was used for making stiffeners in many kinds of fashionable clothing both male and female, but mostly female. At first it was used for bodices, bonnets and hooped skirts, but fashions change. Hooped skirts and crinolines were succeeded by stays and bustles, and still whalebone was supreme. But these at last went out of fashion so that whalebone was less in demand. Since those days 'the disgusting habit of covering oneself all over with water every morning' has been growing steadily so that the demand for whale oil rather than baleen has increased.

In the century and a half from 1750 to 1900 the price of whalebone varied between 10 cents per lb. and as high as $6·70 per lb. while the oil varied only between 2 cents and 50 cents per lb. (Brandt, K., 1940). In the eighteenth century whalebone was so valuable (about 30s. per lb.) that a Dutch whaling expedition could pay its entire expenses and make a handsome profit from a couple of Greenland Right whales yielding 3,000 lbs. of whalebone each. A large whale produced a ton and a half of whalebone plus about 9½ tons of oil, the latter worth about £900 (£16 a ton) at the value of the pound in those days. At its best whalebone was nearly fourteen times more valuable than the oil, so that the Greenland whalers often took only the baleen and threw the rest of the carcass away. In 1863 whalebone was worth $1·50 a lb. but slumped to 65 cents in 1868 owing to the American Civil War. In the seventies it recovered to $1·35 and eventually reached $4·50 in New York. In the eighties a New Bedford agent made a corner in whalebone and forced up the price to $6·0 and more (Hawes, C. B.,

1924). But the buyers then turned to substitutes which not only landed the agent with vast quantities of unsaleable whalebone but caused a slump in the price from which it never recovered, and is not now likely to owing to the invention of plastics.

Until the end of the nineteenth century there were many subsidiary uses for whalebone, for umbrellas, whips, walking canes, helmet frames and covers for telescopes. The bristles were used for brushes, especially chimney sweeps' brooms, and the membranous skins of the baleen plates for stuffing upholstery. Not much whalebone is sold today though it still goes into the making of riding crops, top boots and Guardsmens' bearskins. In Durban in 1930 the baleen plates used to be laid in the sun to dry and I was told that they were sold to a German firm who made sausage skins out of them.

The skin or hide of Rorquals has no commercial uses but the whalers often used to cut round the penis at the base, strip off the skin from the organ and dry the great glove-finger which resulted to make a bag for golf clubs. A golf bag from a Blue whale is creamy white flecked with irregular stripes of blue-grey while that from a Fin whale is creamy white without any flecks, but I cannot say I ever thought the finished article a very beautiful object.

Whale Meat

The flesh of whales has been used as human food for a thousand years, and probably longer. In the Middle Ages there was a flourishing porpoise fishery along the northern coast of France, the Netherlands and the Norwegian fjords. The meat was eaten on the continent and was exported to England where it was considered a great delicacy. King Henry VIII is said to have had a great liking for it. It is out of fashion now but the flesh of small whalebone whales, especially Sei, small Fin and Piked whales, was regularly on the market in Norway during World War II when protein foods were scarce. In England the flesh of Blue and Fin whales was imported from the Antarctic and put on the market in the early years of the war, but it was not a success. Housewives would not buy it, not surprisingly, because not enough research had been done on its preservation and refrigeration. It did not travel well and developed an unpleasant 'whaly' taste. Also it was sold in the fishmongers' shops where large slabs of red meat put the public off.

The country where whale meat is eaten more than anywhere else is Japan. This small, overcrowded island country suffers from a chronic shortage of protein foods. It is the meat for human consumption rather than the oil which forms the main objective of modern Japanese whaling both in the Antarctic and from land stations in the home islands. The meat is sent from the Antarctic deep frozen at $-25°$ C. and is prepared for the market in many ways, in cubes, in strips and canned. The Japanese often eat it raw, as they do chicken and fish, with seaweed or with soya sauce. Served like this it is, to at least one humble member of the consuming millions, somewhat revolting.

During World War I the Californian Grey whale was put on the market in the United States. A thousand whales, giving 7 tons of meat each, were marketed by the U.S. Bureau of Fisheries in California. It was a great success and the price rose from 10 to 20 cents a pound between 1916 and 1919.

The meat of small Rorquals is the mainstay of the whalers' diet in the Antarctic, but that of the Sperm whale is dark and greasy and quite inedible. At South Georgia whenever a small Rorqual arrived at the whaling station the butcher, a strapping young Norwegian, appeared with his boy assistant carrying an affair like a wooden stretcher with two handles at each end. If he was satisfied that the meat looked good and fresh as many rectangular blocks as possible would be cut for him from the back muscles. Each block measured perhaps 3 by $1\frac{1}{2}$ by 2 feet and weighed about 30 lbs. The butcher laid the blocks of meat on his stretcher two or three deep and he and his assistant bore them away with rather uncertain steps, for the load must have weighed more than 3 cwt., all solid flesh. Outside the butcher's shop, which was not really a shop but a shed where pigs and poultry were slaughtered and prepared and sausages were made, the blocks of whale meat were hung on hooks in the open air for three or four days before they were given to the cooks.

We were usually allowed to take a slab of meat for ourselves and we carried it back to the laboratory. It felt damp and warm to the touch but not at all slimy. After hanging in the cool air outside our building for three or four days it turned black on the outside and was ready to eat. It made excellent steaks and a single block of it fed six of us for several days. It was quite as good as beef although the flesh is somewhat coarse grained, but it contains no fat or gristle and comes from an animal even more sweet and clean than that which gives us beef.

A great deal of prejudice still exists about whale meat, largely induced by the fact that it is red. Since it comes from the sea most people expect it to be white with the idea that the whale is a fish at the back of their minds. In the Antarctic, not unnaturally, the sight of the roaring, stinking, steaming charnel yard where the carcasses are cut up, running with blood and littered with guts and ordure, used to upset strangers a good deal. I am sure a visit to a slaughter house would similarly put many people off beef and mutton.

I recall an occasion at South Georgia when an old transport ship flying the Greek flag came into the harbour and lay forlornly at anchor off our jetty awaiting some repair or other. We heard that the skipper was an Englishman and so asked him to dinner. He arrived carefully dressed in his best suit with many creases showing that it had lain in a drawer for a very long time. We had chosen the menu with great care. There was dried lentil soup, fried whale steaks with onions, dehydrated potatoes and tinned mixed vegetable cubes, followed by a choice of pêche Melba, made with tinned peaches and tinned milk, or biscuits and mousetrap—a meal fit for a king, we thought.

During the soup we conversed light-heartedly. 'I visited the whaling station this morning,' our guest said. 'What a disgusting sight! They tell me the Norwegians actually eat the meat of whales, but then I suppose the Norwegians will eat anything.'

After his second helping of whale meat he said, 'What excellent beef steak! How on earth did you manage to get it out here?'

Over the pêche Melba we told him. Our guest turned a pale shade of green and, excusing himself, went outside to lose his entire dinner in the snow.

It may have been the same mixture of prejudice and visual repulsion which caused the British Greenland whalers to suffer terribly from scurvy, and indeed to die of it, without ever thinking of eating the flesh of the Greenland Right whale which is said to be the most palatable of all and which would have prevented the disease. The Dutch Greenland whalers did eat flesh of the Right whale and kept the scurvy at bay.

We found that all young Rorquals gave equally good meat, though many people say that the flesh of the Sei whale is the best. Above a body length of about 65 feet the flesh of all whales becomes too coarse grained and stringy to be pleasant.

Scrimshaw

The large conical teeth of the Sperm whale give an excellent ivory which can be fashioned into chessmen, counters, mah-jong chips and so on. The whalers carve the teeth into all sorts of shapes and scratch

Left:
Humpback
whaling
off the
coast of
Western
Australia.
The gunner
signals to
the
helmsman.

Below:
A hit.

Above: A catcher arriving at Grytviken, South Georgia, with catch. Government buildings and 'Discovery' laboratory in the background.

Below: The plan in operation at Grytviken. A Blue whale being hauled up.

designs on them which they outline in dye or ink. The Yankee Sperm whalers used to while away long passages home, lulls in the hunting or tropical calms by carving teeth during their watches below into elaborate designs. This was known as 'scrimshaw' work and it very often had a beauty and originality of its own. I have seen a Narwhal's tusk made into a walking cane decorated with scrimshaw in geometrical patterns that seemed to be derived from an American Indian origin. At any rate it represented many long hours of patient work by a sailor sitting on his box bunk by the light of a swinging Sperm oil lamp, or on the deck in the tropics under slack sails, the ship lazily rolling and scattering the flying fish.

Ambergris

Perhaps the strangest, and for a long time the most mysterious, of all whale products is that known as 'ambergris' or grey amber which comes from the Sperm whale and has long been used by the makers of fine scents because in alcoholic solution it has the property of fixing or retaining perfumes. It has been known to mankind since the time of the ancient Egyptians who used it in their temples as incense. In India it was believed to be an aphrodisiac, like so many other substances, and in the Middle Ages in Europe it was also used for this purpose, but it was also a medicine for dropsy and other diseases. Burton, in his *Anatomy of Melancholy*, recommends ambergris as diminishing the exhausting effects of a purge.

Until the middle of the eighteenth century ambergris had always been found in the form of lumps washed up on the shore, but its origin was quite unknown. Although it has nothing whatever to do with the resinous amber from the Baltic Sea, which is the solidified and fossilized gum of coniferous trees, yet there seems to have been some confusion between the two substances in the past. The Arabic word *ambar* means 'a great fish', but it also means the resinous amber. A manuscript found on board a Dutch East Indiaman captured at sea in the seventeenth century stated that 'ambergris is not the scum or excrement of the whale, but issues out of the root of a tree, which tree howsoever it stand on land alwaies shoots forth its roots towards the sea' (Beale, T., 1839). Other explanations of the origin of this mysterious substance were that it was extruded by submarine volcanoes or that it resulted from the droppings of sea birds. Sir Richard Hawkins thought that it was 'a liquor which issueth out of certain Fountaines in sundry Seas, and being of a light and thick substance,

5

participating of the Ayre, suddenly becometh hard, as the yellow Amber of which they make make Beades . . .' (quoted in Hawes, C.B., 1924). Marco Polo knew that whalers pursued the Sperm whale for ambergris but it was not definitely known to originate in the Sperm whale until an American, Dr. Boylston of Boston, discovered the fact in 1724. He said the Nantucket whale fishermen found it 'contained in a cyst or bag, without any inlet or outlet to it . . nowhere to be found but near the genital parts of the fish'. In the same year an Englishman named Paul Dudley wrote to the Royal Society claiming the discovery. 'But truth,' he wrote, 'is the daughter of time; it is at length found out that *occultum naturae* is an animal production and bred in the body of the spermaceti whale' (Beale, T., 1839).

The best and most valuable ambergris is that which is found floating in the sea, but it originates in the intestines of Sperm whales where it is occasionally found as slimy lumps, smooth and rounded, up to the size of two fists or a baby's head. It is a grey or black substance with rather the quality of pitch but lighter than water and not sticky. When first taken from the intestine the lumps have a faecal smell, but if kept they darken as they dry, lose the faecal smell and take on a faint, quite pleasant earthy perfume. The physical properties of ambergris are as follows: it melts at 60° C. and burns with a pale-blue flame. It is soluble in absolute alcohol, in ether, in fat or in volatile oils. The alcoholic solution is fluorescent in sunlight with a characteristic yellowish-green rim on the surface of the solution. When heated it gives off an agreeable odour, and on the heated point of a knife vaporizes completely away (Fraser, F. C., 1937).

When cut through, a lump of ambergris shows a kind of marbling on the cut surface, and in the middle there is always found the undigested remains of the hard chitinous beak or beaks of squid. In the larger lumps entire beaks are sometimes found.

It is not known exactly how or why these lumps are formed in the Sperm whale's intestine but it would seem that the indigestible beaks set up some sort of irritation of the lining of the intestine causing it to secrete a mucous substance around the irritant. In due course the mucous masses are voided into the sea through the rectum (not through the mouth as is sometimes stated) and are thus found floating. However, the general health of the animal does not seem to be affected in the least, for no whale from which ambergris has been taken has ever appeared to be at all sickly. Floating in the sea the lumps change colour and assume their pleasant earthy scent.

On account of its virtues and uses ambergris was in the past immensely valuable. It used to be a beachcomber's dream one day to find a big lump of it on the beach and become a millionaire overnight. Today, owing to the competition of other scent-fixing agents, the price of ambergris has slumped somewhat. In 1954 it varied between £4 and £20 per lb. During the 1953–54 whaling season a huge lump 5 feet in length weighing 926 lbs. was taken from a healthy bull Sperm whale by Dr. Robert Clarke (1955) while on board the British whaling ship *Southern Harvester*.

In 1930, working at Durban, we thought we had made a rather similar find and a startling scientific discovery into the bargain. Unfortunately, as it turned out we had made neither. It happened that one day a large Blue whale arrived at the whaling station and, when it was opened, there were taken from its intestines about twenty faecal nodules of various sizes, some not much larger than a cricket ball and the largest about the size of a baby's head. They were yellowish-brown in colour, exactly like the liquid faeces among which they lay. They were slimy with mucus and had a faecal smell. We opened one or two and found inside each one bunches of black baleen bristles from the whale's mouth.

'Ambergris!' we said.

'Ambergris from a Blue whale? I do not think so,' said the Norwegian station manager. His colleague, who was the foreman, gave the lumps a much shorter name. 'Fauch!' he exclaimed in disgust, and we agreed.

Nevertheless the manager locked the lumps in an outside shed and allowed us to keep a very small piece, about the size of my fist, for ourselves. In a few days this had dried and changed colour. It was now dark grey, had lost its unpleasant smell and gave off instead a faint, sweet, earthy perfume.

'Ambergris!' we said again.

The manager rather nervously opened the shed where the other lumps were stored, as though expecting a time bomb to go off, but, sure enough, they had undergone a similar change to ours. He now transferred them to the office safe but still maintained that they could not possibly be real ambergris because it had never before been found in any whale but a Sperm. He allowed us to keep our lump which we had cut in half. The cut surface showed a marbling and in the middle was a small bunch of black baleen bristles.

When we got back to London the following summer I sent both

halves of the lump to the government analyst in Fetter Lane. They were by now dry and hard and had a waxy consistency but the faint, rather pleasant earthy smell persisted. In due course the analyst reported that this was not true ambergris but had several of the physical properties of it. There seems, however, to be little doubt that the concretions in the intestine of our Blue whale had been formed in a similar way to that in which true ambergris is formed in the Sperm whale. The lining of the Blue whale's intestine had reacted to an irritation set up by the indigestible horny baleen bristles, which the whale must have accidentally swallowed, and had formed mucous concretions around them. They would have been voided into the sea if the whale had not been harpooned.

CHAPTER 4

History of Whaling

The history of whaling is made up of a number of chapters each covering a few centuries and all more or less repeating the same pattern. They resemble the one which has now come to an end in the Antarctic. Each began with new discovery and hopeful enterprise, passed through a phase of fierce competition and ruthless exploitation with improving techniques and ended at length in diminishing resources, exhaustion and failure. Man has been both blind and ignorant in the pursuit of the whale, for although whales have been hunted off the coast of Europe certainly since the ninth century it never occurred to anyone even to describe them until the end of the seventeenth, when porpoises and dolphins were dissected and described anatomically. No anatomical account of the great whales exists prior to that of the great John Hunter who described the Greenland Right whale in 1797.

The first accurate and graphic accounts of the natural history of the great whales were given by the famous Arctic whaling captain, William Scoresby Junior, who in 1820 wrote *An Account of the Arctic Regions*, a classic treatise which not only describes the habits and natural history of the Greenland Right whale but deals for the first time with the whales' food and environment. Scoresby was the precursor of the oceanographers of today, especially those of the modern 'Discovery' Investigations, directing his acute and inquiring mind towards the same ends.

In 1839 Thomas Beale published his *Natural History of the Sperm Whale* but Rorquals were not adequately described until 1874 (Scammon, C. M.) and 1904 (True, F. W.). The first scientific study of the natural history of Rorquals was that of my colleagues, N. A. Mackintosh and J. F. G. Wheeler (1929), who for the first time applied the techniques of modern fishery research to a population of whales in Antarctic waters. Since then a great deal of research has been done, up to World War II by British and Norwegian scientists and after it by Japanese, Russian and Dutch scientists as well.

Mankind has probably hunted the whale, as he has caught fish, since the dawn of his history. In northern Norway there are cave pictures of Neolithic Age showing porpoise hunting probably dating from about 2200 B.C., and in kitchen middens of even earlier date the romains of whales have been found, and stone harpoon heads. The Cretans hunted dolphins in the eastern Mediterranean about 3000 B.C. but the Mycenean Greeks believed them to be sacred and did not hunt them. About 1000 B.C. and up to Roman times the Phoenicians carried on a highly developed Sperm and Right whale industry in the eastern Mediterranean, based on Joppa, and it is probably in this Sperm whaling that the story of Jonah originated.

Porpoise hunting has been going on along the northern coasts of Europe since the ninth century and still lingers in places today. Probably larger whales were also taken because in A.D. 890 Ohthere, a Norwegian, made a voyage to the White Sea and on his return visited King Alfred of England to whom he related that he had seen whales 'eight and forty ells long'. Since an ell is 45 inches this makes the whales 180 feet long and one must suspect that this is just another of those travellers' tales.

Whaling in Northern Waters

The first people in Europe to carry on whaling as an organized industry were the Basques, inhabitants of the French and Spanish Biscay coasts around the Pyrenees. The industry, founded on the Biscay Right whale, was fully developed by the twelfth century but probably dated from much earlier, possibly the tenth century when the Basques may have learnt the craft from Norse whalers. The Basque whaling tradition set the pattern and devised the methods which were to be used by whalers right up to the end of the nineteenth century when other methods, based on the invention of the explosive harpoon, superseded those of the Basques. But the tradition still lingers. To this day the coats of arms of as many as six Basque towns have a whaling motif. That of Biarritz shows a *chaloupe* harpooning a whale. Many whaling terms in use today have a Basque origin, for instance the word 'harpoon' itself is derived from a Basque word *arpoi* of which the root *ar* means 'to take quickly'.

The Basque industry probably began when the people of coastal villages combined to cut up and render down the carcasses of whales which were occasionally stranded on their beaches. They extracted the oil by boiling the blubber in pots on the beaches, using it as a lighting and heating fuel, and ate the flesh if it were fresh enough. These occasional accidental strandings were so profitable for the villages nearby that the inhabitants took to forcing the whales ashore, going out after them in boats, making noises to drive them towards the beach and then killing them with lances. By the twelfth century whaling was an organized business. Stone look-out towers were built along the coast and continuously manned during the winter and early spring when the Right whales approached the coast. Other whales, Blue and Fin, were probably seen but in their open boats the Basques could not take them because they were too swift and their carcasses sank. The Biscay Right whale is a slow, leisurely swimmer and its carcass floats, so it could be dealt with by means of the light gear available.

When the tower look-out saw a whale blowing in the bay a bell was sounded and fires of damp straw were lit on the watch towers to warn the surrounding villages, for this was a strictly co-operative effort. All the able-bodied men and boys from as many as twenty villages might be called upon to share in the labour and reward of cutting up a single whale.

On sighting the whale the men of the village, or villages, to whom the look-out tower belonged, put out from the shore in their *chaloupes* ('shallop', 'scallop', *escalope*—all the same word related to our word 'shell' and the Scandinavian *skal*). These were light, shallow draught rowing boats with a harpooner, steersman and ten oarsmen. The harpooner darted his harpoon, often called an 'iron' by English whalers of a later date, into the whale. It was an arrow-headed prong which was not intended to kill the whale but only to make it fast to the boat by means of the harpoon line which it carried out. When the whale was fast the harpooner went aft to the steering oar while the steersman came forward into the bows in order to deliver the lethal blows with the lances. These he thrust into the whale after the boat had been hauled close to it by the harpoon line. After the kill the carcass was towed into the shallows and stripped. Oil, whalebone and meat were shared out among all the helpers but the tongue, an especial delicacy, was the prerogative of the church.

In time the Basques took to pursuing the Right whales out to sea.

Possibly the whales became wary of approaching the coast, but it is also possible that the high price of whale products and the increasing skill of the local boat builders made it more and more worth while to hunt for whales farther and farther out on the high seas. During the thirteenth and fourteenth centuries the Basques built large vessels for whaling and kept a monopoly of European whaling until the end of the sixteenth century. Meanwhile the Icelanders were whaling quite independently of them, having also learnt the trade from the Norsemen. They hunted the Greenland Right whales which they called *Sletbag* or *Slettibaka*.

From about 1538 the Basques were voyaging as far away as Newfoundland, fishing as well as whaling. They brought back cod fish, dried and salted, which they supplied to practically the whole of Europe. Such long and dangerous voyages called for large ships of 700 to 1,000 tons known as 'caravels'. They were about 50 feet long with a very high towering poop, the *castilette*, high prow and bulwarks (Sanderson, I., 1958). They had three masts, the tallest being the mizzen, about 80 feet high, carrying a crowsnest. They were square rigged on all masts though the foremast, right forward, may sometimes have been rigged fore and aft. The bowsprit was about 40 feet long and carried another sprit, below which another small sail could be set

These were sturdy, seaworthy and capacious ships and must have been most uncomfortable for a long voyage. They were very top-heavy and when sailing light were heavily ballasted with sand so that they must have wallowed horribly. They carried a ship's company of about fifty men but no one, not even the captain, had a cabin nor any appointed place to sleep. They must have closely resembled the large, long-distance Chinese junks which are seen around Hong Kong to this day. These too have three masts, the mizzen square rigged, the fore and main right forward and right aft. Their only sleeping accommodation is a kind of shelf under the high poop with the deck head only a foot or so above the bare planks on which the sleeping crew must lie. Almost the entire space within the hull is taken up by a capacious hold.

Each caravel carried one shallop inboard but on long voyages the ships often sailed in convoys or fleets, and then as many as five shallops might be carried per ship, but never more than two per ship were used at one time (Sanderson, I., 1958).

The Basque sailors made these long and stormy voyages across the

North Atlantic and far north to the Arctic with primitive navigating instruments, the astrolabe, the quadrant and the sand clock. Before 1500 the Biscay Right whale had begun to grow scarce so that the Basques came to rely more and more on the Greenland Right whale, the *sletbag*, and had to go far afield into Arctic waters to find it. The whales they caught were towed into some sheltered bay, stripped and the blubber boiled in pots on the beach. At the end of the sixteenth century it became usual to boil out the oil aboard ship. This was a perilous business because the pots stood over a brick furnace based on the sand ballast amidships, so that the fire risk was considerable (Sanderson, I., 1958).

Now other nations, notably the Dutch and the English, began to get into the whaling trade and Basque whaling began to decline. The Biscay Right whale had almost completely disappeared by the end of the sixteenth century both from the Biscay region and from the Newfoundland banks. Although it is always said that Basque whaling exterminated the Biscay Right whale in these seas it is difficult to believe it, because by modern standards the numbers of whales taken were so small. Only 700 to 1,000 whales were taken during the hundred years from 1517 (Harmer, S., 1928). This is for the whole of the Basque industry, and the total for a single town, Lequeito, for the same period was only 35 whales.

In 1583 Newfoundland passed from French into English control and it became more and more difficult for the Basques to fish on the Banks, and so they took to privateering which they found more profitable. They also took jobs as whalers in the ships of their Dutch and English rivals.

About this time the dream of finding a north-west or north-east passage through the Arctic to the fabulous wealth of Cathay and the Indies began to fire the imagination of both Dutch and English adventurers. If it could be found, a way to the East would be opened which would avoid oceans dominated by the sea power of Spain. Martin Frobisher in 1576 made the first voyage with the avowed object of finding a north-west passage. He was followed by John Davis, a west country sailor who gave his name to the strait between Greenland and Labrador, and in 1610 by Henry Hudson who sailed into what was later called Hudson Bay in the first *Discovery* of all. Her crew mutinied and cast Hudson, his young son and one other adrift in an open boat, and they were never heard of again.

Meanwhile expeditions also went north-eastwards in search of a passage to the Orient. The Dutchman, Jacob van Heemskerk, sailed in May 1596 in command of two vessels, Willem Barendsz being the pilot of one of them. They steered due north and came to a bleak snowbound land of spiky mountains, which they accordingly named Spitsbergen, and spent the winter on Novaya Zemlya. The Dutch can thus claim to have discovered Spitsbergen though it had probably already been sighted by an Englishman, Sir Hugh Willoughby, who made a voyage to Russia in 1553. The Basques had undoubtedly been whaling around the island very much earlier, but left no record of their voyages.

These and many other expeditions to the far north brought back reports of the large numbers of Greenland Right whales to be seen in these waters, and great interest was aroused in Dutch and English financial circles.

The first English ship to be fitted out for Arctic whaling was the barque *Grace*, 35 tons, of Bristol which sailed for the Newfoundland grounds in April 1594 for 'train oil and the fins of whales', the latter meaning whalebone (Hawes, C. B., 1924). She found no whales but salvaged some 'fins' from two wrecked Basque ships and searched along the coast of the Gulf of St. Lawrence looking for stranded whales. Not finding any she fished on the banks for cod and returned home in the autumn.

The Muscovy Company now began to interest itself in the attempts to find a north-east passage. It had been established by royal charter as long ago as February 1555 and was one of a number of such companies formed at this time in order to develop trade with different parts of the world. Others were the East India Company, the Levant Company and the Hudson Bay Company. The Muscovy Company was established mainly to develop trade with the Baltic countries and Russia and its full title was 'The Company of Merchant Adventurers of England for the Discovery of Lands, Territories, Isles, Dominions and Seignories, unknown and not before the late Adventure or Enterprise by sea or navigation commonly frequented'. In 1576 the company obtained a monopoly from the Crown to 'make train oil and kill whales' for twenty years, but its first ships fitted out for whaling did not sail north to Spitsbergen until March 1610. They were the *Lionesse* and the *Amitié*, each of 70 tons. They whaled at Deere Sound, Spitsbergen, finding 'great store of whales', but instead of boiling out the blubber ashore they brought back cargoes of it in casks, and since the voyage from Spitsbergen took many weeks the blubber was not in very good condition when it arrived and must have stunk very badly indeed. The company's officers were not pleased.

These early English whalers carried 'Biskayners' (Basques) on board who were 'expert men for the killing of the whale', and so did the Dutch ships which entered the trade shortly after the English.

The following year the Muscovy Company sent the barque *Elizabeth*, 50 tons, and she was successful in bringing back 'the first Oyle that was ever made in Greenland'. English whalers continued to call Spitsbergen 'East Greenland' long after it had been named by the Dutch. In 1612 the company, thus encouraged, sent four ships of larger size, but imagine their horror and disgust on arriving at Spitsbergen to find 'interlopers' already there. These were a Dutch ship and two other English ships not belonging to the company and a Basque from San Sebastian. This seemed frightful impertinence, especially since the Muscovy Company had been given the monopoly by the Crown. The English whalers never accustomed themselves to the presence of mere foreigners on the whaling grounds even though both they and the foreigners at first employed 'Biskayners' to show them how to kill the whales. The English continued to call the foreigners, especially the Dutch, 'interlopers' and from that first encounter onwards continual squabbles and acts of piracy took place on the whaling grounds. The whalers sometimes destroyed each other's shallops on shore and even seized each other's ships, fought over whales and burnt down buildings.

It may be that the English dreaded or were jealous of their formidable rivals, for the Dutch were well and truly in the whaling business from 1612 onwards and remained in it, going only for the Greenland Right whale, until the latter half of the nineteenth century, outlasting even the American Sperm whalers. In 1614 they formed the *Noordse Compagnie* to fish and trade along the coast of Greenland, Spitsbergen, Novaya Zemlya and Bear Island. Instead of sending north small cockle shells of 50 to 70 tons, as the English did, they sent well found ships of 250 to 400 tons carrying fifty men each. They had Basque harpooners and blubber strippers ('flensers') and at first set up their try pots in sheltered bays. The whalers of competing nationalities made use of different bays or landing beaches, the same ones season after season though raids on each other's beaches were not at all uncommon.

The number of Dutch ships on the whaling grounds increased steadily from 14 in 1614 to 52 in 1621. In 1623 the Dutch fleet included large freighters carrying timber and stores with which a permanent shore settlement was built at Spitsbergen. It was a fairly good equivalent of a modern whaling station with a slipway for hauling up the whales, oil cookeries, warehouses and bakeries. It became, in fact, a fair-sized town with living quarters, a church and a fort. It was named Smeerenburg—Blubbertown—and it housed a temporary population every season of over a thousand men. At breakfast time in Smeerenburg the blast of a horn announced to the fleet that hot rolls and white bread were now available fresh from the oven. Civilized amenities were preserved by the Dutch whalers, ashore at any rate.

While the Dutch whaling effort flourished English attempts in the early seventeenth century were not successful and petered out in 1625, the Muscovy Company fading out about that time. There may have been several reasons for the failure of these first English ventures, ships too small and ill found, officials of the company interfering constantly in the ships' navigation and management, often sailing in them and issuing orders to the captain and crew, and, lastly, no attempt made to co-operate with the whalers of other nations. The Dutch, on the other hand, were highly efficient and introduced a great many improvements in technique which have lasted to this day. The wooden whale slipway was one of these. They also started grading the oil and experimented with rendering down other tissues than the blubber.

The main period of Dutch dominance was the century from 1626 to 1726, but after about 1630 the Right whales began to get scarce in the bays around Spitsbergen. Until about then ships had usually anchored and remained at moorings while their whales were being cut up and rendered down on a beach nearby. Alternatively they towed them to Smeerenburg and dealt with them there. But now the whales began to leave the coast and slowly Smeerenburg fell into disuse, although it continued to be the main Dutch base for some fifty years until 1676. Since the whales were now found and killed on the open sea they were also cut up at sea. The blubber was then packed in casks and taken back to Holland in the same way as the early Basques did it. Up to 1642 about 30 ships a year sailed from Dutch ports to the Spitsbergen whaling grounds, usually escorted by warships because of raids by pirates and privateers, but in that year the *Noordse Compagnie* lost its monopoly on the expiration of its charter and the annual number of ships sailing for the grounds rose to two hundred.

The Right whales continued to retreat before the invaders of their cold sanctuary until at last they had to be sought along the borders of the pack ice itself. About 1720 they had become so scarce in the north-eastern Arctic that the Dutch whalers began to sail through the Davis Strait to the west coast of Greenland and Baffin Land.

The catches of the Dutch Greenland Right whalers were, like those of the Basque whalers, very much smaller than those of today. In the 46 years from 1675 to 1721 the total catch of the entire Dutch fleet amounted to 32,906 whales (Sanderson, I., 1958), an average of 715 whales a year. If, say, 200 Dutch ships visited the whaling grounds each year the catch would have been only three or four whales per ship per season. Scoresby (1820) quoted seven whales as being a highly successful result for the year 1736. In that year 191 Dutch ships caught 857 whales—a catch of 4½ per ship. However, the small catches were enough to give big profits because of the high price of whale products. In a period of ten years at the beginning of the eighteenth century the Dutch whalers made a gross taking of 26 million florins and a gross profit of 4 million florins.

The Dutch did not have things quite all their own way after the collapse of the first English attempts because the Hanseatic League joined in the trade and from 1640 competed with the Dutch until driven off the grounds in 1709. In 1634 the French government made a claim to Spitsbergen and forbade French Basques to serve aboard Dutch ships so that the whalers employed Friesians from the German islands who have to this day a long tradition of hunting the smaller whales, dolphins and porpoises.

The Dutch whaling ships were three-masted barques, square-rigged with various fore and aft sails for manœuvring when the shallops were out in pursuit of their quarry. They were squarely built, deep-draughted ships with raised poop and fo'c'sle (Sanderson, I, 1958). Life aboard was tough, the food filthy and the water foul and the crews' quarters, like those in all whaling ships until quite recently, often stank. At four o'clock a breakfast of coarse ground oats with rancid butter was dished out and other meals during the day were according to the work. Pickled meat or dried cod was the diet, dried peas and mouldy bread. The water was stored in barrels which had previously been used for whale oil and was often scarcely drinkable. But the Dutch ate whale meat, which must have come as a welcome relief, and in this they differed from the English whalers who would not touch it. When they got ashore at Spitsbergen, Jan Mayen or elsewhere they slaughtered huge quantities of birds and took thousands

of their eggs, a job for which they detailed all the small boys on board
the ships. They also kept them busy gathering supplies of a cabbage-
like plant that grows on Spitsbergen, and thus they kept free of the
scurvy.

The Greenland Right whale, like the Biscay Right, is a slow swimmer
and its carcass floats and it was an easy prey for the Dutch whalers
whose methods of approach and killing were similar to those of the
Basques, naturally since they employed Basques for the job. Later
the English used the same methods. Five shallops were carried on
each ship, light, shallow-draught boats about 30 feet long. Each
carried a harpooner, a steersman and five oarsman.

From about 1770 onwards Dutch whaling began to decline for the
Greenland Right whale had by then become very scarce in any open
water. By the end of the century it had become scarce not only
off Spitsbergen but also off West Greenland and Baffin Land. The
whales retreated into the ice whither the whalers did not venture to
pursue them. About 1820 the Dutch mostly gave up whaling and
went sealing instead and the last Dutch whaler sailed in 1860.

The Dutch did not exterminate the Greenland Right whale though
in the course of a century and a half they certainly made a contribution
to this end. The job was almost completed by the British who revived
their whaling fleet and came back into the trade at the end of the
eighteenth century. The year 1711 saw a wild speculative boom in
London which produced the South Seas Company inviting speculators
to invest in all sorts of schemes connected with the South Seas. One of
them, by no means the least practical or likely, was for whaling in those
seas and enough capital was attracted to build a fleet of whaling ships.
Other schemes were much less promising—'a wheel for perpetual
motion' and 'a scheme of great profit, but nobody to know what it is'.

The idea of starting up a British whaling fleet again was prompted
by the high prices being paid for imported whale oil and whalebone
produced mainly by the Dutch and Germans. In view of past sad
experiences of whaling by British ships it was a wise precaution to
petition parliament beforehand for exemption from duty for all whale
products imported by the South Seas Company's ships.

A whaling fleet of twelve ships sailed in 1725 crewed by very
expensive experts from Holstein who cost the company £3,000 in
one year. In spite of the prospectus the ships did not go south but
headed north to Greenland and the Arctic and failed to find any
whales. The company sent out more than two dozen ships in eight

years and they ran into debt to the tune of £180,000 by 1732, exemption from duty notwithstanding.

The company then decided to appeal to the government for further financial assistance which, rather surprisingly, was granted, but the England of Sir Robert Walpole was corrupt, rich and prosperous. All whaling ships of 200 tons and more were granted a bounty, or government subsidy, of 20s. per ton. In 1740 this was increased to 30s. per ton and later to 40s. By then (1749) England was at war with Spain ('Jenkins's ear'—'they will soon be wringing their hands', etc.) and whalemen were given exemption from the press gang.

This financial assistance, known as the 'bounty system', gradually put British whaling on its feet. Whaling fleets began to build up, Hull being the principal English whaling port and Dundee the principal Scottish one. In 1760 thirty-five ships sailed for the Greenland grounds from Hull, London and Whitby and by 1770 nearly double that number. In 1788 there were 216 English and 31 Scottish whaling ships in northern waters. Unlike the Dutch the British whalers did not hesitate to follow the whales into the pack ice where they found them plentiful but shy, three Hull vessels taking 27 in one day.

The heyday of British Arctic whaling lasted from 1780 to 1819. The ships were specially strengthened for navigating in pack ice but there were many heavy losses in the ice. A voyage lasted about five months but the ships were provisioned for nine in case they might be caught in the ice. Fearful slaughter was done to the whales and not even the calves were spared, so, not surprisingly, after about 1860 whales became scarce and the fleet began to decline. The first steam whaler, the *Empress of India* of Peterhead, sailed for the Arctic in 1859 but steam arrived too late to be of much use and British northern whaling practically ceased in 1875 though it still lingered in Dundee. In 1910 a Dundee ship caught 18 whales but in 1912 one ship sailed from Dundee and came back without any catch.

Southern 'Bay' Whaling

Towards the end of the eighteenth century it was noticed by voyagers in southern seas, and by convict ships on the Australian run, that the bays and estuaries of Australia, Tasmania and New Zealand were full of Right whales very like the Biscay Right whale if not identical with it. This is now known as the Southern Right whale and is held to be identical with the Black or Biscay Right whale. Accordingly it became the custom to equip convict ships with whaling gear and, after they had unloaded their unhappy cargoes, they went whaling along the Australian coasts. In 1792 twenty ships returned fully loaded with whale oil.

Thus began the 'bay' whaling along first the Tasmanian, then the Australian and then the New Zealand coasts. It was done in the same way as the Basque bay whaling two centuries earlier. At first the whales were so numerous that their 'snoring' (spouting?) kept the Governor awake in his residence at Derwent River Inlet, Tasmania (Sanderson, I., 1958). They arrived there regularly in June and then moved up the Australian coast. In 1794 bay whaling started in New Zealand, where the British whalers had a tough time with the Maoris, who were cannibals and ate quite a number of them. The Right whales moved north up the New Zealand coast through Cook Strait from May to October and then on north to the Chatham Islands. At first most of the whalers came to New Zealand from Australia and, after dropping a shore party in some chosen bay, went on up the coast to collect other cargoes, such as timber or flax, returning to pick up the shore whaling party at the end of the season.

The bay whaling in the Antipodes was immensely profitable to start with. The Southern Right whale gives an oil of very high quality and the blubber was boiled fresh, not after storage for weeks in barrels like much of the oil from the Arctic. But soon the business became very crowded. As Sperm whaling began to decline in New Zealand and Australian waters early in the nineteenth century the Yankee whalers joined in the bay whaling and there were some Frenchmen as well. In the eighteen-twenties the Southern Right whales began to grow scarce and by 1841 were failing to turn up when and where expected. By 1850 southern bay whaling had ceased altogether.

Whaling in the Americas

In the New World, meanwhile, whaling had been going on long before any Europeans arrived. The Indians along both the eastern and western seaboards of North America used methods very much like those of early whalers anywhere. It probably began with stranded whales which were so fortunate for every locality where they turned up that the Indians took to keeping watch for them. When a whale was sighted a great fleet of bark canoes put out, armed with bone-headed harpoons and lines made from vegetable fibres. The line was probably attached to a log or baulk of timber which made it difficult for the whale to 'sound' or deep dive. Norse whalers used seal-

Above: Floating factory *Salvestria*, 1940. A whale carcass astern.

Left: The plan deck of a modern factory ship, Fl.f. *Balaena*, in operation.

Flensing a male Humpback whale at a shore station in Western Australia.

skin bladders for the same purpose. The Indians killed their whale with flights of arrows and towed it ashore to be cut up. They took the Southern or Biscay Right whale and the Humpback on the east coast and the Californian Grey on the west using every part of the carcass, the oil for lighting and heating, the flesh for food, the bones for building and the baleen for personal adornment.

When the first settlers arrived in New England it was decreed that a stranded whale automatically became the property of the landowner on whose foreshore it lay. But, again, stranded whales were such a blessing from Heaven, providing heating and lighting for the whole community for weeks, that the settlers soon began to chase the whales in the bays, taking part with the Indians in the hunt and using the same methods with some innovations of their own. They used rowing boats in place of canoes, iron harpoon heads instead of bone and set up windlasses on the beach for hauling the carcasses out of the water. On Nantucket Island they planted tall poles with cleats on either side so that the look-outs could climb to the top. They kept watch between November and April when the Right whales passed down the New England coast in the autumn and north again in the spring.

As early as this, the end of the seventeenth century, the settlers introduced the co-operative or 'lay' system so that everyone was paid a share, settlers and Indians alike. This system has persisted right through the days of the Yankee whaling and is in use at the present day. In the early New England days the Indians were paid in kind, in clothing, powder and shot, in whale oil and, most important of all and never left out, in liquor.

Soon these early American whalers took to following the Right whales out to sea, just as the Basques had done, but the whales themselves were becoming shyer and scarcer so they probably had no alternative but to go after them. Quite often disputes broke out because in bad weather carcasses were apt to get lost and drift ashore whereupon the owner of the land along the foreshore would claim that the carcass was a stranded whale and his property. One day a dead Sperm whale was found by Indians on a beach on Nantucket Island. They said it was theirs because they had found it, but the English settlers said it was theirs because they had bought the land along the foreshore, while the government said it was unclaimed property and therefore belonged to the Crown. Meanwhile someone had stolen the teeth. Thus the Nantucket Islanders became familiar with the Sperm

6

whale whose oil was believed to be a cure for almost all known diseases.

The Nantucket Islanders were now beginning to build larger ships with which to pursue the Right whales, for they had to go farther and farther out to sea to find them. From rowing boats fitted with a single lateen sail the boats grew early in the eighteenth century into sloop-rigged, decked ships of 30 to 50 tons between 14 and 40 feet long (Sanderson, I., 1958). They were fitted out for cruises of five to seven weeks.

One day in 1712 a Captain Christopher Hussey, while lost at sea in an open boat, struck and killed a Sperm whale. He was cruising for Right whales near the shore 'and was blown off some distance from the land by a strong northerly wind when he fell in with a school of that species of whale and killed one and brought it home' (Hawes, C. B., 1924). This was the first Sperm whale to be taken practically since the days of Jonah. Right whales were now rapidly disappearing, so the whalers soon began going only after Sperm, though at first they contented themselves with taking one per trip, stripping it at sea and taking the blubber home in a few barrels. Thus in a small way began the great American Sperm whale fishery, which was soon to cover all the oceans with a fleet outnumbering those of all the other nations put together until its inevitable decline in the middle of the nineteenth century.

Nantucket Island was at first by far the greatest whaling centre on the American coast and by 1730 twenty-five whaling boats were based there. By 1755 Joseph Russell, a farmer, had built the first Sperm oil factory at Bedford, Massachusetts, later called New Bedford. It was supplied by a fleet of 50-ton sloops which made voyages of two or three months as far as Newfoundland and Virginia. These were comparatively short trips, known as 'plum-pudding voyages' presumably because the ships were home for Christmas, but by 1775 some 60 sloops were sailing from New Bedford each year as far afield as the Falkland Islands. New Bedford now rivalled Nantucket as a centre of whaling which also spread to other New England ports, Mystic, Martha's Vineyard and Boston.

The demand for the products of the Sperm whale on both sides of the Atlantic sent the price of oil up to £40 a ton and New England whaling became very prosperous in spite of pirates who roamed the seas, preying specially on whaling ships which were small and slow. But in 1775 the American War of Independence began and temporarily ruined the young American whaling industry because the ships could not go to sea for fear of capture by the British. Whaling ports were raided and the warehouses were choked with unsold oil. Nantucket almost starved and the condition of the islanders became so grave that twenty-four of their ships were allowed to go whaling by special permit issued by the British admiral. A few were captured and burnt, permits or no permits. By the end of the war the American whaling industry, once so prosperous, was quite dead—though not for long.

After the war the New England ports soon began to rebuild their whaling fleets. The whales, after a brief rest during the war, had become more plentiful off New England shores and by 1788 the number of whaling ships sailing from ports in Massachusetts had again reached a hundred. In 1791 five American ships rounded Cape Horn into the Pacific, where Enderby's ship *Amelia* of London had preceded them three years previously. Whaling voyages now extended up the west coast of South America as far as the Galapagos Islands and as far west as New Zealand.

Unfortunately this new prosperity was short-lived because the British government, already subsidizing its own whaling industry by means of the bounty system, put a duty of £18 per barrel on foreign oil. This closed the British market to the Americans and caused a slump in the price of American Sperm oil. New England whaling ports closed again and quite a number of the captains took jobs in British and French ships, moving their families to Canada or France. In 1789 France offered a market to American oil and business boomed once more, but larger and larger vessels had to be built because the whales were now becoming scarce in Atlantic waters. Whale ships were now barque-rigged and equipped for voyages of two or three years. At this point the island of Nantucket, cradle of American whaling, fell out of the race because its harbour has a bar across the entrance which could not be crossed by ships with a draught of more than ten feet. New Bedford became the chief whaling port of America and kept that position for nearly a century.

But now lean times came again upon the American whaling industry, always susceptible to the changes and chances of European politics. The first blow was the French Revolution (1793) which closed the French market as well as the British to American Sperm oil. The second was the Embargo Act of 1807. Privateers, mainly French, preyed ruthlessly on the high seas in those days and losses to them were so heavy that insurance became prohibitive. Accordingly Congress passed the Embargo Act which ordered all whaling ships to stay in port because the United States had no navy with which to protect them. The third blow was the outbreak of the war of 1812 during which the American whaling fleet was almost entirely destroyed by raids on the ports or taken as prizes by the British fleet. Again American whaling practically ceased, but, again, not for very long.

Yankee Sperm Whaling

After the war of 1812 whale products increased greatly in importance and value. Sperm oil was needed for lighting and heating all over the world. The Americans got their industry going again and during the middle of the nineteenth century the Yankee Sperm whaling entered upon its golden age. The 1812 war had left only about 40 whaling ships afloat but by 1821 there were 84 in commission (Sanderson, I., 1958) and from then on they increased in numbers steadily, sailing to the ends of the earth after the Sperm whale. They rounded Cape Horn into the Pacific and by 1835 there were a hundred whaling ships off Japan. They sailed past the Cape of Good Hope into the Indian Ocean and found large numbers of whales off Madagascar and the Seychelles. The great period of American Sperm whaling lasted from 1835 to 1846 and in 1842 there were 594 ships from the U.S.A. whaling on the high seas, more than three times the number of all the other nationalities put together (Harmer, S. F., 1928). The British, their biggest competitors, came a poor second. The peak year was 1846 when there were 729 American Sperm whalers on the high seas and 70,000 men were employed in whaling. Frank Bullen in *The Cruise of the Cachalot* records that you could not sail for twenty-four hours on the main Indian Ocean shipping routes without coming upon a whaler chasing or stripping a whale. From 1835 to 1860 the yearly production of Sperm oil totalled about 118,000 barrels and the total value of the whale products landed annually in the U.S.A. was $70,000. As an example of the sort of profits the whalers made at this time one ship, *Lagoda*, earned $652,000 in twelve years and her owners in one year paid a dividend of $363\frac{1}{2}$ per cent. She had cost less than $500 to build (Sanderson, I., 1958).

Yet if owners and skippers grew rich in this trade the same cannot be said of their crews. It was a hard and brutal life with poor pay (20 cents a day), bad conditions and worse food. Although the lay system operated on all whaling ships the share which went to the crew was very small indeed. In *The Cruise of the Cachalot* the author wrote—'Each of us were [*sic*] on the two hundredth "lay" or share at

$200 per tun, which meant that for every two hundred barrels of oil taken on board we were entitled to one, which we must sell to the ship at the rate of £40 per tun or £4 per barrel.' Supposing the ship got back to her home port after three years at sea with 20,000 barrels as a result of killing 800 Sperm whales, the crew would then share among themselves the price of one hundred barrels, that is £400. Among, say, thirty men this works out at about £13 each, less all deductions for clothing, tobacco and so on after three years' work before the mast. Needless to say the prices at which the crew were compelled to buy these necessities were unreasonably high. Cruel and inhuman officers used to abuse and maltreat their crews so as to goad them into insubordination for which one of the mildest penalties was the forfeiture of the man's share of the profits. Severer penalties were the rope's end, the knout and the cat-o'-nine-tails.

Yankee Whaling Ships

The whaling ships were heavy wooden vessels of about 350 tons, 'bow and stern almost alike, masts standing straight as broom sticks and bowsprit soaring upwards at an angle of about forty-five degrees' (Bullen, F., 1898). They were barque-rigged with decks flush fore and aft, square sails on fore and mizzen, fore and aft sails on the main. Sometimes they were ship-rigged, as was the *Cachalot*, with square sails on all three masts. Our own *Discovery*, a Dundee whaler, was barque-rigged. Right in the centre of the deck, occupying a space about 10 feet by 8 feet was a square erection of brickwork. This was the try works, two huge iron cauldrons over brick grates, surrounded by a trough of water. The officers' quarters aft were fairly spacious and comfortable, often with beds slung on gimbals to counteract rolling and with sprung mattresses. The captain's cabin housed a vast double bed because the skipper very often took his wife with him on whaling cruises. Needless to say the crew's quarters in the fo'c'sle were cramped and comfortless and often verminous. There were three tiers of narrow board bunks running into the angle of the fore-peak. A small oil lamp swung from the deckhead and heating was by means of an oil stove. Towards the end of the days of American Sperm whaling some of the ships had done as much as seventy or eighty years in the trade, at sea all the time apart from occasional refits.

In *Two Years Before the Mast* a meeting with a Yankee whale ship was thus described—'As soon as her anchor was down we went aboard and found her to be a whale ship, the *Wilmington and Liverpool Packet* of New Bedford, last from the "offshore ground" with nineteen hundred barrels of oil. A "spouter" we knew her to be as soon as we saw her by her cranes and boats, and by her stump top-gallant masts, and a certain slovenly look to the sails, rigging, spars and hull; and when we got on board we found everything to correspond— spouter fashion. She had a false deck, which was rough and oily, and cut up in every direction by the chines of oil casks; her rigging was slack and turning white; no paint on the spars or blocks; clumsy seizings and straps without covers and homeward bound splices in every direction' (Dana, R., 1834). Everything, in fact, to shock a smart young deckie eighteen months at sea.

The ship's complement of a whaler consisted of a captain and four mates, four or five harpooners and about thirty seamen. They were a polyglot mixture. The harpooners were nearly always Portuguese from the Azores or Cape Verde Islands who had a special aptitude for whaling. The seamen were of all races and nationalities, many of them youngsters who had drifted from farms into the whaling ports. There were many negroes who also had an aptitude for this trade and often became officers. One, named Paul Cuffee, became a skipper and finally a well-to-do owner of whaling ships.

Each ship carried four or five boats or shallops slung from cranes on the bulwarks and one or two spare boats were carried bottom up on a gallows on deck. They were similar to all other whaleboats, clinker built of cedarwood planks over white oak frames, about 30 feet long, narrow and double-ended with a small deck at either end. They were exceedingly light, easily handled and seaworthy, as they had to be, fitted with centre boards drawn up when not in use into a midships casing. They also had a mast and sails. At sea, except in the most severe weather, each boat was slung outboard on its davits with all whaling gear ready so that it could be lowered at a moment's notice.

Each boat was manned by a harpooner, a steersman and four oars-men. The steersman was usually one of the mates and in command of the boat. He steered it by means of a sweep 19 feet in length which was more efficient for steering than a rudder, but the pulling oars were shorter than this, 9 to 16 feet long. The bow thwart was occu-pied by the harpooner who took the bow oar. This thwart carried a three-inch hole for the insertion of the mast and was supported below by a solid baulk of wood. On the port side the rear plank of the foredeck had a notch in it of the girth of a man's thigh, the so-called 'clumsy-cleat', in which the harpooner could brace his thigh when he stood up to hurl the harpoon at the whale.

The forward plank of the afterdeck was likewise supported by a baulk of wood but it extended upwards above the afterdeck to form a pillar about eight inches high and six inches in diameter. This was called the 'loggerhead'. Round it the running line, attached to the harpoon and secured to the keel of the boat, could be made fast by means of several swift turns whenever necessary. The four oarsmen were the bow (though in fact the harpooner pulled the bow oar until he stood up to face the whale), the midships oar, tub oar and stroke. The bow oarsman was always the most experienced and trustworthy of the oar hands and his was a place of honour since he had charge of the lances and had to unsheath them for the final kill. The midship oarsman was the strongest man of the boat's crew and he pulled the longest oar, 16 feet in length. The tub oarsman had at his side the tub in which the harpoon line was coiled and it was his job to see that it came free without getting entangled and to keep it wet, since the friction of its passage over the fairlead in the bows could generate a heat which might set it on fire. The stroke oar had to set the time and pace and to keep the harpoon line clear as it ran out and coil it down handsomely as it came in.

The Kill

At sea the masthead look-outs were manned continuously during the hours of daylight. The look-out positions were not barrel crows-nests as they are today but merely pieces of planking on which the feet could rest, one on each side of the mast, and a couple of iron half hoops, rather like a pair of large spectacles, which came about waist high. The look-out on the mainmast was manned by a harpooner and a seaman, that on the foremast by a mate and a seaman. There was a bounty of ten pounds of tobacco free to the look-out first to give the famous cry—'Thar she blows!'

Then the skipper or the mate hailed the masthead.

'Where away? What do you call her?'

'Sparm whale, sir. On the port quarter, three miles to windward! Ah! Thar she white-waters!'

The ship would then down helm and come up as close to the whale as possible and, with no fuss, every man knowing his job, the boats were lowered, probably two or three with an officer in the stern of each with the steering oar, the oarsmen in their places, the harpooner at the bow oar. The officer was called the 'steersman' and the harpooner the 'boat steerer'.

If the whale were to leeward the mast was stepped, the large sprit-sails set and the boats sailed down upon their prey, but if it were to windward a long hard pull would be needed which might last for hours. The men were not allowed to look over their shoulders as they rowed or sailed lest the sight of the awesome monster should unnerve them. When at last the boat had come up to the whale the mast was unstepped and the boat brought into position for the harpooner to strike.

Two harpoons, or 'irons', lay ready in the bow pointing forwards, resting in a wooden fork called the 'crutch'. Each consisted of a rough, strong shaft of hickory about six feet long ending in a spear of soft iron about $2\frac{1}{2}$ feet long. The head was not arrow-shaped like that of the Dutch harpoons but was a fine steel blade with one edge broad and the other razor sharp, swivelled on a steel pivot on the shaft and held fixed by a wooden peg which broke on contact with the whale. The two harpoons were connected by lengths of line called 'forerunners' to the same whale line, 720 fathoms of manilla rope $1\frac{1}{2}$ inches in circumference. This was coiled down in tubs in 200-fathom lengths.

When the boat was in position the steersman cried to the harpooner, 'Stand up and face her!' Then the harpooner took up one of the irons and, when he judged the moment right, plunged it into the shining, streaming cliff of the whale's side as high up as possible behind the flipper. To strike the whale successfully with the iron called for great skill and strength and the harpooner was by no means always success-ful, sometimes more than one iron being required. If all failed a shower of abuse descended on the head of the harpooner from the steersman. But once 'fast to the fish', as they said, the harpooner picked his way aft in the rocking boat and the steersman came forward into the bows. This perilous change of place was traditional in all small boat whaling, American, Dutch or English, for it was always the steers-man's duty, as officer in command of the boat, actually to kill the whale. The harpooner now took the steering sweep and became the 'boat steerer' while the steersman took up his position in the bows ready for the kill and directed the boat's movements.

All the boats in the chase attacked the whale and cast their irons at it, but usually one boat successfully got fast before the others, who backed away and stood off to lend a hand if needed. Sometimes more than one boat got fast, and then they played the whale together. Indeed it sometimes happened that two boats from different ships got fast to the same whale in which case the two boats had by law to share the proceeds.

When struck the whale usually 'sounded' or made a long, deep dive, throwing up its great tail flukes and carrying out a long length of line which whipped out of the tub and went smoking over the bow fair-lead. On the other hand it might make off at speed towing the boat or boats behind it. As soon as the first wild rush of line slackened off a quick turn or two was taken round the loggerhead so that the rope led taut and dripping into the water, down to the suffering monster invisible beneath. It was the whalers' task now to play the whale like a giant fish, taking in just enough slack to prevent bights of line from getting round the body of the whale or round the boat. Sometimes the whale ran away with the full 720 fathoms' length of the harpoon line so that the other boats had to stand by to bend their lines on to that already fast to the fish.

In due course, after minutes or as much as half an hour, the whale had to come to the surface again in order to breathe. The boat now drew on to him, hauling in and coiling down the line, while the steersman stood ready in the bows with his lances. They were 'slender spears of malleable iron about four feet long, with oval or heart-shaped points of fine steel about two inches broad, their edges kept as keen as a surgeon's lancet. By means of a socket at the other end they were attached to neat handles or lance poles about as long again, the whole weapon being thus about eight feet in length and furnished with a light line or "lance warp" for the purpose of drawing it back when it had been darted at the whale' (Bullen, F., 1898, p. 13).

When ready the steersman sent his lances home, three or four if possible, aimed into the side high up, somewhere below the hump where the heart is. Now the boat had to back away quickly for the whale, mortally wounded, began the terrible and pathetic death agony, known as the 'flurry', thrashing the water with its tail in fear and pain, snapping with its jaws and wallowing in a smother of foam, crimsoned with its blood. If the boat did not back away quickly enough it was liable to be struck by the flailing tail flukes or snapped by the rod-like jaw. Although there were instances of 'ugly' whales trying to bite boats or turning upon them apparently in fury it is doubtful if a Sperm whale could deliberately deal a blow with its tail. Since it has no natural enemies one must doubt whether it would understand that it was being attacked. Its last thrashing movements are almost certainly blind and involuntary, as are probably the clashings of its jaws.

Sometimes the whale had to be approached and attacked a second time and there, too, lay danger from a sudden gigantic movement of the tail or head, and certainly casualties often occurred. This is how Dr. Robert Clarke (1954, pp. 332–33) described the drama of the Sperm whale's end as he himself witnessed it near the Azores:

'The movements of the flurry may be large in dimension but they are carried out slowly, with the labouring exertion of an exhausted animal. The struggle is heralded by the spouting of blood from the blowhole due to the mounting haemorrhage of the lungs. At this stage, called by the old whalemen "red flag" or "chimney afire", the respiratory beat is still sufficiently strong for the exhaled air to atomize the blood, so that the blow is a red mist. The whale struggles at the surface describing a somewhat circular path. The head rears more and more from the water, rising at an abrupt angle between six and fifteen feet into the air whilst the gape of the open mouth increases. The jaws now clash shut as the head falls sideways back, making a splashing withdrawal to a few feet beneath the surface. Next the whale rounds out, as though in an effort to sound. First the snout emerges and then the hump, and then the flukes rear out, but when these are still far from the vertical they fall back and smite the water with a report which, on a calm day, can be heard for miles. The head again emerges and pushes upwards, the jaw clashes and much the same labourings as those described take place once or twice again. The circular path is maintained, but the exertions become less and less large in scale. The spout of blood is no longer a mist but a broad, low cascade welling at the blowhole. If it has recently been feeding the whale vomits squid, sometimes very large, in whole or part. So much blood has been lost that the welling at the blowhole has ceased before the last convulsion takes place. The flukes may sweep a little in a slow, flat arc on the surface, and the head start to rear once more. Now the head splashes back, the body rolls out on one side, with the head awash and the jaws gaping and the stout blunt flipper sticking stiffly upwards. It is dead "fin out".

'A belief of the American whalemen was that the Sperm whale always dies towards the sun, that is, the head, as it rears in the circular path of the flurry, is always directed towards the sun. I have watched the flurry closely in three whales and noticed that this happened on each occasion.'

Now began the long arduous task of towing the whale back to the ship. The whale line was passed through a hole cut in one of the flukes and all boats' crews, towing in line ahead, bent to the oars. The pulling might go on for many hours but the ship, which had been keenly watching the chase and kill, bore towards them.

Brought safely back to the ship, the carcass was secured alongside by chains. Meanwhile a staging of planks, the cutting stage, had been erected over the bulwarks on the lee side and the work of cutting off the blubber in strips began at once. The cutting was done by the officers, using long-handled spades, standing on the cutting stage with the carcass in the water beneath them. When the blubber had been removed the head or 'junk piece' was severed from the carcass and lifted on board where the 'case' or spermaceti reservoir was slit open, letting the white, congealing, soft wax run out. The stripped carcass was cast adrift and left to the cloud of screaming sea birds. The strips of blubber were next cut up into 'horse pieces' about 18 inches long and 6 inches across and fed into the try pots beneath which the furnaces were fuelled by means of refuse and scraps from the carcass. When boiled enough the oil was poured into casks and stored below. The whole business took about three days of hard work and a whale of moderate size gave about 30 barrels. During the whole of the working-up time the ship drifted free with the wheel unmanned and no look-outs posted, but at night with cressets blazing which could be seen for many miles.

This was the hazardous, hard life the Yankee whalemen led. Not all of them got safely back to their homes, for there were many casualties, due not only to the hazards of whaling but to the dangers of lawless foreign ports.

The Decline of Yankee Whaling

After 1846 Sperm whales began to become less easy to find. They had been slowly diminishing during the twenties and thirties when the Yankees in the Pacific took to supplementing their catches with Southern Right whales, first around the Antipodes and later in the Sea of Okhotsk and through the Bering Strait. On the Californian coast they wreaked slaughter among the slow, amiable Grey whales.

American whaling, then, was already on the decline when it was struck by a further series of misfortunes. The first was the Californian gold rush, which drew away many of the likely lads from the whaling ports to try their luck prospecting. In 1857 America was unsettled

by the growing dispute about slavery and a financial slump sent down
the price of whale products. Capital to equip whaling expeditions
became difficult to raise. But in 1859 the greatest and most lasting
blow was struck at the whaling fleet. This was the discovery of
petroleum and the production of oil from mineral sources which
competed with Sperm oil and, in the end, drove it off the market as a
fuel and illuminant. In 1861 came the American Civil War and the
end of the golden age of whaling. Confederate commerce raiders,
especially the famous *Alabama*, captured or destroyed many whale
ships which belonged to Federal ports and practically drove the
whaling fleet off the seas.

In 1856 there were 635 American whaling ships on the oceans of
the world, but none at all during the years of the Civil War. After the
Civil War the price of whale products rocketed again and the number
of ships rose once more to 253, but by then a really serious decline
in the stock of Sperm whales had set in. The ships had to scour the
oceans for them and supplement their catches where they could with
other whales which were also growing scarce. Harmer (1928) writes—
'Sperm whaling reached its zenith in 1837, more than twenty years
before it had petroleum as a competitor. The decline from that year
to 1860 was due to the destruction of whales in excess of their rate of
reproduction.'

American whaling still lingered for a time, following the Greenland
Right whale north of the Bering Strait. In 1880 the first American
whale ship under steam sailed north, but she was too late. There were
not enough whales and the operating costs of the ships were too high.
In 1905 there were still 51 registered American whalers and a few kept
on until 1925 when two schooners were laid up at New Bedford.
Today there is only one American whaling ship, and she is embedded
in concrete at Mystic, Connecticut, where the old whaling town has
been lovingly preserved.

Japanese Whaling

On the other side of the globe Japan emerged during the nineteenth
century from the mist which had for so long hidden her from the
eyes of the western world. Until the arrival of Commodore Perry
and the United States Navy in 1853 Japanese laws had forbidden
citizens to travel abroad or foreigners to visit the islands whose
culture had remained unchanged for hundreds of years.

The predecessors of the present inhabitants of the Japanese islands were a people known as the Hairy Ainu because they wore beards and had hair on their bodies. They were not a seafaring people and probably did not hunt the whale. Yet before their day, in what corresponds to Neolithic times in Europe, whaling was taking place from the island of Sakhalin by the use of canoes made of skins stretched over a framework of withies. Bladders made of sewn skins or stomachs buoyed up the lines, which were woven from vegetable fibres. In fact this was probably much like primitive whaling anywhere else, among the Norsemen, Eskimoes or American Indians. Stone round houses of this date have been found in Japan containing whale bones.

Between this very early Japanese whaling and the beginning of the seventeenth century there are no records. The inshore, small boat whaling which we see depicted on Japanese prints probably dates from about 1606 when it was started by one private family named Wada of the town of Daichi, Kyushu (Budker, P., 1958). The most famous whaling pictures were by Yamada Yosei, published in 1829, but they show a technique so elaborate that it could not possibly have just suddenly begun and must have been learnt from people older than the Hairy Ainu.

The Japanese inshore whalers took Biscay Right whales, Sperm and Rorquals, especially Humpbacks, and also, farther north, Grey whales. They had look-outs stationed on the hills of the many wooded islands and signalled the species, position and direction of travel of the whales migrating southward down the coast in late winter and northwards in the spring and early summer. When one was sighted a regular armada set out from the shore (Budker, P., 1958). In the earliest Japanese whaling only harpoons and lances were used but in 1674 nets were introduced. There were 20 chasing boats 42½ feet long with eight oars and auxiliary sail. Each was manned by a headsman (boat-steerer), 13 men and a boy. There were six net-carrying boats of the same size but with 10 men and eight oars. There were six boats of the same size which helped the net boats to manœuvre. In addition there were four larger towing boats, another for the leader of the expedition and another for the second-in-command.

The crews stood up in the boats, facing forwards, pushing their oars as Oriental people do, instead of sitting down facing aft and pulling them. The net boats spread the nets across the channels between the islands and the chasing boats then manœuvred so as to drive the whale into them. When it was exhausted by its struggles in the net it was attacked with lances. One of the seamen of especial strength and bravery then dived into the water, swam to the whale and drove a long sword into its heart, or as near as possible. He then made a hole with a knife in the nasal septum between the blow-holes so that a rope could be passed through it. In the meantime most of the little men who swarm in Japanese prints had jumped into the water to await the end of the convulsions. When dead the whale was lashed between two towing boats and conveyed ashore. Every part of the carcass was used; the blubber was rendered down in iron pots; the meat—more important to the Japanese than the oil—was graded and sent to market; the intestines were thoroughly washed out and cut into small pieces as special delicacies; the bones and residue were dried and ground for use as manure; the baleen was washed, ironed and dried for bristles, stiffeners and for much the same uses as in the west.

This method, depicted in minute and realistic detail in old engravings, persisted until early in the twentieth century when the Norwegians arrived with up-to-date whale catchers.

The Harpoon Gun

Until the middle of the nineteenth century commercial whaling in the western world had concerned itself with Right and Sperm whales, and also with the Californian Grey. When these began to become really scarce the whale ships turned to the Bottle-nosed whale, and there was also a commercial fishery for Narwhals and White whales, but these were all of small importance compared with the whale fisheries which preceded them.

The great family of the Rorquals all this time had gone scot-free. They were 'wrong' whales and nobody could approach them or deal with them. They swam too fast and when dead their carcasses sank so that, with the equipment then available, they could not be towed. But now, in the absence of other prey, the whalers began to cast envious eyes upon the Rorquals, especially the Norwegians along whose coasts herds of them passed unmolested every year.

The problem of the Rorqual's speed was solved when steam was introduced. A whale could now be chased at 10–12 knots but it could not be killed, for hand harpoons and lances could not be thrown from the deck of a moving ship. In 1868 this problem, too, was solved by the invention of the modern harpoon gun.

Experiments had been going on for half a century with explosive lances and darting guns of various sorts able to fire a harpoon at the whale. Two Americans invented a sort of bazooka, the muzzle end of which rested on one man's shoulder while another pulled the trigger. It fired a harpoon with a rope attached coiled down in the boat, but it was an alarming instrument, apt to blow up, and the whalers did not take to it. The Yankee whalers did develop lances with explosive heads and Bullen in *The Cruise of the Cachalot* (pp. 146–148) described a contraption called 'Pierce's darting gun' but 'none of the harpooners could be induced to use it'.

The modern harpoon gun was invented by a Norwegian sealer turned whaler named Svend Foyn who was born in the little whaling port of Tønsberg in 1803. He had his own ship specially built and carried out experiments and trials with her for four years (Budker, P., 1958). This was the *Spes et Fides* (known as *Spisse* to the Norwegians), 86 gross tons and 94 feet 10 inches long. She was schooner rigged with free-edged sails, that is, without booms, and auxiliary steam. She had a movable board like a door abeam of the mainmast on each side, resembling an otter trawl board, which could be lowered over the side to take way off the ship and act as a brake, but it was not a success and was soon done away with. At first there was a battery of harpoon guns on the bows but they were reduced to one after experiment. The *Spisse* made her first cruise off the coast of Finmark in 1864 and when the first harpoon was fired Svend Foyn caught his foot in the line and was dragged overboard, but he was soon rescued and recorded in the log-book his thanks to the Almighty for his deliverance. He was a very God-fearing old man and in his correspondence and log-book he repeatedly apostrophized the Deity while devising this hideous weapon for the destruction of the largest and most innocent of the Deity's creatures.

After four years of trial and experiment the *Spes et Fides* made a successful whaling trip in 1868 and caught thirty Rorquals. The single swivel gun, mounted on a bow platform, fired a muzzle-loaded harpoon with two barbs. Later the explosive head was introduced so as to kill the whale while at the same time holding fast to it. The line, which was attached to the shank of the harpoon, ran up the foremast and down again into the forehold, passing over a slung pulley below the masthead. The pulley was slung on rubber 'sandows' which took up the strain as the ship rolled with a whale at the end of the line. In due course the rubber was replaced by powerful springs which are in use today.

Having killed the whale with this apparatus Svend Foyn was faced with the problem of what to do with it since the carcass immediately sank. He solved the difficulty by pumping the carcass up with compressed air, a cumbersome operation in those days with a hand pump and compressor, but today it is done with an electric pump. Svend Foyn assumed that since whales swim head first they should naturally be towed head first, but here was another problem because the head, being the heaviest part of the carcass, hung down in the water while the lower jaw hung lowest of all, causing the mouth to gape. Further, there was nothing on the flat head to which a towing line could be fastened. All this seemed an insuperable difficulty until some bright intelligence on board the *Spisse* suggested towing the carcass tail first so that the inflated body would float behind like a balloon, and this is how it is done to this day, the ribbed belly swollen and protruding from the water and the mouth agape with the tongue lolling out.

The modern harpoon gun does not differ much from that invented by Svend Foyn, though refinements have been introduced. In order to carry it a special type of small, fast ship, the whale catcher, came into existence. While they have become larger, more powerful and faster in recent years whale catchers remain little more than a harpoon gun mounted on a platform with a powerful engine and very manœuvrable hull behind it.

Although Svend Foyn patented his deadly invention in 1868 it was not taken up by Norwegian whalers until 1880. It gave them world-wide supremacy in whaling which lasted until the fifties of this century when the Russians and Japanese arrived on the scene and the southern industry collapsed through overfishing. It took the glamour but also the danger and hardship out of whaling and has led the way to the mass slaughter of Rorquals which has all but exterminated them in their turn.

Norwegian Whaling

Whaling now became land-based again, that is to say, the carcasses were not cut up and rendered down at sea as they had been in the days of the Right and Sperm whalers. Instead fleets of whale catchers carrying harpoon guns were based on whaling stations on shore like Dutch Smeerenburg in the seventeenth century and hunted over the neighbouring seas, bringing their catches back to the stations to be dealt with.

The first Norwegian whaling station was set up at Svolvaer in the Lofoten Islands, and then others opened at Tromsö and on the coast

of Finmark. Here Fin and Sei whales are abundant close in to the
coast, feeding on shoals of herring, so that the catchers, which were
small in those days, were able to hunt by day and lie in port over
night. *1905*

In the nineties these stations did well, starting from small beginnings. Their catches rose from about a hundred whales a year to over
two thousand in 1896, and stations opened in Iceland, the Shetlands,
the Hebrides and the Faroes and, a year later, in Newfoundland.

Early in the new century trouble arose with the Norwegian fishermen, a very large and politically important section of the community.
They put forward their belief, not based on evidence but on prejudice
and perhaps on jealousy, that whaling drove migrating shoals of fishes
away from the coast. Feeling ran very high and there were riots in the
fishing ports. The Norwegian government gave way and in 1904
placed a ban on the taking and landing of whales along the entire
coast of Norway. This forced the whaling companies, which had
already invested large sums in capital equipment, ships, gear and
trained personnel, to set up whaling stations on foreign shores and
they soon spread all over the world. By 1910 Norwegian whaling
stations were to be found dotted about the globe in many remote and
lonely places. They were in Alaska, on the coast of Chile, on the
Galapagos Islands, on the remote coast of Western Australia, in many
parts of Africa and in many other outposts and islands besides. Only
in Japan was a slight difficulty encountered for the Japanese government, in a burst of xenophobia, forbade whaling by any but Japanese
nationals, but the Norwegians were not deterred. They used Japanese
crews with two skippers and two mates, one of each Japanese and
nominally in control, the others Norwegian and actually in control.

This northern Norwegian whaling for Rorquals was short-lived.
From 1906 it declined rapidly owing, once more, to the disappearance
of the catches. By 1912 whaling had almost ceased in the northern
hemisphere, but meanwhile the whalers had begun to turn their eyes
southwards.

Modern Whaling

Since the thirties of the nineteenth century when James Weddell,
an English sealer, reported many whales in the Antarctic sea which
bears his name, exploring ships had been returning with similar reports
from various parts of the Antarctic. The whales they saw were all
Rorquals. In 1892 an expedition of four small steamships belonging

7

to the Tay Whale Fishing Company went to the Antarctic to look for Right whales which Sir James Clark Ross in the forties had claimed to have seen in large numbers. They found none, but saw many Rorquals and, after wintering in the Falklands, took some seals and returned home. In the same year two Norwegian expeditions went to the Antarctic also looking for Right whales. One was that of Captain Carl Anton Larsen in the *Jason*, a small sealer which Nansen had used for his landing on East Greenland in 1888. No Right whales were found but Larsen's reports stimulated H. J. Bull of Tønsberg to lead an expedition in the whaling ship *Antarctic*. This also found no Right whales but made the first landing on the Antarctic continent in South Victoria Land and returned to Norway convinced that an expedition fitted out for the capture of Rorquals would be successful. Accordingly in 1901 Captain Larsen again went south, this time in command of the *Antarctic*. This was the Swedish Antarctic Expedition led by Otto Nordenskjöld, which spent two winters on the northern tip of the peninsula of Graham Land. The *Antarctic* foundered in the ice but her Swedish crew were rescued by an Argentine naval vessel which took them to Buenos Aires. Here Larsen formed a company, the *Compania Argentina de Pesca*, registered in Buenos Aires, in order to carry on whaling from a station on the island of South Georgia. This he established in a bay which he called *Gryt Vik* or Pot Bay because the sealers, who used to operate there, had left their round iron blubber pots on the beach. Today, for some reason, the definite article has been added to the name of the place and it is called *Grytviken*, The Pot Bay. Larsen had failed to interest anyone in Europe in this venture but it was an immediate success and by 1911 seven other leases had been granted by the Falkland Islands government for whaling stations in South Georgia. At first the stations caught only Right whales and Humpbacks but by the outbreak of World War I these had disappeared and the stations' catchers were obliged to go a day or two farther afield in search of Blue and Fin whales.

Now we have reached the beginnings of modern whaling. The first floating factory ship was the *Admiralen*, which arrived in the Falklands in 1905. There she caught mostly Sei whales but in January 1906, finding that her catchers had to go ever farther afield to find any whales at all, she moved to the South Shetland Islands (Deception Island). Here she caught Blues, Fins and Humpbacks but met with a great deal of bad weather and returned to the Falklands at the end of February. In the years following World War I the number of floating factory ships increased and in 1923 Captain Larsen led a whaling expedition, in the factory ship *Sir James Clark Ross* with five catchers, into the Ross Sea on the other side of the continent. It returned with a cargo of 17,500 barrels of oil and in the two following seasons increased this to 32,000 and 40,000 barrels. This led the way to the extension of pelagic whaling along the pack-ice edge eastwards from South Georgia to the Ross Sea and to the slaughter from 1934 onwards of an average number of whales exceeding 30,000 a year.

CHAPTER 5

At the Whaling Station

At the station of the *Compania Argentina de Pesca*, founded by Captain Larsen at Grytviken, South Georgia, in 1904, there were five whale catchers in the summer season of 1929–30 and they hunted within twelve to twenty-four hours' steaming from the north-eastern coast of the island. This was the number of catchers permitted to each station under the terms of their government licence. There were four other stations working at South Georgia that year so that throughout the hours of the long southern daylight twenty-five catchers combed that comparatively small area of sea.

As far as possible the catchers brought their whales back to the whaling station at night, turned round in the harbour and went straight out again on the hunt so as to get on the whaling grounds by daybreak. From time to time, however, they were obliged to go alongside the jetty for an hour or two in order to refuel, or for some other reason, so that there were always one or two boats out of step with the rhythm, bringing in occasional whales during daylight hours. Their catches lay like monstrous, ribbed balloons in the murky waters of Grytviken Harbour until work began at the whaling station at five-thirty in the morning.

Wheeler and I had an arrangement with the foreman, a fatherly old man who stumped about with a whale hook and from time to time drew from his pocket an immense silver watch. He had agreed that when there were whales waiting in the water to be dealt with he would himself personally run up a tattered red flag on the mast of the coaling hulk so that we could see there was work awaiting us. When we saw through field glasses the flag fluttering from the mast of the hulk at half past four in the morning we knew we had to turn out. In mid-season it was almost always there, sometimes only faintly visible through whirling snow.

Wheeler, and our assistant, Saunders, and I gulped a cup of cocoa, brewed on a 'primus', and put on our whaling clothes. These comprised, in addition to overalls and as much warm clothing as the weather justified, a pair of sea-boots with wooden soles and heels studded with steel spikes an inch long. These gave a foothold on the slimy, slippery surface of the boards of the whaling 'plan', but they made progress very difficult anywhere else. I myself wore a pair of rubber thigh boots with wooden soles and heels, and they made progress anywhere even more difficult. We each had a belt on which we slung a heavy sheath knife. All these accoutrements hung on pegs in a rough room off the laboratory when not in use and, when we judged they were about ripe for it, we boiled them in kerosene tins over primus stoves. As the season wore on we heard quite a lot of complaints about the whaly aura which accompanied us and when the *Discovery II* arrived at Grytviken in January 1930 we were not welcome on board in our whaling clothes.

Thus arrayed we crossed the harbour in our motor-boat, reaching the whaling station in time for the start of work at five-thirty. Sometimes it was snowing heavily or blowing a gale from the scree-covered mountain slopes, or raining in torrents so that the mountains spouted water, but at other times, especially around Christmas, it would be a still, clear morning of pale, pastel shades with the many high snow peaks wearing caps of cloud and looking as though God had just said 'Let there be light'.

The official time for the start of work at the station was six o'clock, when the hooter blew and the men came streaming out of their barracks, but the three blubber strippers or 'flensers', as they were called, came on the scene half an hour earlier so as to have the first carcass ready stripped when the working gangs turned out. Otherwise the men would be obliged to stand about expensively doing nothing for about half an hour.

As we arrived alongside the station jetty we could see how many whales had come in overnight. Sometimes there were only one or two, but in the middle of the season, when each catcher was bringing in its quota of six or seven per trip, there might be as many as twenty carcasses lying there in the early morning, their grooved underparts upwards, swollen with the compressed air pumped into them, and now still more inflated by the gases of their own decomposition. The heads and tails were invisible beneath the greasy water so that they looked like enormous pumpkins. Multitudes of seabirds surrounded them, tearing at the blubber, fighting and screaming. At midsummer they speckled the surface of the harbour like leaves and their chatter and screaming, audible from afar, continued without ceasing day and night. This vast population of scavenging seabirds was entirely sustained by refuse from the whaling stations. Now that whaling in South Georgia has come to an end countless thousands of sea birds must have perished.

The 'Plan'

The central feature of every whaling station was the 'plan', a Norwegian word meaning a plain or level place. It was an open space about two acres in extent and, in spite of its name, not really level but sloping gently towards the sea where there was a slipway up from the water. This was the great charnel yard where the whales were stripped and dismembered and their fragments fed into the boilers. Its floor was boarded over completely like the deck of a ship, the boards always thick in grease and slime even when no work was in progress. Without the long spikes which all workers on the plan wore in their boots it was impossible to walk on it. Many steam winches with stout steel hawsers stood along the landward side and one especially powerful winch, wound with very heavy steel cable, faced the slipway. It was this which hauled the carcasses out of the water. On the two other sides were the sheds of corrugated iron that housed the boilers, one for the boilers for the blubber and opposite to it another for the meat boilers, with bucket hoists to the boiler tops. At the back of the plan was a raised staging about twenty feet above the level of the boarded floor. On this platform were winches and four steam saws, while a slipway sloped up to it from the plan. This was where the whales' final obsequies took place. Skull, jaws, backbone and ribs were all hauled up here to be cut up by the steam saws after the flesh had been stripped from them. Underneath the staging were the bone boilers into which the sections of bone were tipped. This was the 'bone plan', a kind of smoking high altar above the rest of the sacrifice.

All the other buildings of the whaling station, the administrative block, the living quarters, the ship repairing shops, the stores and so on lay disposed around the central plan, but at some distance from it, like a small town. The manager's villa was as far removed as possible, a Norwegian-style wooden house with a flag on a mast, in this case the Argentine flag. At Grytviken there was a small wooden church, the most southerly in the world.

The plan could accommodate two carcasses at a time, sometimes three if they were small ones. They were hauled up one at a time and each one was stripped of its blubber, or 'flensed', by a gang of three specially skilled men, the flensers, whose sole job was to remove the blubber from each carcass in three long strips. The stripped carcass was then winched across to the other side of the plan to be dealt with by another gang of three men called 'lemmers'. The next whale then immediately came up the slipway to be flensed. The lemmers' job was to butcher the carcass, to sever the head and ribs from the backbone, to carve off the back muscles and remove the viscera. By the time the last of the meat from the first carcass was being loaded into the hoists, and the skull and backbone were being hauled up to the bone plan, the second one had been flensed and was being handed over to the lemmers, while a third was coming up the slipway from the water. Thus it went on all day except for half an hour's break for breakfast at eight, an hour for lunch at twelve thirty and half an hour for coffee at three. The final knocking-off hooter blew at six. By that time each day at midsummer twenty or even more whales had disappeared into the boilers and when the plan was working to capacity it was a gory scene. Flesh and guts lay about like small hillocks and blood flowed in rivers amid the racket of the winches and the thrashing of the rotary knife that sliced the blubber. Steel wires whipped and tautened in all directions while clouds of steam from winches and boilers arose as from a giant cauldron.

As we approached the plan the Chief Flenser, Hans Hansen, was walking down towards the slipway pulling behind him the heavy cable from the main winch with a ponderous shackle on the end of it. He was the most important man on the plan, more important than the old foreman with his watch. He decided in what order the carcasses should be dealt with and his decision largely regulated the work on the plan. He was a stocky, broad-shouldered man with a sandy walrus moustache and small, bright, china-blue eyes. He was a very accomplished sail maker of the old school and, if you gave him half a bottle of whisky, he would run you up a suit of sails for the dinghy, a sea bag or a drogue or a golf bag from a whale's penis. Attached to the shackle on the heavy steel cable he was now hauling down the plan there was a heaving line which he carried looped over his right arm. In the meantime the station motor-boat, with its decked-in diesel

engine tonking rhythmically, was busy towing whale carcasses towards
the slipway in twos and threes. Hansen pointed to a cow Blue whale
carcass and heaved his line accurately to the boy on the deck of the
motor-boat. The boy hauled the shackle and cable to the boat and
attached them to a steel wire sling round the whale's tail. The flukes had
been cut off by the crew of the catcher at sea in order to make handling
easier so now only a triangular stump of the fluke remained on each
side round which the sling was made fast.

At a signal from Hansen to the winch the hawser rose out of the
water and became taut, dripping. The tail rose first out of the water
and moved slowly and rather jerkily up the plan. There was an overhead coal railway above the seaward edge of the plan at Grytviken,
straddling the slipway on a high wooden bridge which made a hazard
which the whales had to overcome on their way to their last rites.
Sometimes a flipper, or the battered, spent harpoon still sticking in
the back of the carcass, would foul the posts of this bridge and then
everyone stood back and waited for the bridge to come down, bringing
the railway with it, with pleasant anticipation of disaster. But it never
did, though the flipper often smacked back with a force that it was as
well to stand clear of.

The Carcass

The huge fusiform dead thing with cliff-like sides almost always
came up lying half on its back and half on one side. Only occasionally
did it, owing to some trick of balance, come up on the plan lying on
its front so that the flat triangular head, and the long smooth back with
its back fin, were uppermost. Lying half on its back it had the grooved
throat and chest uppermost, facing sideways left or right, one oar-like
flipper sticking up in the air, the other underneath the body. The
blowholes were under the head and so not visible. The lower jaw and
voluminous rough-surfaced tongue fell sideways, the tongue lolling
out so as to expose the foremost baleen plates, blue-black on either side
of the narrow black palate, making a V-shaped trough lined by coarse
black bristles.

The eye, right at the corner of the mouth, had neither lid nor lashes
and was open, as in life, but glazed now and opaque. The ear-hole
was a tiny aperture not much larger in diameter than a human little
finger. It was above and behind the eye, but below it from this aspect
since the carcass was lying on its back. There was no outer ear of any
kind and the hole was quite flush with the surface of the head. On

the edge of the upper jaw one could see small, inconspicuous bristles arranged in groups, all that remains of the hairy pelt of the land mammal.

Behind the grooved thorax and the belly was the genital opening lying in a groove and in front of it, within the groove, the clitoris, a curved organ like a finger about three inches long. Owing to the pressure of the compressed air inside the belly the genital groove was gaping open so that the clitoris was protruding. On either side of the genital groove the nipples too were protruding like rounded bosses from the slits in which they are normally concealed in a cow that is not nursing.

In the bull Rorqual the penis is a smooth, cylindrical organ tapering to a conical tip. In the flaccid condition, not erected, it is withdrawn into a slit in the belly wall and is almost invisible. Indeed there has often been confusion in the whaling returns between young bulls and cows for this reason. When erect the organ is extruded from the slit and, in large Blue bull whales, it may be eight or ten feet long. A large bull usually comes up on the plan with the penis extruded but flaccid, trailing its pointed tip along the boards. In both whalebone and toothed whales the penis bears a striking resemblance both in shape and structure to that of cattle and other even-toed Ungulates.

So there it is, this poor hulk, its skin already soiled by birds which have been pecking at it all night, streaked with slime and ruled with a longitudinal greasy high-water mark, the result of lying all night in the fouled and polluted water. It was difficult to believe that less than twelve hours ago this impersonal mass was a living animal, snorting through the fields of ocean. In an hour's time nothing would be left of it at all. The improbability of its appearance somehow made it more difficult to believe that it was ever a living creature. This, and the impersonality of living things after death have, I think, made men callous about killing whales. The marine environment, too, is another factor. It is so mysterious and secret. If a whale in life were as familiar and near to us as a stag or a horse a more humane view would long ago have prevailed about whaling. We only get a close view of whales after they are dead, and then they look so very dead! The fact is that death, whether of an animal or human being, is death—totally impersonal and not in the least like sleep.

Flensing

When the carcass came to a halt on the plan, its tail near the hauling winch and its snout near the water's edge, the two other flensers arrived on the scene carrying their long-handled flensing knives. The flensing knife has a curved blade of fine steel, about four inches across, on the end of a wooden handle some four feet long. The blade was always kept razor sharp and every man had his own knife which he kept sharp himself or saw to it that it was kept sharp. His initials were carved on the shaft of the handle and he carried in his belt a hone with which he freshened up his knife from time to time, pausing in his work and lubricating his hone with spit. Some could spit squarely on to the face of the hone holding it at arm's length. Practice made perfect, no doubt. Each of us three had a flensing knife borrowed from the old man who presided over a sort of armoury with a grindstone where all the knives were kept and repaired. He was in general charge of knives. We also each carried a hone but no amount of spit would keep my knife sharp. At intervals, which varied with the amount of use I made of my knife, I used to pay the old knife grinder a visit. It cost me a tot of whisky a time but for that I came out of his shop with my blade shining like the crescent moon and keen as the sword of Saladin.

The flensers peeled the blubber off every carcass in the same way, in three long strips. Hansen made a cut along the back just above ground level from the tail to the snout, the blubber parting abruptly under his knife with a crisp satisfying sound. Fritz, the second flenser, made another similar cut along the belly, the pleated chest and throat. Hartvig, the third flenser, ran his knife right along the uppermost side of the carcass in the middle line, walking along its shining flank and side fifteen feet above the floor of the plan. These three cuts went just through the firm white blubber layer to the red muscle beneath, but did not cut the flesh, or very little. When they had been completed the blubber was in two upper strips and a third underneath the carcass which was lying upon it as though upon a blanket. The two uppermost strips were drawn off the carcass from before backwards by wire hawsers from the winches. Almost simultaneously they arched upwards and backwards with a crackling sound, leaving the white connective tissue undercoat on which the blubber lies. The flensers aided their progress with sweeping but gentle strokes of their knives to and fro transverse to the long axis of the strip, as one does on a much smaller scale when skinning a rabbit. Each strip came away cleanly in one piece because the whale wears its blubber like a garment, and the thick layer of white connective tissue underneath it enables the blubber to vary in thickness. When the blubber has been removed the connective tissue layer invests the carcass like the pith of an orange.

The actual living skin of the whale is very thin (5–7 mm. in a big one—Slijper, E. J., 1962) and so cannot be made into leather or hide nor used commercially at all. It contains neither sweat nor sebaceous glands and so is cool and dry and not in the least slimy to the touch. It secretes a thin cuticular outer layer which, when the skin is dry, can be peeled off like thin tissue paper.

When the two strips had been peeled off back to the tail, like two lengths of skin from a banana, the flensers broke them off with a stroke of the knife and they lay with their white undersides upwards side by side alongside the blubber shed. Here they were cut into rectangular blocks, looking like cheese or bacon, the 'horse pieces' of the old-time whalers. These were fed into an aperture in the wall of the shed at ground level where a circular knife noisily revolved and sliced them up into sections which were carried up to the tops of the boilers by a moving conveyor. All this was the work of the blubber boys. In the old whaling days this was unskilled work and was done by boys but in my day at the Pesca station the blubber boys were stout Argentines of Polish extraction who chattered as they wielded their whale hooks in a mixture of Spanish and Polish.

The carcass was now turned over so as to remove the third strip of blubber on which it was lying. When this too had been peeled off the carcass was naked except for its white shift of connective tissue. The flensers had finished with it and it was pulled across to the other side of the plan, one wire at the head and another at the tail, in order to be butchered by the lemmers. Already the next carcass, chosen by Hansen, was jerking up the slipway.

Lemming

The Head Lemmer, short clipped moustache and hard blue eyes under an old peaked cap shiny with grease, spoke no English but swore a lot in Norwegian. He was a man of great strength, as he had to be, and a flensing knife in his hands looked as light and precise as a surgeon's scalpel. His first job was to cut out the tongue and remove the lower jaws or mandibles from their attachments to the skull.

The Tongue

The tongue of a Rorqual is a huge cushion of connective tissue, full of elastic fibres. It contains practically no muscles and very few blood vessels so that the whale cannot move its tongue. It used to be thought that the tongue could be inflated by being engorged with blood when the whale was feeding and pressed against the roof of the mouth so as to sweep the food off the baleen bristles and back into the throat, but it is now realized that this cannot be true. In life the tongue seems to be just a great rigid cushion and its precise function is not certain. In the Rorqual foetus the tongue has a free tip but in the adult this disappears and the tongue is attached everywhere to the floor of the mouth. In toothed whales the tip of the tongue is free throughout life and the tongue itself is more muscular, but it is still not certain what exactly its function is. It carries no taste buds in any whale so that, like all animals that swallow their food whole, the whale does not taste what it eats.

When the tongue had been cut out of the mouth it lay on the plan like an enormous, shapeless jellyfish, covered with wrinkled, bluish-black skin. Its oil yield is low so it was often left lying about until the meat and viscera were being cut up, and then it went into the boilers with them. As the water drained out of it the tongue gradually spread outwards like an amoeba and became a menace to safety because its elastic tissue was remarkably mobile and if, inadvertently, you happened to step on it the wobbly tissue immediately slid away like a million banana skins. You were liable to go down on your backside in the muck and slime, which was a cause of great mirth to everybody. Very unlaughable accidents, however, have often happened as a result of this, broken limbs or cuts from falling on knives. On our way south the voyage through the tropics was enlivened by hair-raising stories of men slipping into boiler tops, flush with the deck, with several tons of tongue tissue running down on top of them.

As the tongue was being cut out the lower jaws came away together as a pair like a huge Gothic doorway. They are slung from the base of the skull by cushions of muscle which the lemmers cut through easily. This left the triangular head and upper jaws exposed upside down and bare right back to the throat. We could see how small the throat was, just as Kipling said, not more than four or five inches in diameter.

The Baleen

The head, with the two rows of baleen plates, one on each side, forming a trough lined by black bristles, made an isosceles triangle with the eyes at the basal angles and the throat in the middle of the base line.

Each species of whalebone whale has a different number of baleen plates in the upper jaw, different in shape and size for each species. They are made of exactly the same horny substance as our hair or finger and toe nails, growing in the same way at the base and wearing away elsewhere, especially along the inner edge. It is said that a whale completely renews its plates within the space of seven years. The plates hang down from the upper jaw in continuous series one behind the other about $\frac{1}{3}$ inch to $\frac{3}{4}$ inch apart. Each is a triangle, the longest side facing inwards and slightly curved, frayed out into a mat of long bristles. The plates are shortest in the front of the jaw, largest in the middle and then diminish back to the jaw angle.

Right whales have long slender baleen plates, very fine and flexible, frayed out into soft, silky bristles. The Greenland Right whale has about 300 on each side with an average length of 10 feet and a maximum of $14\frac{1}{2}$ feet (Slijper, E. J., 1962). Rorquals have shorter and broader plates, the Blue an average of between 318 and 326 on each side with an average length of $3\frac{1}{2}$ feet, rather coarse in texture and bluish-black in colour (Mackintosh, N. A. and Wheeler, J. F. G., 1929). The Fin has an average of between 356 and 392 on each side with an average length of $2\frac{1}{4}$ feet. They are black or bluish but about 150 on the right side in front are cream coloured. The bristles are usually the same colour as the plates except in the Sei whale which has dark grey plates but white bristles of fine silky texture.

The baleen plates owe their strength and flexibility to their structure. Microscopically they are built up of close-packed hollow tubes embedded in a matrix. The tubes run through the whole length of the plate and form the bristles so that each bristle is really a hollow tube. The plate is thus a bundle of tubes and this ensures great tensile strength, lightness and elasticity, and is a type of structure frequently used in engineering.

These microscopic details, of course, cannot be seen with the naked eye and the plates look quite solid. Each plate is crossed by a series of wavy transverse ridges which had long been thought to represent a periodicity of growth and might possibly give a clue to the age of whales (see Chapter 8).

The lemmers removed the baleen plates as two continuous strips by cutting along the jaw through the tissue beneath their bases. At South Georgia these were the only parts of the carcass which were not used and they were dumped out at sea when convenient by the motor-boat. A submarine feature made of baleen plates must by now exist off the northern coast of the island.

The Skull

Next the head came off, the lemmers cutting through the fibrous jacket surrounding the articulation of the skull with the first neck vertebra. The articulation consists of two rounded bosses of bone, the occipital condyles, with the entrance to the brain case between them.

Like all mammals whales have seven cervical (neck) vertebrae but so flattened and compressed that no sign of a neck can be seen from the outside. Unlike dolphins and porpoises, in which the neck vertebrae are fused together, Rorquals and Sperm whales have them separate. Removing the head from the neck was a tough job, always done by the head lemmer himself, who spat on his hone and wiped the sweat from under the peak of his cap on even the coldest morning. The head came away quite suddenly, pulled by a wire at the snout.

On the rear or occipital aspect of the skull the ear bones were visible. Each bone, known as the tympanic bulla (or petro-tympanic bone), looked like a conch shell adhering to the base of the skull. It is actually a hollow flask or bony capsule which surrounds part of the middle ear and is quite loosely attached to the bony body of the skull by means of a peg so that it can be easily removed. The outer aspect of the bulla, after removal, may, at a stretch of the imagination, be taken to resemble a human face. A little painting up, and the addition perhaps of some tufts of hair, and it is sure to bear a fancied and not very complimentary resemblance to somebody on the station, usually the manager if possible.

During all these butchering operations great quantities of blood came cascading out of the carcass. It was now pouring out of the headless trunk from the great arteries and veins of the neck, flowing over our boots to make an ever-growing scarlet margin to the greasy water of the harbour. In spite of this apparently vast volume of blood measurements have shown that the ratio of blood to body weight in whales is not really very different from that in other mammals, 6·6 per cent in the horse, 8·1 per cent in the sheep and 6·5 per cent in the Blue whale (Slijper, E. J., 1962).

The Thorax

The lemmers now began to open the headless trunk, beginning with the thorax, exposing the heart and lungs, and then passing to the belly to expose the stomach and viscera. First they cut away the ribs on the uppermost side so as to open the thoracic cavity, a wire from a winch keeping a strain on the uppermost flipper. When the ribs came away they took the heart and lungs with them. Rorquals have only a small, reduced breast-bone to which the first pair of ribs is attached so that a cut along the middle line severed the ribs of opposite sides from each other. The lower ribs were left like a great scallop shell attached to the backbone, containing a dark pool of blood. This was next separated from the backbone and whisked away, spilling its blood out between its severed ribs as it went.

As in all mammals the thoracic and abdominal cavities of a whale are divided from one another by a sloping muscular wall, the diaphragm. In whales this is much more obliquely placed than in other mammals and in its upper part lies almost horizontally. The cavity of the thorax itself is relatively wide dorsally so as to accommodate a heart which is wide but not really large for the size of the animal. The lungs again are small for the size of the body, comparatively only about half as big as those of other mammals (Slijper, E. J., 1962). They lie high up in the widest part of the thoracic cavity with their longest surfaces pressed against the backbone, not extending downwards towards the breast as the lungs do in land mammals or man. Thus the lungs of a whale occupy a position similar to that of the swim bladder of a fish and act as a buoyancy chamber, raising the centre of gravity of the body in much the same way.

In most mammals the trachea or windpipe opens into the throat at the glottis and is a tube reinforced by incomplete rings of cartilage. Lower down it divides into two branches, the bronchii, one to each lung. In whales there is a small third branch which goes directly to the fore-part of the right lung, a peculiarity also seen in cloven-hoofed ungulates (except camels). Many of the cartilage rings of the windpipe are fused together in whales so as to form cylinders or sleeves, giving the tube extra strength.

These details cannot be easily seen on the plan because the contents of the thorax come away in a jumbled heap. The heart looks very big, some six feet wide and weighing half a ton, and the lungs are a pair of shrivelled sacs covered by a yellowish jacket of connective tissue, the pleura. If you make a cut in the lungs with a flensing knife, the spongy red tissue inside exudes a crimson froth.

The Abdomen

After opening the chest and carrying away the ribs, the next task
was to open the belly. The cut which took away the uppermost ribs
was now carried on backwards and downwards obliquely to the vent,
and thence vertically down to the ground. This was to allow a great
flap of the belly wall to fall down like a drawbridge, when out should
roll quite cleanly all the guts, the stomach, liver and intestines, and in
the cow the uterus with its contained foetus. In practice this never
quite happened.

The instant an animal dies decomposition begins, first of all in the
gut. As time goes on the gases generated by bacterial action, which
causes decomposition, inflate the organs, especially the intestines and
stomach, so that they press against the abdominal wall and the belly
swells like a balloon. None of the whales we saw on the plan had
been dead less than about seven hours, many for twelve or more, so
that their insides were always in varying states of decay, the gut
pushing against the belly wall. As the keen edge of the lemmer's knife
slid through the rather thin belly muscles the pale whitish blue intestines
bulged out between the red lips of the cut. One touch of the knife,
purposeful or accidental, on those protuberances and an explosive jet,
a fountain or cascade, according to the extent of the wound, shot out
throwing orange liquid intestinal contents six feet and more from the
carcass. One could not always be certain of avoiding this malodorous
shower bath which was often atomized by the force of the explosion
and blown far and wide by the wind.

When the flap of the belly wall fell down the intestines pushed out
and came clear, coil upon coil of whitish motor-tyre inner tubes,
tinged with blue. A slash with a knife here and there showed them to
be infested with the long, beaded, ribbons of tape worms fixed by
minute heads to the intestinal wall.

Our first whale was a cow and the folds of the uterus fell out at
the rear before the coils of the intestine emerged. At first sight they
looked like a disarranged curtain of bluish-white and pinkish-white
satin, and they tumbled out disorganized in fold upon fold like the
coverings of a bed. Nearly all the cow whales we saw were pregnant,
carrying the usual single foetus which we could discern as a curved
shape outlined under the coverings of the uterus, rather as though it
had fallen out of bed wrapped in folds of the bedclothes.

In all whales the bull's testes are internal, lying within the abdominal cavity, and not descended into a scrotum as in most land mammals. They are a pair of sausage-shaped objects, in the young Rorqual smooth and white and about six inches long, but enlarging greatly at puberty. In a big Blue whale they may be 2 feet 6 inches in length and weigh 75 to 100 lbs. each. Inside they are the same as those of all mammals, a maze of small tubules the walls of which generate the spermatozoa, no larger in a Blue whale than in a man.

Here we may note that almost all the organs of the Rorqual's inside have a whitish appearance with bluish or pinkish tinges. This is because they are sheathed in thick coats of connective tissue. The liver and heart are red but the heart is covered with a good deal of white connective tissue and fat. The kidneys, composite organs made up of huge numbers of small red kidney units, are swathed in white connective tissue. Bluish and pinkish tinges are due to blood vessels showing through the coverings. Provided the tissues are fresh, which they hardly ever were on the plan, and nothing is damaged, so that no blood or faecal or other matter has been spilt, the inside of a whale, like that of any animal or man, is clean and almost odourless. Unpleasant odours begin to build up from the moment decay sets in. When we saw them the organs were all damaged and their contents strewn broadside.

As long as there were carcasses waiting at the slipway the butchering on the plan did not cease for a moment until the hooter blew for the various pauses for meals and for the final knocking-off time at six o'clock. It was our job to dive in and make what observations and notes we could while ribs, guts and muscles were being ripped apart. As we worked the carcasses were torn asunder and reduced to heaps of meat and sections of bone with flesh adhering to them. In less than an hour from the time that each one came up the slipway and flensing began nothing was left of it and all trace of it had vanished up the meat hoists into the boilers, up the bone slipway to the steam saws, into the blubber conveyor. The last of every one was the long stripped backbone snaking up to its last rites on the bone plan. The men who worked with whale hooks hauling the meat and guts towards the hoists were by then armoured and shining with oil and blood up to their thighs.

Each morning the sun was well up by the time the fifth or sixth carcass was jerking its way out of the scarlet water. A spiritual feeling was now beginning to manifest itself in my inside when suddenly, with a rising jet of steam from its position on the blubber shed, the hooter blew for breakfast. Abruptly silence descended upon the

8

charnel yard as the men streamed back to their quarters, leaving their knives and whale hooks exactly where they stood at the very moment when the eldritch but welcome shriek began. Now the gulls descended screaming upon the crimson disorder. They, like us, had half an hour in which to fill themselves to repletion and get back again, they to their rooftop perches and we to our arduous, malodorous tasks.

CHAPTER 6

The Rorqual

Our work on the plan had certain primary objectives, and the observations and the notes we made were all directed towards them.

Firstly, we had to note the length and sex of each carcass and, of course, the species. This would establish growth rates and sex ratios and the proportion of young to old whales in the population. The changes in the average size of whales caught would give a clue to the effect of whaling on the stock of whales in South Georgia waters. From such statistics, collected over several years, analyses of the population could be made with regard to species, size and sex and changes noted from one season to another. For such analyses it was important to establish certain critical points, one might almost call them milestones, in the life of every individual whale not only at South Georgia but all over the Antarctic. One such was the length at which the whale reached sexual maturity or puberty, and another was that at which it reached full physical maturity, or, in other words, became fully grown so that all growth had stopped. We also had to make certain bodily measurements so as to record changes in bodily proportions as the whales grew. If the proportions were different in southern from those in northern whales it might be that southern Rorquals belong to an entirely separate population, even a different species, from northern ones.

Secondly, we had to look at the stomach of every whale we saw since what the animal was feeding on, or if it were feeding at all and how much, were facts of obvious importance in an investigation of this sort. Thirdly, we had to look at the genital organs, the uterus and its contained foetus, the ovaries and testes, which would give us some information about the whale's breeding cycle.

External

Before each carcass was stripped we had to inspect it thoroughly on the outside, looking for external parasites and special markings which might tell us something about the past history of each whale. We noted the presence of whale lice and barnacles on the skin, and those strange tassel-like creatures which hang outside the blubber and are the females of a Copepod crustacean (*Penella*). They are greatly modified and very degenerate and live with their heads buried in the blubber while the males and young stages are believed to be free-living but have never been seen.

These creatures all attach themselves to the whale's skin in the tropics but die off in cold Antarctic waters. Their presence or absence, therefore, their abundance or scarcity and the extent to which they seemed to be in course of rejection by the whale, all gave a clue as to whether the whale was a new arrival in the south or had been in the Antarctic for a longer time.

Every carcass bore certain curious and, in those days, mysterious markings whose presence and numbers also gave the same sort of indications. They might also give some hint of how many visits the whale had made to tropical waters. For these were evidently the healing scars of wounds inflicted in the tropics. They were white, oval, healed cicatrices seen most abundantly on the flank, belly and tail regions. On many whales, especially larger, older ones, there seemed to be several grades or generations of these marks, newer, more distinct ones overlying older, fainter ones.

For a long time these were a great puzzle and no one knew what could be the cause of them, though they were familiar enough to the whalers. They had never been noticed on any species of whale which spends its whole life in cold waters, like the Greenland Right, the Narwhal or the White whale.

Whales taken at tropical stations bore open wounds, like bites in the blubber, of which these at South Georgia were the healed scars. At Durban we saw what looked like the marks of teeth.

It has now been established that in some whales at least the wounds are caused by lampreys, eel-like creatures with suctorial mouths and with horny teeth with which they bore into the skins of fish. A Canadian biologist at a whaling station on Vancouver Island found wounds on Fin and Sei whales which showed tooth marks corresponding to the teeth of the Canadian lamprey. He also saw lampreys dropping off the whales back into the water as the carcasses came up the slipway (Pike, G. C., 1951).

Puzzling features, however, remain. The lamprey inhabits shallow inshore waters and estuaries and is never found far out at sea. While the whales around Vancouver Island might well be attacked by them close inshore among the islands it is hard to see how the great ocean-going Rorquals could come under such massive attack by these creatures as the numbers of their scars seem to indicate. Rorquals seldom approach the coast but mainly spend their lives hundreds of miles out at sea.

Consul Olsen, who first described Bryde's whale (1913), reported that creatures called hag-fish caused wounds in the skin of that species of whale at Durban. At Saldanha Bay, Cape Province, what looked like hag-fish had been noticed attached to whales at sea but they dropped off as soon as the whales were captured. Hag-fish are related to lampreys but are entirely marine. They are elongated, eel-like, slimy fishes with suctorial mouths armed with sharp horny teeth. They live buried in mud or sand at depths down to 300 fathoms with only their heads protruding. They seem to feed mainly on dead or dying fish on fishermen's lines or in their nets, boring through the skin into the body cavity. It is certainly possible that the wounds on the flanks of whales may be caused by these fishes, but the same sort of difficulty arises since hag-fish, like lampreys, are mainly coastal though they do occur in deeper water. If this is indeed the explanation of these wounds one would have to assume that all Rorquals, since all seem to be heavily attacked, must pass through water with a depth of 300 fathoms or less at every, or almost every, visit to tropical waters. But this seems very unlikely since there are few places along the coasts of tropical Africa or South America where the 300-fathom line is not close in to the shore. At present, therefore, the exact origin of these wounds remains an unsolved problem.

These parasites and markings are acquired in the tropics, but there is one which is acquired in the Antarctic and shed in warmer waters. This is the yellow film which covers the skin of Blue and Fin whales from mid-season, about Christmastime, onwards. It forms more thickly on Blue than on Fin whales and is thickest and most complete on fat whales with thick blubber, especially towards the end of the season. Indeed at one time Blue whales which bore this yellow discoloration, often from snout to flukes, were believed to belong to a different species known as the 'Sulphur-bottom' whale.

The film is now known to be made up of unicellular plants (diatoms) with skeletons of silica like those which compose the mass of the plant plankton. Several species are found in the film on the bodies of whales (Hart, T. J., 1935) and the commonest of them forms a film on ice floes in the Antarctic pack ice. The plants reproduce themselves by means of spores so that the whales become infected with them when they visit the ice. A slight infection of film was a sign that a whale had visited the pack ice edge fairly recently. It is known that the infection takes about a month to develop so that a faint spattering of yellow might indicate that the whale had been about that time in Antarctic waters. A heavy infection meant a fairly long stay in the south, hence its appearance late in the season. Blue whales tend to be more heavily infected than Fin because they frequent the pack ice edge while Fin whales, on the whole, keep away from it. In tropical waters the yellow film disappears, the plant cells dying and dropping off the skin.

So much for the outside of the carcass. By now there was little time left in which to see it anyway, but before the two strips of blubber came away one of us measured the thickness of the blubber layer on the flank in as nearly as possible exactly the same place on every carcass. This would give a measure of relative fatness throughout the season. It involved stepping astride the taut steel hawser pulling on the blubber strip. We often had to straddle taut wires like this but it was a dangerous thing to do because if something were suddenly to give way and the wire to whip back at a critical moment a broken limb or even castration (so they jocularly assured us, as though that would have been a great joke) might well have resulted. 'D'you want to lose them?' they shouted. But we thought it was all in the cause of science.

The Stomach

After the lemmers had begun to dismember the carcass our next concern was the stomach. A study of feeding habits and diet was of obvious importance in the study of a population whether of whales, fishes or any other living creature.

When the intestines fell out from the abdominal cavity we were able to examine them thoroughly throughout most of their length. Those of a dead Rorqual measure about four times the length of the body, but considerably less in life because the intestinal muscles relax and stretch after death. This compares with man, $6\frac{1}{2}$ times the length of the body, and with the lion, 3·9 times. But in the sheep the intestine is 30 times the length of the body and in the seal 16 times (Slijper, E. J., 1962). Herbivorous animals tend to have long intestines and carnivorous animals short ones, while omnivorous animals such as man have intestines of intermediate length. A man has 154 inches of intestine when alive, stretching to about twice that length when dead.

The stomach remained largely hidden when the abdominal cavity was opened on the plan because of the flap of the belly wall which fell down on top of it. Parts of the liver also hid it from view. Only a small part of it could be seen protruding like a bag from which, in a whale recently fed and with a full stomach, the shrimp-like crustaceans known as 'krill' which form the Rorquals' exclusive diet, came spilling out like corn from a bin*. From a full stomach a mound of it representing a ton or more spilt out and you could stand in it up to the knees. In a whale recently fed the krill was as good as fresh. From the examination of several hundred stomachs of Rorqual whales at South Georgia, along the ice edge and over great stretches of the Southern Ocean it can be said that this pink and orange, pop-eyed shrimp-like creature 2½ inches long or less is the sole diet of whalebone whales in the Antarctic. At South Georgia only very occasionally was anything else whatever discovered among the mass of krill in various stages of digestion, and that had evidently been engulfed by accident.

A large number of the stomachs we saw at South Georgia were full, from what we could see of them, and all of them had the remains of at least some krill. A very few were empty, containing nothing but gallons of sea water possibly swallowed during the death agony when the whale drowns. In some cases where the stomach appeared to be empty we found krill entangled upon the baleen bristles, the whale having evidently vomited up the contents of its stomach when struck by the harpoon.

At South African stations, on the contrary, the proportion of empty stomachs was high and when there was any food at all it was only in small quantities. It consisted of small pelagic crustaceans related to the krill but not identical with it, for the krill does not live in tropical waters. Usually it was too far gone in digestion to be identified. Evidently, then, Rorquals gorge themselves to repletion upon krill in Antarctic waters during the summer but practically starve during their migrations to the tropics. This is an example of that

* See photo page 160.

mutual exclusiveness of sexual and feeding activity which is wide-spread in nature and found in groups as far removed from one another as fish and insects.

Although a whale's stomach can never be seen properly on the plan we know that it has in fact several chambers, somewhat resembling the stomach of our domestic cow, the sheep and other cloven-hoofed Ungulates.

In carnivores and in omnivores, including man, the stomach is a single bag (Fig. 6), but its lining is differentiated into three sections. The first, near the oesophagus or entrance, has no digestive glands. The central section does have digestive glands and here digestion takes place, while the third or pyloric section has glands which secrete an alkaline mucus.

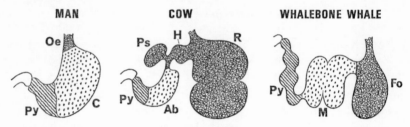

Fig. 6 DIAGRAMS OF STOMACHS OF MAN, COW AND WHALEBONE WHALE
(From Slijper, E. J., 1962)

MAN C Central section, Oe Oesophageal section, Py Pyloric section.
COW R Rumen or paunch, H Honeycomb bag, Ps Psalterium or Manyplies, Ab Abomasum, Py Pyloric section.
WHALEBONE WHALE Fo Forestomach, M Main stomach, Py Pyloric section.

In the domestic cow (Fig. 6) the first or oesophageal portion of the stomach is represented by three chambers, the rumen or paunch, the smaller 'honeycomb' bag and the psalterium or manyplies (many folds). None of these has digestive glands and their complicated arrangement, with the paunch full of bacteria, is a mechanism for breaking down the quantities of cellulose in a herbivorous diet. Digestion begins in the cow's small central stomach, the abomasum, corresponding to the central part of the human simple bag. The rear portion of this small chamber corresponds to the human pyloric portion.

In whales (Fig. 6) the stomach has three distinct chambers. The first or fore-stomach is much the largest with a capacity in a big Rorqual of about 200 gallons and capable of holding a ton of krill.

This is about four times the capacity of the domestic cow's stomach (Slijper, E. J., 1962). This portion has thick muscular walls and no digestive glands and it is this, though only part of it, which is visible on the plan. Like the paunch of ruminants it is the chamber where the food is broken down before digestion. It contains no bacteria but its thick muscular walls probably squeeze the food, the hard shells of the krill no doubt helping the breaking down process. The fore-stomach, like the cow's paunch, is a flask-shaped bag with its entrance and exit high up and close together so that it is a trap for large particles which are not released until digested, or reduced to a suitable size. The next chamber corresponds to the cow's abomasum or the central section of the human stomach. In Rorquals it is incompletely divided into two sections while the third, or pyloric portion, is a long narrow passage, its walls constricted to form four narrow chambers.

One is often asked if a whale could have swallowed Jonah. From the above it is evident that a man could easily be contained in a Rorqual's fore-stomach, but it is difficult to see how he could get there since the oesophagus, the gullet, is nowhere more than five inches in diameter, though capable of distension to ten inches. Killer whales are believed to swallow seals whole and Sperm whales swallow giant squids, though these are soft-bodied creatures perhaps at most two feet in diameter, and most of their immense length (30 feet or more) consists of tentacles. At a stretch, perhaps, one might imagine that a Sperm or a Killer might swallow a man, but not that he could survive the experience. Budker (1958) quotes the story of a man who fell overboard from the whaler *Star of the East* off the Falkland Islands in 1891 and was swallowed by a Sperm whale. When the whale was opened on the deck the following morning the flensers noticed movements in the stomach and the man was cut out still alive but with the exposed parts of his skin bleached white. The story, however, seems a very tall one. In the first place he would have suffocated in the stomach within a few minutes and, in the second place, he would have been lodged in the muscular fore-stomach where no digestive action takes place so it is difficult to see why his skin should have been bleached or, in fact, affected at all. On the whole the story of Jonah, I think, must be treated as an allegorical fable, like that of Adam and Eve and the Serpent.

We sometimes took samples of krill, if in fresh enough condition, back to the laboratory in order to measure them and note any change in size as the season advanced. There were in most seasons two distinct sizes of whale food in the stomachs. Large and small individuals were sometimes present together in the same stomach but often in different masses within it as though they represented meals of different shoals. In some seasons there was a change from large to small krill in the middle of the season, and it was evident that the smaller ones represented a younger brood which was supplanting the older large ones in the seas around the island.

The Reproductive Organs

Next we had to examine the reproductive organs which would give information about the sexual season and breeding habits. A knowledge of the sexual cycle would throw light on the rate of recruitment of the population, that is, the numbers of whales likely to be added to it to replace those taken out of it by whaling. We wanted to know the time and duration of the mating season, the number of young born at a birth, the average frequency of births during the lifetime of a cow whale. Further, we wanted to find out the duration of pregnancy, the season of giving birth, the size of the young at birth, the growth rate of the infant, the length of the nursing period, the size of the young at weaning.

If it were possible to keep whales alive in tanks most of these facts could be found out by direct observation, by simply breeding whales and watching them. But we cannot keep Rorquals alive in tanks, though direct observations have been made on dolphins and their breeding habits at Marineland and other oceanaria in America. But in dealing with the great whales we have to do our best by examining large numbers of carcasses and the unborn foetuses taken from them.

The gigantic body of a Blue whale begins life as an ovum $0 \cdot 1 – 0 \cdot 2$ mm. in diameter, no bigger than that of a mouse. The ovaries or egg glands of mammals are relatively very small organs behind the kidneys. Those of a rabbit are about $\frac{3}{4}$ inch in length and those of a human being about $1\frac{1}{2}$ inches. In young Rorquals the ovaries are small, soft and compact, about 6 inches in length, and together do not weigh more than 2 or 3 lbs. At puberty, however, they increase very greatly, their size and weight thereafter depending on their sexual condition. In Blue and Fin whales puberty is reached at an age of about five years. In a resting, inactive state the ovaries may be a foot to eighteen inches long in a cow Blue whale and weigh between 20 and 60 lbs. together.

The mammalian egg or ovum, after being shed from the ovary, is fertilized in the narrow curved oviducts. These are tubes, one on each side of the body, leading back to the right or left horn of the womb and their walls undergo rhythmical contractions which draw the ovum into the oviduct and along it into the womb. Farther back the right and left horns of the womb join to form a single median chamber, the vagina.

This is the arrangement in Ungulates (hoofed mammals), carnivores (dogs, cats, etc.), lower monkeys (lemurs) and in whales. In bats, higher monkeys (apes, chimpanzees) and man the two horns of the womb are coalesced into a single chamber (Fig. 7).

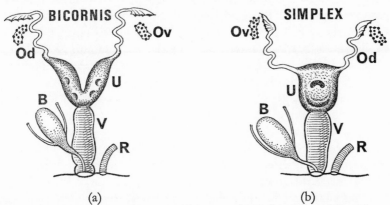

(a)   (b)

Fig. 7 (a) Uterus in Ungulates, Carnivores and Whales (*Uterus bicornis*)
(b) Uterus in Old World Monkeys, Bats and Man (*Uterus simplex*)
U Uterus, V Vagina, Od Oviduct, Ov Ovary, B Bladder, R Rectum.

The fertilized ovum grows into an embryo implanted in the lining tissue of the wall of the womb by means of its special attachment, the placenta. Shortly before an ovum is shed from the ovary the womb gets ready to receive it, increasing in size, its lining becoming soft and engorged with blood. At the same time in many female animals a condition familiar to us as 'heat' occurs, the purpose of which is to attract the male, and in such animals it is only during the 'heat' period that the female will accept the male.

The majority of animals have a recurring breeding season during which the ovary sheds eggs and 'heat' occurs. Usually the eggs are shed from the ovary spontaneously one at a time, independent of coition. Thus the dog, for instance, has two breeding seasons or 'heats' per year during which between four and seven eggs are shed and, if they are all fertilized, produce the same number of puppies. The domestic cat has two or three, rarely four, breeding seasons a year, but the shedding of eggs depends on coition taking place. If successful coition occurs between four and twelve eggs are shed about thirty hours later, and the average number of kittens in a litter is four.

In man and the primates there is no sexual season and one, though very occasionally more than one, egg is shed once a month independently of coition. If more than one egg is shed twins, triplets or multiplets may result.

If, in man or any other mammal, no fertilization takes place when the egg is shed it is voided and the womb returns to its normal resting condition, until the next shedding which may be later in the same season or not until the next one. In the human being this process whereby the womb sheds its lining and returns to its normal condition is called menstruation, since it takes place once a month.

We know, from the condition of the ovaries of Rorquals examined in South Africa, in South Georgia and round the Antarctic that the cows shed their eggs during the winter in the southern hemisphere from May to June, when they return to tropical waters well fed after a summer in polar seas. This, and August to November in the northern hemisphere, is the breeding season. The eggs are shed successively from the ovaries, one at a time, until fertilization occurs. There is little outward sign of 'heat' except that cows in an active state have the external sex parts somewhat swollen and protruding. Naturally, this was seldom seen in southern waters but more often at South African stations.

Among animals which roam about together in herds, like cattle or whales, or live gregariously like rabbits, it is very rare indeed that fertilization does not take place at 'heat' and the female become pregnant. How many eggs would be shed before the end of the breeding season if no fertilization occurred we can only find out by artificially segregating the sexes, as indeed happens to our unfortunate domestic animals and pets. As we have seen the dog sheds up to seven eggs at a 'heat'. The cat does not shed eggs in the absence of the male. The domestic cow sheds only one egg at 'heat' and the sheep two. In whales we have no means of knowing how many eggs would be shed in the absence of the male but it is probable that every Blue or Fin cow is fertilized after shedding a maximum of three eggs per season.

It is not certain how whales copulate, largely because of the difficulty of observing the performance at close range. There have been a number of eye-witness accounts but one is always a little doubtful about them. Whales doing anything at all make a vast confusion of spray, and all that can really be seen is a number of dark shapes cavorting in the water. Most accounts are of things seen from a moving ship which makes them even more doubtful. Some witnesses profess to have seen Humpbacks and Sperm whales embracing each other upright in the water, the Humpbacks with their long flippers around each other. Others say that Humpbacks, Sperm and Californian Grey whales lie horizontally on the surface belly to belly. Humpbacks have been seen slapping each other playfully but resoundingly with their long flippers. There have been no eye-witness accounts of the love-making of Blue or Fin whales and Slijper (1962) thinks that the resemblance between the penis of the Rorqual and that of the domestic bull suggests that whales take very little time over it, like all the even-toed Ungulates.

In all mammals the eggs are produced from vesicles in the ovary, the follicles. As soon as an egg has been shed the vesicle from which it came swells up to form a large knob on the surface of the ovary, the yellow body (*corpus luteum*). If the egg is not fertilized this subsides but leaves a hard scar. Meanwhile another vesicle enlarges and prepares to shed the egg within it. But if fertilization successfully occurs the yellow body enlarges and in Rorquals becomes a roughly spherical object about the size of a baby's head attached to the ovary by a neck. It is now called the '*corpus luteum* of pregnancy'. After the birth of the calf this disappears but leaves a scar which is believed to persist for the rest of the life of the cow. Every egg shed from the ovary in whales thus leaves a scar behind it and its shedding is permanently recorded. If we knew the number of eggs shed at each mating season we should have in the ovaries an indication of the cow's age, an important piece of information from the point of view of population analysis. Unfortunately we do not know this with certainty.

It was easy to spot the large, rounded lump of the corpus luteum of pregnancy as we dived for the ovaries among the disarranged folds of the uterus and its blanket-like supporting membranes. We soon became quite expert at ovary hunting, disregarding the whalers warning shouts indicating danger from wires. As soon as we saw the ovary with the big swelling on it we knew that the whale was almost certainly pregnant and that there must be a foetus in the horn of the uterus corresponding to the ovary with the swelling on it. Towards the end of the season the foetus was large enough to be obvious and visible within the folds of the uterus as an elongated shape. Indeed

late in the season, near their birth time, it was often so large that
the womb could not contain the monstrous child within it and the
foetus slid out on to the plan, rupturing the bag of the womb and
dragging its membranes like a scarlet veil behind it. At the beginning
of the season, however, the foetus might be less than a foot long yet
even so it made an easily visible lump and could be dragged out by
the tail or by the spirally twisted umbilical cord. At South African
stations it was a different matter for there, soon after the mating season,
adult Rorqual cows were carrying very small embryos not much more
than an inch or so in length. Even at that length they were not too
difficult to find for even an embryo an inch long with its membranes
is an object 'about the size of a thrush's egg' (Mackintosh, N. A. and
Wheeler, J. F. G., 1929). We laid the two horns of the uterus on the
plan and slit them carefully along their length and in one curved horn
or the other were sure to find the tiny whale wrapped in its delicate
membranes white against the soft red lining of the womb.

The great whales have only one young at a time since, like the
horse, primates and man, they normally shed only one egg at a time.
Like man they very occasionally shed two, and even more rarely a
higher number, resulting in twins or even multiplets. When I was
at South Georgia a Fin whale at another whaling station was found
to have a litter of five foetuses inside it, though some of them looked
unlikely to be born alive. This was such a rare event that work on
the plan was held up while the whalers had their photographs taken
alongside the phenomenon.

Like the embryos of all mammals that of the whale is attached
to the wall of the womb by means of a membranous placenta. In many
mammals (carnivores, monkeys and man) the union of the placenta
with the tissue of the womb is so intimate, though there is no mingling
of the mother's and embryo's blood streams, that at birth the placenta
tears away the lining of the womb and there is much bleeding at
birth. In whales, as in Ungulates and the lower monkeys, the union of
the placenta with the womb is less intimate so that the embryo with its
membranes slips out easily without rupturing the lining of the womb.

As a routine we measured the length and noted the sex of every
foetus after we had dragged it from its mother's belly. The lengths
of foetuses, if there are enough of them, plotted against the dates
on which they were taken give a growth curve of the foetus in the
womb (Fig. 8). From this we can establish the duration of pregnancy,
the season of birth and the length of the newly born calf. Pregnancy

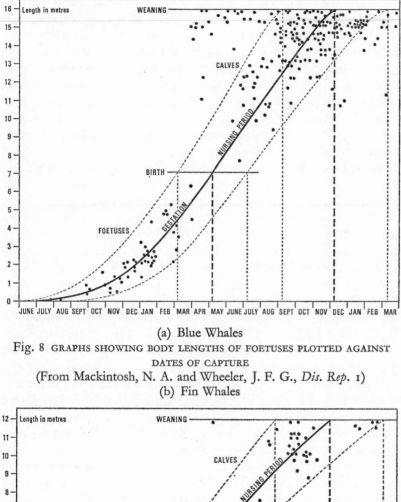

(a) Blue Whales

Fig. 8 GRAPHS SHOWING BODY LENGTHS OF FOETUSES PLOTTED AGAINST
DATES OF CAPTURE
(From Mackintosh, N. A. and Wheeler, J. F. G., *Dis. Rep.* 1)
(b) Fin Whales

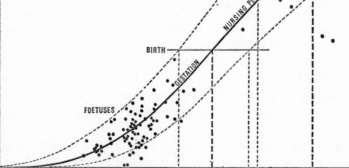

lasts from the mean date of finding the very smallest foetuses on the plan to that of finding the very largest. The season of birth must obviously be soon after the very largest foetuses are found and the size of the calf at birth will be somewhere between that of the largest unborn foetus and that of the smallest young whale examined on the plan. The duration of the nursing period will also be the lapse of time between the mean date of finding the largest foetus and that of seeing the smallest young whales. There is, of course, a gap in the visible record here because, since calves were not killed, we never actually saw a suckling calf on the plan.

From the smallest to the largest foetus there is a lapse of ten months (Fig. 8) for Blue whales and eleven and a half for Fin. This is the duration of pregnancy. Blue whale cows which conceive in tropical or subtropical waters when on 'heat' from May to August give birth from March to June the following year on their way north once more after nourishing themselves and their babies for ten months on the Antarctic fields of krill. Fin whales which conceive during the same pairing period give birth from May to August the next year.

The Blue whale calf weighs about two tons at birth and the Fin somewhat less. At a length of about a foot, three or four months old, all the organs of the adult are formed except the baleen plates, the ventral grooves and the skin pigmentation, and all the rest of the period of pregnancy, some six or seven months in a Blue whale and seven to eight in a Fin, is taken up with prodigious growth at the rate of about two and a half feet in a month. The baleen plates do not develop until well after birth, near the time of weaning, when the calf has to feed for itself. All that can be seen of the plates in the foetus is a series of transverse ridges close together in the upper jaw, giving it a comb-like appearance. In both jaws of the young foetus up to about 10 feet long the rudiments of teeth can be seen like small buds beneath the skin. They disappear when the foetus is about six months old and the baleen plates begin to appear. They are evidence that the ancestors of whalebone whales had teeth in both jaws.

Nearly all observations on the actual birth and on the suckling of calves have been made on Bottle-nosed dolphins at the Marineland Oceanarium and elsewhere and it has been presumed that they are similar among Rorquals. The young calf is born tail first and slips out easily enough because of the light attachment of the placenta. In the Bottle-nosed dolphin the birth process (parturition) takes about half an hour and other cows have been observed taking a sisterly interest in the labour. The baby Rorqual (Blue or Fin whale) is twenty to twenty-five feet long at birth and arrives in its watery world with all its faculties fully developed and enough muscle power to swim alongside its mother. At Marineland the mother dolphin was seen to support her baby up to the surface so that it could take its first breath. Since the mother's teats do not protrude it is believed that the milk is squirted forcibly into the calf's throat by cutaneous muscles of the breast which, as we saw, is in the inguinal position. The calf's tongue is free and muscular at the tip so that it can press against the nipple and make a funnel for the milk.

Whalers know well that the cow whale shows great devotion to her calf, and will shelter it and interpose her body between it and any possible enemy. If the calf is wounded she will swim beneath it and try to bear it up, and if it is killed she will not leave the spot. Old-time whalers used to take advantage of this and often killed the calf first in order to get the mother.

From our measurements of foetuses and young whales, and from records in the British Museum (Natural History) the duration of the nursing period in Blue whales is known to be seven months (Mackintosh, N. A. and Wheeler, J. F. G., 1929). They wean their calves about Christmas time at a length of about 60 feet. Fin whales nurse for about six months and the calf is likewise weaned at Christmas time at a length of about 40 feet. At weaning, when the calf ceases to suck and begins to feed for itself on krill, an abrupt increase in the size of its baleen plates takes place. Up to that time they are weak and comparatively feeble.

The Blue whale is thus pregnant for ten months and nurses its calf for seven while the Fin whale is pregnant for eleven and a half months and nurses for six, so that pregnancy and nursing occupy seventeen months in both these Rorquals. After the breeding season, whether or not there has been fertilization and pregnancy, the ovary goes into a resting state and sheds no more eggs until the next breeding season. If fertilization and pregnancy have occurred, and they almost always have, the resting state lasts for some five months after the calf is weaned. Pregnancy, nursing and resting, therefore, occupy twenty-two months so that most Rorquals probably mate and become pregnant every other year. The percentage of mature cows which we found to be pregnant at South Georgia was around 50 per cent which itself suggests pregnancy every other year. If the majority became pregnant every year the percentage would have been near a hundred and if every third

9

year near 30 per cent. Some possibly do skip two years and a few
unlucky ones are not allowed to enjoy a resting period for occasionally
a cow has been found to be pregnant while still nursing.

We did not see many nursing cows during our work on the plan,
naturally, since it was forbidden to kill them, but the gunners occasionally took them by mistake, often in a fog or a twilight when the calf
could not be seen. The mammary glands, on either side of the middle
line just in front of the genital opening, were greatly swollen during
nursing and were large oval breasts with slightly protruding nipples. The
milk flowed freely from them, sometimes spouting in a fine jet. Once
we collected some and had it for breakfast with our porridge. It was
sweet and very fatty and, on the whole, spoilt a good plate of porridge.

When we had weighed and measured our poor unborn young it
was dragged away to the meat boilers by means of a whale hook stuck
callously in the blowhole, and that was the end of all the marvellous
care and preparation which nature had lavished on what was to have
been another splendid living animal. What penalty, I used to wonder,
would the gods in due time inflict for such a sacrilege?

The male reproductive organs tell us less about the breeding cycle
than the female. In many mammals, such as the carnivores, the male
is continually sexually active and is able to mate with the female at
any time, as man is also. In others, such as the deer, the male has a
season of 'heat', corresponding to that of the female. In the stag this
is called the 'rutting' season. At this time the testes are active, filled
with seminal fluid, and the male becomes combative, fighting with
other males. Between rutting seasons he is quiet and the testes are
inactive. In Blue and Fin whales, but not in Sei, there seems to be a
rutting season at the beginning of the winter, corresponding to the
female 'heat', but there is no evidence that the male becomes combative at this time. In April and May the testes are filled with seminal
fluid containing active spermatozoa and, since the time of rutting is
slightly in advance of the female season (May–June), the male must
store the spermatozoa until he makes contact with the female. The
spermatozoa of a Blue whale are no larger than those of a man.

The internal position of the whale's testis is probably related to the
streamlining of the body, but must have another significance since
some land animals likewise have abdominal testes, for example, the
elephant, the sloth and the armadillo. It may be related to the temperature at which the spermatozoa exist in the oviduct. In animals
with a testis hanging in a scrotum the spermatozoa are at a lower

temperature than that of the body cavity and cannot survive long at the higher temperature of the oviduct. In those with a testis inside the body the spermatozoa are at the same temperature as the rest of the body and can therefore be stored in the oviduct to await the arrival of the ovum.

Maturity

Now we had done all we could on the innards of that particular carcass and they had been hauled off to the meat hoists. We must now wait a little while before we could make our final observation. This was the determination whether the whale was fully grown (physically apart from sexually mature) or not. Just as it was important to know what proportion of sexually mature and immature whales the population contained, which could be found out by inspecting the ovary or testis, so it was also important to assess the proportion of old, fully grown whales. It allowed a still further division of the population into categories and would assist in measuring the rate of recruitment of young whales to the stock.

The signs of complete growth are visible in the backbone of mammals, which is a chain of bony cylinders. Naturally we could not see it in our whale until all the innards had gone and the great masses of the tail and back muscles had been stripped off. Then it lay almost naked like a long serpent waiting to be hauled up to the bone saws.

At the fore and after face of each of the cylinders (vertebrae) which make up the backbone of a mammal there is a bony plate or disc which, in the young animal, is separated from the cylinder by a thin partition of cartilage (the fore-runner of bone).

In man, owing to his erect posture and the mechanical stresses to which it subjects the backbone, these discs often become displaced or distorted (slipped) in later life with painful effects on the nerves which enter and leave the spinal cord between the cylinders or vertebrae. These often take the unpleasant form which we call lumbago or rheumatism.

When the animal becomes fully grown the cartilage partitions between the discs and the cylinders are replaced by bone and the discs join up with the cylinders throughout the length of the backbone. In order to find out whether or not this had happened in each sexually mature whale we had to examine the backbone as soon as the big masses of the tail muscles had been stripped away. This was the final act of dismemberment of the carcass.

The method of judging whether a Rorqual had reached complete physical maturity or not was devised by Wheeler (Wheeler, J. F. G., 1930) and was used by us on every sexually mature whale we saw at South Georgia and Durban and has been used since in many factory ships. The bony discs join up with the cylinders starting simultaneously from the tail forwards and from the neck backwards. But the process goes faster from the tail end than from the neck and completes itself at about one-third of the length of the thorax from the neck.

When the tail muscles had been stripped from the underneath of the backbone we each climbed upon the hillocks of red flesh armed with a small axe, and struck at the undersides of the backbone across the junctions of the vertebrae so as to lay bare a small white patch of bone. If fusion of the disc and cylinder had not taken place a fine, pink, wavy line of cartilage could be seen on the cut surface. If it was almost but not quite complete a white line could be seen, and if quite complete there was no sign of any join at all on the plain white bony surface exposed by the axe. Because of the speed with which we had to dart in while the backbone was actually on the move up to the bone slipway we had only time enough to chop in three or four places along its length, but this was enough to enable us to judge how far forward or backward the process of fusion had gone.

These hazardous and, for the whalers, laughable activities marked the end of that carcass so far as we were concerned. The backbone slid away up the greasy slope of the slipway to the bone plan where the steam saws screamed like witches. In the middle of the season, around Christmas time, during late December and early January, we were kept busy on the plan from five-thirty in the morning until the hooter blew for knocking off at six o'clock in the evening. We dealt with about twenty whales a day on the plan and were kept busy writing up our notes in the laboratory until past midnight. But in the early part of the season, in October and November, and towards the end, in late February and March, things were slacker. After the middle of March there might be only one or two whales a day at the whaling station and we were finished before breakfast. Then we could go sailing or fishing or climb about on those great bleak mountains whose screes swept the shores of the bay like skirts.

CHAPTER 7

The Chase

The Whale Catcher

The chief instrument for the pursuit and capture of whales is the catcher or chaser boat. Like all the rest of the equipment of modern whaling it has now reached a size and efficiency undreamt of in the early days. For some years after the introduction of the harpoon gun whale catchers were small sailing ships of less than 100 tons with auxiliary engines. Today they average between 700 and 900 gross tons, have diesel engines of about 2,000 h.p. and a speed of 18 knots. Forty years ago catchers had a gross tonnage of about 500 tons, a length of about 125 feet, were driven by oil-fired steam engines and had a speed of about 14 knots.

The general build and shape of the hull is the same today as it was then, cut away at the waist of the ship so that the main deck is always awash amidships. The draught is very shallow so that, aided by her balanced rudder, the vessel is very easily manœuvrable and can turn completely round in her own length in a few minutes. From the low open waist the lines of the hull sweep upwards to a high, outwardly flared bow which supports the platform on which the gun is mounted. Thus the gun platform is kept clear of spray which is thrown far outwards. A sloping gangway leads from the wheelhouse or bridge to the gun platform and at the crucial moment the gunner, who is the captain of the ship, walks down it to take his stand behind the gun. The steel foremast, strengthened to take the weight of the harpoon line on an accumulator pulley, has a barrel look-out beneath the truck.

The Harpoon and the Gun

Like the ship that carries it the harpoon gun has not changed very much in recent years, but has undergone improvements. It still does not differ greatly from that invented by Svend Foyn. It is of the cannon type, 45 inches long with a 3-inch bore, and rotates on a movable swivel which can turn in any direction. It has a glycerine recoil and an effective range of about 25 yards. The harpoon is 5 feet in length, made of steel, and weighs about 160 lbs. Its shank or shaft is $3\frac{1}{2}$ inches in diameter and is split throughout most of its length, having a narrow slot running down its centre which gives it flexibility with strength and has another purpose as we shall see shortly. A conical explosive grenade screws on to the fore-end of the shaft and contains a time fuse which explodes it three seconds after the shot has been fired (Matthews, L. H., 1931). Immediately behind the head of the shaft the harpoon carries four swivelled barbs which, when the harpoon is loaded into the gun, are lashed back to the shaft with twine. When the harpoon head strikes the whale and explodes the lashings break so that the tension of the harpoon line deflects the barbs outwards, anchoring the harpoon in the flesh. The gunner aims at the back of the whale between the shoulder blades, a target which is exposed for less than a second, and, if the shot has been correctly aimed, the explosion shatters the backbone in which the harpoon becomes lodged. Sometimes the explosion inside the whale can be heard from the deck of the catcher. But if the shot misses its mark, as often happens since both target and gun are in motion, and strikes in the wrong place, the agonies that the victim must endure do not bear thinking of. If the shot is well and truly aimed death is instantaneous, but if not the struggling beast may have to be hauled close and given a second or even a third shot.

Svend Foyn's gun was muzzle-loaded with a charge of 350 lbs. of black powder rammed home, but in 1925 a breech-loading gun was introduced with a charge of 14 oz. of smokeless powder (Matthews, L. H., 1931). This fires the harpoon itself which is still muzzle-loaded into the barrel of the gun and the harpoon line is attached to a ring which slides in the slot or split running down the centre of the shaft. With the gun loaded and ready to fire the ring hangs outside the muzzle, but as soon as the harpoon leaves the muzzle the weight of the line pulls the ring back to the after end of the shaft.

The Harpoon Line

The harpoon line is in two parts. The line itself is made up of several 120-fathom lengths totalling about a kilometre (three-fifths of a mile) and on its leading end attached to the harpoon, is the fore-runner which is of smaller circumference and has a length of about 80 fathoms. The fore-runner is made of $4\frac{1}{2}$-inch circumference manilla or nylon rope and lies coiled down neatly on a tray in front of the gun when the harpoon is loaded at the ready. It passes from the ring on the harpoon back over rollers under the gun platform and is joined to the harpoon line itself which is $6\frac{1}{2}$ to $7\frac{1}{2}$-inch circumference manilla rope. When the shot is fired the fore-runner is carried out by the harpoon first, followed by the harpoon line, and the enormous, sudden strains involved in playing a whale on the end of the line from a rolling ship are balanced by a series of accumulator springs in the hold, lying on either side of the keel from the forward bulkhead to the after or stokehold bulkhead. From these springs on each side a wire runs up through the deck and over a pulley, sprung from the masthead, to end with another pulley high up on the mast and over this the harpoon line passes. The line is thus double sprung, once at the masthead and again within the hold. From its pulley below the masthead the line runs down to the drum of a winch on deck, thence into the hold where it is coiled ready to run out.

After the whale has been struck it is played very much like a big fish. The mast acts like a fishing-rod with the harpoon line as the fishing-line and the winch on deck as the reel. But the analogy is not exact because the mast is not flexible and all the play is provided by the accumulator springs.

One often hears whale hunting light-heartedly described as one of the most exciting sports in the world, but the word 'sport' hardly fits it. In the first place the quarry has no chance and is run down to the point of total exhaustion and mercilessly gunned to death. Most experienced gunners are good shots, able to hit at first shot between the shoulder blades at about 25 yards range, but there are many inex-perienced ones in the game who make a botch of their shooting. I once saw a gunner expend four harpoons on a whale, finally despatch-ing it at the fourth shot hauled close at 15 yards. Even an experienced gunner, especially in bad weather, fog or twilight, may need more than one shot, the second one after an agonizing struggle. Secondly, there is not the slightest risk to the hunter in the whale chase for he is safely perched aloft in his armoured sea chariot. Though there have been casualties to whale catchers, especially in the early days when they were small and cranky, these mishaps are usually due to the hazards which beset any small ship at sea in the polar regions. They

have been holed or marooned in the ice, or have turned turtle in heavy
weather through icing of the hull and rigging, but these are all mishaps
which are common to both whalers and fishermen.

A Trip in a Catcher

I made several trips in catchers during my time in the Antarctic.
During the first one I was terribly sea-sick, for there can be few motions
in the world more upsetting than the whirling dervish dance of a whale
catcher. She rolls and pitches at the same time and there seems to be a
rotary component in her performance which imparts giddiness as well
as nausea, and a profound longing for easeful death. Let no one under-
rate this dreadful malaise which has incapacitated many an earnest
marine biologist and fisheries scientist.

If one felt the urge to make a trip on a catcher, which was usual
in the days of one's Antarctic apprenticeship because it was all part
of the adventure, the correct procedure was to broach the subject
at one of those rather heavy sessions at the manager's villa when, in
an overheated room redolent of past similar occasions, one sat around
with the gunners, drinking in stolid silence the cheapest possible
whisky provided by the manager, usually poured from bottles of a
much more expensive brand. In spite of the heat from a tall stove
in one corner of the room the red-faced, paunchy men were swathed
in heavy clothing, and the conversation, mostly in Norwegian, was
about the bad weather and the gloomy prospects for catching whales.
There were long silences in the midst of which they lifted their glasses
and said '*Ja! Skøl!*'

Choosing an appropriate moment you said that you would very
much like to take a trip on a catcher, and the thing was done. For the
gunners usually enjoyed having a passenger and so did the crew. It
made a change and a new face.

My first trip was aboard the *Morsa*, one of the newest boats of the
Compania Argentina de Pesca. She was an oil-burning steamship of
about 400 tons with a speed of fifteen knots, very spruce and handsome with her grey paint and two white stripes on the funnel, but
formidable, her lines long and flowing and her menacing gun perched
high and downward pointing on her bows.

I had been told to watch out for her and go on board in the evening
next time she came in to refuel. She returned from hunting about
four o'clock one fine afternoon, towing four whales and making a
great swirl of white foam skirts. Seconds after she had passed her

bow wave curled and broke as a series of small rollers on the shingle beach outside our building. I saw her drop her catch and go to the oiling jetty, so I packed a sea bag, not forgetting a bottle of whisky, and went aboard. The ship seemed to be deserted, but presently a seaman appeared.

'Go up, please,' he said, indicating the companion ladder to the bridge. He showed me to the gunner's cabin, a small square compartment under the bridge containing a large radio transmitter and receiver, a bunk, a settee and a number of family photographs. It was stuffily unventilated and the air in it felt as though it had been breathed many times over.

'You take the settee, please,' said the seaman. 'The skipper is at the villa, but soon he comes back,' and he left me. I lay down fully clothed, the ship rocked gently at her moorings, the pumps whined and, after removing several layers of clothing, I fell asleep.

The gentle heaving of the settee on which I lay woke me, and then I was aware of the rhythmical beat of the engines. It was getting light and I could just make out a shape occupying the gunner's bunk. I had not heard him return. I put on the layers of clothing I had taken off, and a wool-lined leather cap with ear flaps, and went up on to the open bridge, a small square space with a steering wheel and binnacle surrounded by canvas dodgers. A burly young man with a beard stood at the wheel, bracing his legs to the motion of the ship, the flaps of his wool-lined cap hanging down like the ears of a spaniel.

'*Morgen!*' he said. This is pronounced '*Morn!*' and means 'Good morning'. 'It is good weather!'

For a while I stood on the bridge watching the steep black and green cliffs of South Georgia slip past and fall away in the growing light to reveal the black peaks above them slashed with white. Soon it began to dawn on me with apprehension that I was not feeling very well. Presently I realized with disgust and shame that I was feeling very ill, both giddy and sick. It was no use pretending. I went and lay down again on the settee in the stuffy cabin where the gunner was now a more distinct shape in his bunk, fast asleep. I felt better lying down and slept fitfully but was soon aware of the gunner arising fully dressed from his bunk, putting on more clothes and quietly leaving the cabin. He was a very big man but moved silently. I dozed some more and then the door of the cabin opened, admitting a blast of fresh air.

'*Frokost?* Breakfast?' said the steward, putting his head into the cabin. I sat up and was at once assailed by giddiness and sickness, but managed to crawl down the companion ladder to the mess-room under the cabin. The young mate and the middle-aged chief engineer were there, wedged into the narrow settee space between the bulk-head and the table with the fiddles on it. They were shovelling Nor-wegian fish balls (*fiske-boller*) into themselves, holding their plates up close to their chests and swaying to and fro in their seats in order to counteract the bucketing motion of the ship. They drank strong coffee from mugs secured in the round holes in the fiddles. They were talking rapidly in Norwegian, pausing momentarily to say '*Morn! Morn!*' when I staggered in and flopped into a place at the table. Life is pleasantly informal in a whale catcher—it has to be. The steward, young, affable and agile, but pale and puffy about the face from his unhygienic life, leaned against the jamb of the doorway and joined in the conversation. Soon the engineer said '*Ja! Ja!*' and got up, wiping his hands on the inevitable bit of cotton waste which engineers always seem to have about them. He said '*Tak for maten, Steward*' ('Thanks for the meal, Steward') with a polite little bow as is the Norwegian custom, and went out. I could not face fish balls, which are soft, white and faintly slimy, so I had a cup of coffee and a piece of brown bread, and sat hunched up over the table fighting back my unpleasant symptoms and looking, I am sure, very woebe-gone. When the gunner came in and squeezed himself into a place at the table, he first greeted the steward and then beamed pityingly at me. He had a big, red, jovial face. '*Sjøsick?*' he asked rather unneces-sarily. 'That is a bad sickness.'

Soon I began to feel that fresh air was necessary above everything else so I climbed up to the bridge again and draped myself in a corner, sheltered from the wind by the canvas screens. South Georgia had now become a long, low denticulate line of black and white on our port quarter, wreathed in layers and pinnacles of cloud. Occasional white horses winked on the grey, choppy sea while flocks of whale birds in V-formation sped low across the waves with a rapid, pur-poseful flight. This was supposed to be a good sign, indicating that whales were about. Actually this is a kind of half truth for the whale bird, or *Prion*, feeds on krill so that when flocks of them are to be seen it may be taken as a sign that krill is plentiful, and so probably whales also. The *Prion* nests in burrows on the steep scree slopes of the island but only approaches land after dusk. During daylight it keeps at least ten miles away from the coast because if it comes nearer it is immediately set upon and devoured by that fierce bird of prey, the Skua gull.

Around our dancing ship albatrosses of several kinds wheeled and soared on motionless pinions and grey fulmar petrels pursued us. Every now and then the birds landed upon the surface of the sea to seize a scrap from the galley waste, but soon rose again and hurried after us, overtaking us effortlessly.

Then suddenly from the masthead look-out came the whaleman's old and famous call to action, heard above the beat of the engines and the swish of the bow wave—'*Hvalblåst!*' The man in the masthead barrel was pointing to the horizon on the port bow, his arm and hand still pointing, coming round like the hand of a compass as the ship's head swung twenty degrees. '*Tre finnhvaler!*—Three Fin whales!'

Far away in the direction in which the look-out's arm was pointing I saw one, two, three high thin exclamation marks appear and stand for a second, dark against the lighter grey of the sky, before they faded and vanished.

The gunner appeared on the bridge, even bigger now in a leather coat, and gave the order '*Fuld fart forover!*—Full speed ahead!', which the mate rang down on the engine telegraph. The rhythmic beat of the engine quickened and the ship trembled as she leapt forward from wave to wave, clove through them and pushed wide arcs of foam away from her bows. All eyes, including mine, were sweeping the grey disc of the sea when suddenly the spouts appeared again one after the other, much nearer now and on the starboard bow. Now we could see, as each tall, white plume faded, a black wheel bearing a sickle-shaped fin turn slowly over in the water behind it. Each one with a strange, unhurrying deliberation vanished into the waves.

'Ja! Fin whales,' said the gunner.

An experienced whaler can, in moderately good visibility and with not too much wind, broadly distinguish one species of whale from another at sea by the size and shape of the spout (Fig. 9).

The spout of a Blue whale lasts from three to five seconds and in calm weather a big one may throw up a plume 25 to 30 feet high, rather pear-shaped, widening towards the top. The height, of course, depends on the size of the whale and the strength of the wind. A Fin whale, under similar conditions, throws up a spout that lasts about the same time but is not so high, 15 to 20 feet, and is a slender, graceful feather of spray, not widening so much at the top as that of a Blue. The Sei has a low, short spout, some 10 feet high, lasting for a few

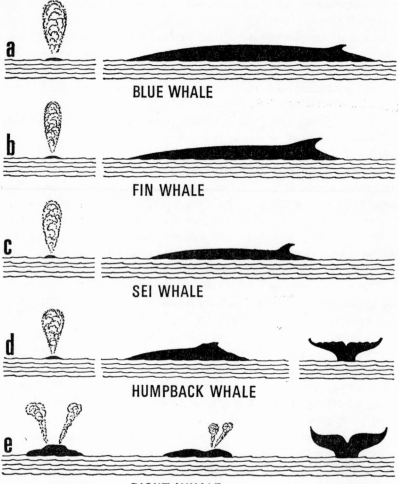

Fig. 9 Diagrams of spout and view of back as seen at sea

seconds. The spout of the Humpback is low, a mere 6 feet, and bushy
in form, while that of the Right whale is double, the spouts from the
two blowholes separate.

But conditions are never ideal and the spout by itself is not a reliable
key to the whale's identity at sea, which is never certain until one can
get a closer view (Fig. 9). Then it can be seen that the back, visible
behind the blow, shows only a small notch of backfin in a Blue,
but a well curved sickle in a Fin and a still higher sickle in a Sei. The

Humpback, owing to the acute angle of its movement up to the surface and down again, presents a hunch-backed appearance in the water as its nickname implies. When it dives or sounds after a series of shallow submersions the Humpback almost always throws its tail clear of the water, a startling, up-rearing T-shape dripping foam. The Right whale also raises its tail from the water when it dives but shows much less of it than the Humpback.

The spout of a whale is a romantic, haunting thing to behold from the deck of a ship. It symbolizes the mystery of the sea itself, the remoteness and unfamiliarity of this strange monster. At one time it was thought to be caused by sea water thrown up by the whale exhaling before it breaks surface. Then it was realized that the whale does not, in fact, exhale before it breaks surface, the blowholes remaining tightly closed until clear of the water. Then it was thought that the spout must be caused by condensation of the warm breath on contact with the cold air, until it was pointed out that whales can be seen spouting just as clearly in the Red Sea. The spout is actually a column of water vapour caused by the act of exhalation and is formed by condensation, not by the contact of warm breath with cold air but by the elementary principle of physics that when a gas expands it cools. At close quarters it is possible to hear the shrill whistle which the breath makes as it is forced out under pressure through the narrow apertures of the blow-holes. Saturated with moisture, it expands suddenly on expulsion from these narrow orifices, cools and drops its moisture as a fine cloud of spray. The trachea (windpipe) is filled with an oily, mucous foam (Fraser, F. C. and Purves, P. E., 1955) which is produced by glands in the air passages at the back of the skull and is found also in the windpipe of rabbits. It has been suggested that this may have the property of absorbing nitrogen and that the spout consists, at least in part, of droplets of this foamy substance expelled from the windpipe.

When the whales blew again they had doubled back and were on our port quarter, so we swung round after them drawing a semicircle of foam and troubled water. They were easily keeping their distance from us. Fin whales, whose cruising speed is 10–12 knots, can put on spurts of 16–18 knots (Gunther, E. R., 1949). Blue whales are faster than Fins of the same size and a big one with a cruising speed of 14–15 knots is believed to be able to put on spurts of up to 20 knots. On a subsequent trip in a catcher we chased a Blue whale running dead ahead for over eight hours at the ship's maximum speed of 15 knots. However, Blue and Fin whales, when cruising undisturbed, will often idle at not much more than 5 knots. Humpbacks are slow swimmers, averaging 4–5 knots, though when chased they can do 10–12 in short bursts. Right whales are very slow, wallowing along at not much more than 2 knots, but able to reach 5 when chased. The great whales are very much slower swimmers than porpoises and dolphins, which can maintain speeds of 20–22 knots for as much as half an hour. All these figures, of course, are very much open to question for it goes without saying that no really reliable observations have ever been made. All figures of speeds are guesses in many cases made by unreliable witnesses from the decks of moving ships, and sometimes in bad weather and poor visibility. People have a remarkable capacity for reporting what they wish to be believed.

In those days, forty years ago, when the maximum speed of a catcher was 15 knots, the gunners used to stalk the whales. They would get as close to a whale or a school as they could without alarming it. When the quarry became alarmed, hearing the menacing beat of the ship's screw, the school would probably split up and the whales would begin to dodge about. The gunner would then choose one of the school and follow it, and it used to be the boast of an experienced gunner that he could predict where the whale would surface next and would be there on the spot waiting for it. It was believed that the beat of the screw was less audible to the whale if the catcher's propellers were made of an alloy called phosphor-bronze, though how much truth there was in this there was really no way of knowing. Modern whale catchers, with a top speed of 18 knots, can run down the fastest whale in straight pursuit and the method of stalking the quarry has been abandoned. The whale is merely run down until it is too exhausted to dive and then it presents an easy target.

The whales we were pursuing blew one after the other several times in quick succession, and then there was an interval of five to ten minutes during which we all eagerly scanned the empty sea, before they reappeared and spouted several times again.

It was evident that the whales had become aware of the enemy pursuing them, for the school dispersed and the next spouts appeared in widely different directions. The gunner chose one of the three that was almost dead ahead and rang 'Full Speed' on his engine telegraph. We set off after our prey again, dancing over the slate-grey waves. The whale at first ran for it, blowing five or six times in fairly rapid succession on the same course, and then vanished in a long 'sound'.

'*Fand!*' said the gunner—an expletive which means 'fiend' or 'devil'. But he did not immediately slow down and we ran on for about half a mile.

'*Sagte!*—slow!' We loitered and then stopped, lying in wait, waves lapping against the hull and things clinking as they swung to the roll. I had forgotten about feeling sea-sick and stood in my corner of the bridge peering over the dodger, scanning the sea like everybody else. We hoped that our whale would surface near us.

Suddenly it broke surface almost alongside us like a great engine coming out of a tunnel. The spout shot up from the open blowholes and I could look down over the canvas dodger as though upon an engine from the parapet above the tunnel mouth. I could see the nostrils gaping within their muscular lips. The spout made a whistling explosion like an exhaust, its vapour drifting over us on the wind with a stench of whale. As the flat head came up the spout ceased but the blowholes did not close at once and we could hear the rush of the indrawn breath before the waves closed over the head. Before it was lost to sight we could see the water foaming between the baleen plates. The gleaming back followed with its sickle-shaped fin and then sank from view in a smother of foam. Where it had been there remained an oval dome of smooth water like polished glass upon the ruffled surface of the sea. It lasted for some minutes, shrinking and slowly losing its shape. This is known as the 'slick' and was at one time thought to be caused by an oily exudation from the whale's skin, but it is now realized that it is the effect of a mass of water kicked up to the surface by the upstroke of the tail flukes as the whale dives.

Now the gunner walked down the sloping gang plank to the gun platform. He wore a long leather coat and peaked wool-lined cap and was a monolithic figure as he stood behind his gun. We were still going ahead at slow speed and the gunner, indicating with his hand a few degrees of starboard helm as though he knew precisely where the whale would break surface next, bent himself behind the gun ready to swing it in any direction.

As the ship moved round slightly the whale broke surface again almost dead ahead and some thirty yards in advance of the bow. The spout stood up from the wide open blowholes. The gunner swung his gun. I dislike loud noises and braced myself against that deafening splitting apart of the air. My ears rang, and through the pall of smoke about the bows I saw the black dart leap forward with its whip of line. The whale took it down and, as the harpoon line ran out, the accumulator pulley beneath the masthead descended slowly with an uneven motion. There was silence, broken only by the rushing sound of several hundred fathoms of line running out almost vertically from the rollers under the gun platform down into the water.

It does not, of course, follow that because the harpoon line appears to lead vertically from the bows into the water the whale has therefore dived vertically. It may go down vertically at first and then the trajectory of the dive may flatten out. The whale may surface a quarter or half a mile away with the line still leading almost vertically into the water from the rollers.

This was what happened, for our quarry broke surface some five hundred yards away on the starboard bow and began his silent, terrible death struggle. If whales could utter cries which could rend the heart their deaths would be less dreadful than this losing battle which our whale was now engaged upon, in silence broken only by the far-off screaming of clouds of sea birds. We could not even hear the thrashing of crimsoned foam as he writhed and plunged, spouting a bloody spray at first, then an upgushing, followed by a bubbling upwelling amid a spreading island of blood. Suddenly the struggle ceased, the red foam subsided and we could see the body lying on its side quite still, one flipper sticking out of the water. The birds busied themselves above and around it with shrill cries.

The question of the cruelty of whaling comes up from time to time in the press and, inevitably, one is often asked about it. The answer is that the explosive harpoon is the most barbarous instrument used for slaughtering animals by any livestock industry, but there seems to be no possible alternative. Some attempts have been made to devise a more humane type of killing instrument and in the whaling season 1949–50 an electric harpoon was tried out experimentally. The idea was to give the whale a lethal electric shock. A small calibre light harpoon was used and the harpoon line carried out a conductor with a monophase alternating current of 220V and 50–80 amps. The whale was supposed to come to the surface 10–15 seconds after being struck in a rigid state with its mouth open. The current was left on for three minutes as a precaution. However, the invention did not catch on with the gunners, for electricity is difficult and tricky at sea. Insulation corrodes on contact with sea water and short circuits are liable to develop. At best the electric harpoon simply did not function at all, and at worst the gunner was liable to receive some of the impulse himself.

Above: Two Fin whales surfacing. In the foreground the "slick" of a third, which has just submerged, can be seen.

Left: A school of Sperm whales surface-ing. In the fore-ground one has spouted and is about to submerge, showing the "hump".

Below: Sperm whales submerging. The whale on the left is throwing up its tail flukes on submerging.

Left: Male Sperm whale 55 ft. long at the Azores. Note the scratches on the snout.

Below: Loaded whale train about to leave the jetty at Durban.

Several tough gunners told me they did not really like their job and had had about enough of it by the time the season came to an end. For a watcher such as myself, not yet inured to this spectacle of anguish, there is the difficulty of imagining that this grotesque creature, plunging and wallowing at the end of the line, is a beast as sentient as a horse and, in its own way, as noble. Its habit of life in its unfamiliar element makes it impersonal and mysterious. What an outcry there would have been long ago, as Sir Alister Hardy has remarked, if herds of great land mammals, say elephant or buffalo, were chased in armoured vehicles firing explosive grenades from cannon, and then hauled close at the end of a line and bombarded again until dead!

Now the winch began to haul our dead carcass close to the ship. For some minutes only the slack line came in, but presently it grew taut and stretched dripping to the whale which began slowly to move towards us while its attendant chorus of birds moved with it. Soon we could see the grin of the baleen plates and the ribbed belly. As it came alongside it had a curious rubbery smell and the shaft of the harpoon was sticking out between the shoulder blades. The gunner had aimed true.

When the carcass was alongside the tail was pulled up to the starboard rail. It was a female Fin whale. The mate now cut off the two tail flukes with a flensing knife and they fell into the water and sank while he cut two notches in the front edge of the remaining stump. This was the ship's indicator mark by which the workers on the plan would know what ship had taken this whale. Each boat cut a different number of notches in the tail stump of its whales up to the number of five. Next the nozzle of an air pump fixed to a long shaft was pushed into the thorax so as to pump the carcass up with air and make it float. The wound made by the nozzle was plugged with cotton waste. Then a buoy with a long pole carrying the Company's house flag, pale blue and white, the Argentine colours, was attached to the tail and the carcass, thus marked, was cast adrift. It would be left to float until we came back to collect it at the end of our hunting. Every whale the catcher took during the next forty-eight hours of hunting would be bouyed like this and all would be rounded up and towed back to Grytviken together, six or seven whales if the hunting was good, towed tail first alongside the bows of the ship. Naturally they would slow her down a great deal and we should crawl home laboriously but triumphantly at three or four knots.

10

In modern whaling radio transmitters are fitted to the buoys and give out continuous signals so that the positions of the buoyed whales are always known. Forty years ago flagged whales were often lost in fog or rough weather, or found only after a long search, by which time they were rotten and gave a poor yield. In those days each catcher, at the end of her two or three days' hunting, had to cruise around collecting her flagged catch, but nowadays a special boat, often an old superannuated catcher, is allotted this humble task in order to save the time of the catcher fleet.

'*Ja! Ja!*' said the gunner when I resumed my place behind the canvas dodger. 'So now you have seen a whale killed! And you are not *sjøsick*, no?'

I was not. I had forgotten all about it. We were now going full speed ahead and looking for another whale. Up from the galley below the bridge there drifted an inconceivably delicious smell. It was lunch time and I was hungry. The pale young steward, who all this time had been unconcernedly attending to his duties, as vitally important as anybody else's, was waiting to welcome us.

Diving

When swimming normally and undisturbed upon its lawful occasions a Rorqual whale makes a series of undulations through the water, blowing—exhaling and inhaling—once at each breach of the surface. A Blue whale breaks surface three to five times at intervals of half a minute and a Fin whale five to six times. These shallow undulations occupy perhaps two or three minutes and then the whale disappears in a deep dive or 'sound' for a longer period of up to ten minutes. When undisturbed it probably does not sound very deep, perhaps 25 to 50 fathoms, and, indeed, there is no reason why it should since the krill it is seeking lives between five fathoms and the surface. Gunther (1949) has described how Fin whales, idling at the surface, can submerge gently in a shallow dive and surface almost horizontally without flexing the body at all.

When Blue or Fin whales are alarmed they make much longer dives or sounds of up to twenty minutes duration, with a limit of about forty minutes. This we saw in the *Morsa*, and it is part of the gunner's skill to get on the spot where the whale will come up from his sound. The depth to which whales may descend during their sounding dives was a matter for speculation by the old Greenland whalers, and William Scoresby (1820) was of opinion that Greenland Right whales must reach great depths, perhaps as much as 800 fathoms, because of the length of harpoon line carried out. But, as we saw in the *Morsa*, the length of harpoon line paid out is no indication of what the whale is doing at the end of it or of where it is, and the same great lengths of line were often paid out in quite shallow water. Racovitza (1903), scientist of the *Belgica* Expedition, did not believe that Rorquals ever descended normally more than about 100 metres (56 fathoms). Definite proof of the depths to which Rorquals may dive was established by a Norwegian (Scholander, P. F., 1940) who fixed pressure gauges (manometers) to harpoons used in hunting Fin whales from a Norwegian whaling station. Counting only whales which came to the surface alive he found recordings between 46 and 194 fathoms, the whales coming back quite unaffected from even the deepest dives. Sperm and Bottle-nosed whales are believed to dive much deeper than this and to remain submerged for longer periods (see p. 225).

When a whale is on the run the sounding dives become less frequent and of shorter duration. It breaks surface more often and blows more frequently. This is its way of panting, for it cannot take deeper breaths, as we can, in order to replenish the air in its lungs but instead has to breathe more frequently.

Whales dive to greater depths and stay under for longer periods than any other aquatic mammal, although seals can dive to more than 100 fathoms and stay down for as long as fifteen minutes. Several questions have interested scientists in this connection. How does a whale manage to hold its breath for so long? How does it take down enough oxygen to last it for forty minutes or longer? What are the effects on its body of the enormous hydrostatic pressures to which it must be subjected during a deep dive?

Land mammals cannot hold their breath for more than a few minutes. A man can only do so for 1½ minutes, although Arab pearl divers, after practice and training, can make dives of up to four minutes. At the end of that time the partial pressure of carbon dioxide in the blood and lungs stimulates the respiratory centre of the brain, the so-called 'vital knot' in the medulla, to take another breath. There seems to be no sure answer to the question why a whale's respiratory centre is not stimulated when the breath is held for periods of half an hour or more. Laurie (1933), who discussed this problem, thought that the difference between whales and land mammals must lie in the respiratory centre itself which, in the whale, must be less sensitive to carbon dioxide tensions in the blood.

As we saw on the plan whales have relatively small lungs which represent only 0·6–0·9 per cent of the body weight, about half the figure for land mammals and man. Yet they can take down enough oxygen to last their huge bodies for the duration of a deep dive. There seem to be several reasons for this. When a man or land mammal breathes normally the lungs are not filled, but only half filled, and even that small amount of air is not changed, for with each exhalation a man expels only two litres of air while the maximum capacity of his lungs is five litres. If he breathes out hard he can expel another litre (1,000 c.c.) but 300 c.c. remain behind even if the lungs are completely collapsed. Whales, on the other hand, can almost completely fill and empty their lungs at every inspiration and expiration. The walls of the tubules and chambers of their lungs are very thick and reinforced with bands of elastic fibres so that they can collapse quickly and completely at each expiration (Laurie, A. H., 1933).

When a human diver takes a lungful of air the oxygen which it contains is held partly in the lungs (34 per cent), partly in the blood (41 per cent) and partly in the muscles (13 per cent) and other tissues (12 per cent). In the blood the oxygen is combined with the red pigment (haemoglobin) in the corpuscles while in the muscles it combines with a substance called myohaemoglobin, which takes up oxygen as haemoglobin does and gives the muscles their red colour. In whales the inspired oxygen is differently distributed, 9 per cent in the air in the lungs, 41 per cent in the blood, 41 per cent in the muscles and 9 per cent in the other tissues (Slijper, E. J., 1962). The meat of Rorquals is very dark and that of Sperm whales almost black owing to the large quantities of myohaemoglobin they contain.

It is also believed that a whale's muscles use up very little energy and so require very little oxygen during a dive. Normally, during the contraction of voluntary muscles (those under the control of the will) lactic acid is produced and it is the oxidation of this which provides the energy for the muscular contraction. In whales this process is believed to predominate during swimming at the surface but during long dives the muscles can contract anaerobically (without the intervention of oxygen) and lactic acid is not produced in such quantities.

Whales, then, can exchange larger quantities of air in their lungs than land mammals and can store larger quantities of inspired oxygen in their muscles, using it very economically when beneath the surface.

During a dive a whale's body has to withstand enormous hydrostatic pressures. In air our own bodies withstand an atmospheric pressure of 14 lbs. on every square inch of surface, but we do not notice it because the pressure acts in all directions and the air in our lungs is under the same pressure. In water the pressure which a sub-merged body has to withstand increases by 14 lbs. (one atmosphere) for every ten metres (five fathoms) of descent, so that a whale at 50 fathoms has to withstand a pressure ten times greater than at the surface, and at 500 fathoms a hundred times greater. All the soft tissues of a whale's body are largely composed of water, like those of any other animal including man, so that they are practically incom-pressible, but the air in the lungs is compressible. Since the lungs are elastic and fill the space they occupy we might expect the air in them to be compressed to a pressure equal to that bearing upon the outside of the body, but they are to a large extent protected by the rib cage, so that there will be a tendency for the stomach, liver and other abdominal organs to be pushed up against the diaphragm which will tend to bulge into the thorax, causing inequalities in the flow and distribution of blood. Blood will tend to engorge the thoracic vessels, flowing from the abdomen, where the pressure is greater, to the thorax, where it is less. Differences of pressure between one part of the body and another must occur when the whale rises or descends steeply in a dive because the fore-end of a seventy-foot whale would be at a pressure different from that at the rear end by one or two atmospheres.

Wonder Networks

The blood system of all whales, especially porpoises and dolphins, is provided with a remarkable arrangement of networks or plexuses, known as the *retia mirabilia* (wonder networks), the function of which is not certainly known but which are believed to regulate the flow of blood. They consist of dense networks of arteries or veins, or both, embedded in masses of fat. The largest and most elaborate of these networks is at the front end of the thoracic cavity where it forms a dense cushion in the shoulder and lower neck region. It continues into the spinal column to form another massive network at the base of the skull. There are other such networks in the pelvic and inguinal regions and around the genital organs, but while those in the chest, neck and skull are made up of arteries those in the pelvic and inguinal regions consist of veins.

In addition to these networks whales have other special arrangements of the blood vessels. Two large spinal veins run beneath the nerve cord in the vertebral column, forming a kind of shunt system so that blood may return to the heart from either the brain or the abdomen by a route alternative to the great trunk veins.

The networks in the thorax and pelvis, and some but not all the other specializations of the blood system, are found in all aquatic mammals, networks being most developed in porpoises and dolphins. These do not dive so deep or so long as the great whales, but they make swift, repeated, shallow dives involving rapid and sudden changes of pressure. It has been suggested that the networks may act as sponges, holding up quantities of blood and redistributing it as necessary so as to equalize the flow from one part of the body to another. The spinal veins allow blood to by-pass the thorax and the heart from the brain to the viscera and vice versa. All these might be mechanisms for preventing differences of pressure from impeding the flow of blood, especially in the thoracic region. Further, it has been suggested that the masses of fat in which the networks are embedded may have a purely mechanical function. When engorged with blood they may swell up and act as cushions, forming padding, particularly in the thorax where pressure on the lungs and heart during a dive would be lower than in the abdomen which is unprotected by the rib cage.

Another problem in connection with the diving of whales which once worried scientists was the fact that they can return safely and swiftly from great depths without suffering from the agonizing and often fatal complaint known as 'caisson sickness' or 'the bends'. This affects men who work under great pressure in caissons or diving suits if they are brought back to atmospheric pressure too quickly. Under increased pressure extra nitrogen is forced into solution in the blood and if the pressure is released suddenly, by bringing the diver too quickly to the surface, the nitrogen comes out of solution in the blood in the form of bubbles in the blood vessels, especially in those around the spinal cord. The diver experiences fearful pains in the joints with stomach ache, head ache and sickness, while bad cases may be fatal. In order to prevent this pressure must be reduced slowly and in stages so that the nitrogen can come out of solution slowly without forming bubbles in the blood vessels.

It is now realized that caisson sickness only results if the body is supplied continuously with nitrogen under pressure during the dive, as is the case with men working in caissons who are supplied with air under pressure for breathing. But if a man were to take in a gulp of air and hold his breath he could return with it as quickly as he liked from any depth because there would be no excess nitrogen to be forced into the blood. The only question of importance would be how he could hold his breath for long enough.

The Ear

We saw in the *Morsa* that the whales were well aware that they were being pursued and could detect the beat of the ship's screw a long way off. Whalers have always assumed without question that whales must have a very acute sense of hearing. In the old days shallops were specially designed to slip through the water with as little noise as possible and no talking was allowed when approaching a whale. The Japanese used to beat on the gunwales of their boats to frighten Humpbacks into their nets and to this day in the Faroes this method is used to scare blackfish into shallow bays. During whale-marking cruises it has been noticed that whales may receive a steel dart in the back with indifference but very much dislike having one plop into the water beside them.

The whale's sense of hearing is second only to that of the bat, whose ears are the most sensitive known. It is the whale's principal source of contact with its environment. The eye probably does not see very much, partly because of its lateral position, widely separated from its fellow and each with its individual field of vision, and partly because the water is almost always too murky. The sense of smell is almost non-existent since there is no sensory lining in the nasal passages. But by means of its exceedingly sensitive and acute ear the whale keeps in contact with its fellows, locates its food, is warned of the presence of enemies and derives its sense of direction.

The human ear can perceive sound vibrations in air which have a frequency of between 15 and 20 kilocycles (15–20,000 vibrations per second), but cats are sensitive to vibrations of 50 kcs., rats and mice up to 90 and bats up to 175 kcs. Dolphins respond to vibrations between 120 and 153 kcs. But the difference between land animals and whales is that while the former use their ears to detect vibrations in air whales use them for detecting vibrations in water. For this purpose they have adapted the auditory apparatus of land mammals which they inherited from their terrestrial forebears.

The human ear can hear sounds rather better under water than in air because water is the better conductor of sound waves. In both media we hear sounds coming to the ear both through the ear drum and by conduction through the bones of the skull. In air we hear much more through the ear drum than by conduction, and since our ears are fairly wide apart one ear hears any sound a minute fraction of a second later than the other one, and from this we obtain a sense of direction. Animals such as elephants, which have ears very wide apart, have correspondingly accurate directional hearing. Under water, on the other hand, vibrations reach our ears more easily by conduction and for this reason we cannot perceive the direction of sounds under water. Nevertheless whales have a very accurate directional sense under water so that sounds must reach their ears through the ear drums and not by bone conduction. Their ears must somehow be insulated from all vibrations except those entering through the ear drum.

The details of the structure and mode of action of the ear of whales have been worked out by two Scotsmen on the staff of the British Museum (Natural History) (Fraser, F. C. and Purves, P. E., 1954, 1960). They showed how the ear is insulated from all vibrations which might reach it by conduction through the bones of the skull or the surrounding blubber. Indeed the whale's ear may be likened to a telephone receiver sensitive to vibrations along one channel only, the wire.

In mammals generally the ear consists of three parts, the outer, middle and inner ear (Fig. 10a). The outer ear consists of the external visible part (or *pinna*) and the short passage (the auditory *meatus*) lined by external skin leading into the skull and ending at the ear drum. This is a tightly stretched vibrating membrane, made of skin, which responds to vibrations coming to it along the *meatus*. All this is the sound-collecting part of the ear.

The middle ear, on the inner side of the ear drum, is an air space entirely surrounded by the bones of the base of the skull and is connected to the throat by the Eustachian tube so that pressure is the same on both sides of the drum. In many mammals the middle ear space has a sort of enlargement or annexe leading off it in the form of a chamber surrounded by a flask-shaped bone, the tympanic bulla, forming a resonating chamber. A chain of very small delicate bones, the auditory ossicles, stretches across the middle ear space from the ear drum to a second vibrating membrane which occupies a hole in the inner wall of the space. This is called the 'oval window' (*fenestra ovalis*) and the auditory ossicles form a sound transmitting mechanism from the drum to the window. The middle ear, in fact, is the sound-transmitting part of the ear.

The inner ear or labyrinth is embedded in a tough bone, the petrosal, at the base of the skull. It contains the spiral system of sound receptors, the vestibule or *cochlea*, which receives vibrations from the oval window, and it also contains the semicircular canal system which imparts the sense of balance. The labyrinth is filled with a fluid which conveys the vibrations of the oval window to the vestibule.

The whale's ear must not only be insulated from conducted vibrations but must also be able to respond to water-borne vibrations which are of smaller amplitude than air-borne ones. There must also be some means of equalizing the pressure on both sides of the ear drum because the Eustachian tube cannot be used for this purpose under water.

All three parts of the ear are recognizable in whales but they are differently constructed from those of land mammals (Fig. 10b). We have seen already that there is no external sound collecting *pinna* since there is no need for it under water where sound waves travel farther and more easily than in air, and it would interfere with the streamlining of the body. The aperture of the ear, as we have also seen, is very small, a hole not much larger in diameter than a little finger. The *meatus* leading from it to the ear drum is long, as much as four feet in large whales, and S-shaped in the vertical plane, thus allowing for seasonal changes in the thickness of the blubber over it. In toothed whales the narrow passage is open throughout its length and filled with sea water up to the ear drum but in whalebone whales the passage has a middle blocked-up portion where it is completely occluded, and then it widens out like a funnel for a distance of about three feet up to the ear drum. This part is occupied by a plug, called the 'wax plug', although it is not made of wax. A very narrow tube to the ear drum runs through the middle of the plug.

This plug has been known to exist since the old Right whaling days when it was thought to be made of ear wax (*cerumen*) similar to that which is secreted in our own ears. Actually it is made of horny material identical with that which forms the baleen plates and the hair, finger and toe nails of other mammals (Purves, P. E., 1955). It is built up of concentric layers of this substance shed by the skin which lines the passage of the *meatus*. It is shed more copiously at certain seasons than at others, giving the plug a laminar or layered structure which has been related to a periodicity in the whale's metabolism. Fraser and Purves (1960) established that the plug is a highly efficient conductor of sound.

In toothed whales the ear drum has the form of a cone which projects

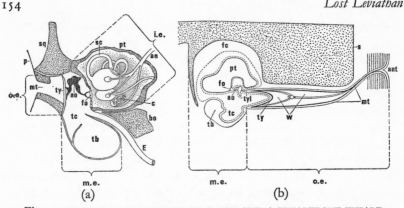

Fig. 10 DIAGRAMS OF THE EAR OF A CAT AND A WHALEBONE WHALE

(a) Cat. o.e. Outer ear, mt External *meatus*, P Pinna, ty Tympanum or ear drum, m.e. Middle ear, ac Auditory ossicles, fo *Fenestra ovalis* (oval window), tc Tympanic cavity, tb Tympanic bulla, E Eustachian tube, i.e. Inner ear, an Auditory nerve, c *Cochlea*, sc Semicircular canals, sq Squamosal (cheek) bone, pt Periotic bone, bo Basioccipital (base of skull) bone.
(b) Whalebone whale. Inner ear not shown, o.e. Outer ear, mt External *meatus*, W Wax plug in *meatus*, ty Finger-shaped projection of ear drum, tyl Tympanic ligament, me. Middle ear, ao Auditory ossicles, fo *Fenestra ovalis* (oval window), tc Tympanic cavity, tb Tympanic bulla, pt Petrosal bone (surrounding the inner ear), fc Foam-filled cavity surrounding the petrosal bone, S Bones of base of skull. (From Dudok van Heel, 1962.).

into the middle ear, but in whalebone whales it is a taut, vibrating ligament, not a diaphragm as in other mammals and man. It forms a conical projection like a glove finger protruding outwards into the passage of the *meatus* where it is embraced and ensheathed by the horny plug (Fig. 10b). The glove finger transmits vibrations to the ligament whence, as in other mammals, they are transmitted across the middle ear to the oval window by the auditory ossicles. These in whales are very heavily constructed and multiply the amplitude of the vibrations communicated to them by the ear drum ligament. So small amplitude water-borne vibrations are converted to large amplitude before they reach the inner ear.

Fraser and Purves think that the horny plug in the external *meatus* is the sole channel by which vibrations reach the ear drum ligament, just as vibrations are conveyed by wires to a telephone receiver, but Dutch scientists, who have also worked on the anatomy of the whale's ear, do not agree and think that some vibrations reach the ear through the blubber (Slijper, E. J., 1962; Reysenbach de Haan, 1956).

In land mammals the tympanic bulla, a sort of resonating annexe to the middle ear, is one of the bones of the base of the skull and an integral part of it, but in whales the flask-shaped bulla fits quite loosely into the other bones at the base of the skull with no actual bony junction so that it can be dislodged quite easily, as we saw on the plan, to make a trophy with a funny face. In toothed whales it is joined to the skull only by ligaments and in whalebone whales it is cushioned by pads of connective tissue. Thus it is almost completely separate from the skull and insulated so that it can take up no vibrations from it or from surrounding bones. This is made even more sure by the heavy solid construction of the bulla itself. As additional insulation the middle ear space is surrounded by air cavities with which it communicates through an opening in the wall of the bulla so that pressure remains the same both inside and outside the middle ear. In toothed whales these cavities run into the base of the skull and in all whales they are filled with an oily mucous foam secreted by glands in their walls. This, as already mentioned, fills the throat and nasal passages and is believed to take part in the formation of the spout.

The air cavities around the middle ear are themselves surrounded by venous 'wonder networks' embedded in fat or connective tissue. These provide a pressure equalizing mechanism. In land mammals the Eustachian tube ensures that pressure in the ear and outside the body is the same. In whales when pressure in the air cavities around the ear gets out of equilibrium with the hydrostatic pressure outside the body the networks can be filled with blood or emptied like inflatable cushions so as to vary the amount of space they occupy in the walls of the air cavities.

The inner ear, deeply embedded in the hard petrosal bone, part of the base of the skull, comprises the same organs as in all other mammals, the semicircular canals and the spiral *cochlea*.

The semicircular canals are very small in whales but are evidently efficient since porpoises, anyhow, have an acute perception of balance. In the *cochlea* the receptor cells at the base of the spiral are large and well developed, and it is these which in all mammals perceive sounds of high tone. They are large in those land mammals which have an acute perception of high tones, such as bats and mice.

This complicated and highly specialized auditory apparatus is evidence of extremely acute hearing. The ears are very wide apart and, as we have seen, are efficiently insulated from all vibrations which do not come through the ear drum ligament. It follows that whales must have an accurate directional sense and must have been able not only clearly to hear the beat of the *Morsa*'s screw but to pin-point its direction accurately.

Intercommunication

Other mammals, such as bats, which have a highly developed hearing apparatus, are equipped to communicate with each other by means of it. They make sounds which can be perceived and understood by their fellows. In bats these are of very high frequency, many of them outside the range of human hearing.

The fact that whales have acute hearing and a highly specialized auditory apparatus led scientists to suppose that they must use it for communicating with one another.

Whalers have known for a long time that the White whale or Beluga can emit screaming noises which caused British whalers in the nineteenth century to call it the 'sea canary'. By far the greater part of the research on this question has been done on dolphins, especially the common American porpoise which we call the Bottle-nosed dolphin. Mysterious noises were first picked up by underwater detection equipment used by the U.S. Navy during World War II, but it was not until after the war that they were recognized as being made by dolphins. They give out low frequency sounds (7–15 kcs.), heard as shrill whistles, and high frequency sounds (20–200 kcs.) heard as a sort of creaking noise. The latter are apparently used for echo-location, like radar, and are often outside the range of perception of the human ear (15–20 kcs.). Bats are known to use high frequency sounds made in the throat for echo-location while flying.

It is now known that many of the smaller whales give out sounds of various sorts, whistles, howls, grunts and squeaks, but it has only recently been established that the large whalebone whales and the Sperm whale also emit sounds. There had been many unconfirmed reports of this. For instance the French research vessel *Calypso* reported that a young Sperm whale uttered a shrill whistle as it collided with the ship's screw. Hans Hass, the well-known underwater photographer, also heard a dying Sperm whale utter a loud squeak.

The first actual recording of the sounds made by Sperm whales was taped aboard the U.S. submarine *Bluegill* on 29th April 1957 (Perkins, J. *et al.*, 1966). The record contained what are known as 'carpenters', hammering noises which result when rhythmical pulses are received from two or more directions at once. The sounds were a series of clicks.

Sounds emitted by a Fin whale were recorded by the Research Vessel *Trident* on 7th April 1964 in a position 125 miles east of Bermuda. Four minutes of intermittent and varied sounds were recorded when the ship was close to two whales which seemed to be communicating with one another (Perkins, P., 1966) and they were a series of clicks and whistles.

The question remains, how do whales make these sounds and what organs do they use to produce them? The assumption is that the larynx is the sound-producing organ, though whales have no vocal cords. Nevertheless, experiments with dead dolphins, in which air was forced through the larynx, produced sounds something like those made by the living animal. Lacking any proof to the contrary it has been supposed that the squeals which toothed whales produce come from the larynx while clicks are believed to come from the nasal passages. Whalebone whales have a blind pouch or sac below the larynx which is suspected of being a sound-producing organ, but again there is no definite proof of this. It is believed that the lungs may be responsible for some of the low frequency sounds emitted by whalebone whales.

In general it seems that whalebone whales emit low frequency moans and screams and it is believed that they use them for communicating with each other. They may perhaps use them for echo-location but the vibrations are thought to be of too low frequency to be of much use in detecting swarms of krill, except very large dense masses.

The clicks made by Sperm whales are believed to be used for echo-location, but only by inference from the very similar sounds made by Bottle-nosed dolphins which are known to use them for this purpose. By inference, too, it seems that the smaller toothed whales have a fairly efficient echo-location apparatus which they can use for navigating and perhaps for locating prey.

CHAPTER 8

Size and Age of Rorquals

Length

Blue and Fin whales of the southern hemisphere are, on an average, larger than those of the northern hemisphere though it is not certain that this is a constant difference between them. If it were absolutely certain that Blue and Fin whales do not cross the Equator to mingle with those on the other side it might be possible to say that northern and southern Rorquals belong to two different species, with the Equator separating two distinct populations. However, this is not certain because Fin whales are sometimes seen in the Persian Gulf and off the coast of India, and they did not come through the Suez Canal. But in the Atlantic and Pacific strays from one side of the Equator to the other are believed to be rare.

The Blue whale is the largest of all whales and the largest animal at present in existence. It is probably not the largest animal that has ever existed because sharks' teeth of Cretaceous age have been found which it is thought must have belonged to fish about a hundred feet long. Adult cow Blue whales are larger than bulls by a difference of 4·6 to 7·6 per cent. In the northern hemisphere the largest Blue whale recorded was a cow of 88 feet 7 inches (27·0 m.) but far larger ones than that have been measured in the southern hemisphere, though not for some thirty years or more now. The largest measured by Mackintosh and Wheeler (1929) in South Georgia was a cow 93 feet 6 inches long (from tip of snout to notch between tail flukes). In 1914 Barrett-Hamilton measured a cow Blue whale 92 feet long (Hinton, M. A. C., 1925) and in 1921 another was taken in the Panama Canal which was said to be 98 feet long and Sir Sidney Harmer (1923) confirmed from measurements of its neck vertebrae that this must have been its length.

The Fin whale, the next largest, does not reach anything like these lengths. Again the adult cow is larger than the bull by differences of from 3·0 to 8·7 per cent so that the sex difference is more marked among older Fins than among older Blues. The largest Fin cow recorded by Mackintosh and Wheeler (1929) at South Georgia had a length of 80 feet 5 inches (24·53 m.), the largest of eight hundred whales. In the northern hemisphere the largest Fin whale was a cow 80 feet 6 inches long (24·55 m.) but this was an uncertain measurement and the largest recorded by True (1904) had a length of 70 feet 8 inches (21·5 m.).

Weight

The weight of such gigantic animals was a matter for speculation for a long time and there was a belief that it could be estimated at about one ton per foot of length. D'Arcy Thompson (1942) calculated the weight of a hypothetical Blue whale from the known weight of foetuses. He assumed that the weight would be proportional to the cube of the length throughout the animal's whole life, as it in fact would if the bodily proportions did not change at all as the animal grew up. A foetus 4 feet 6 inches long weighed 46 lbs. and so D'Arcy Thompson calculated that a whale 45 feet long would weigh 46×10^3 lbs. or about 23 tons. Similarly a whale of 90 feet would weigh 23×2^3 or 184 tons. There is no confirmation of the ton per foot estimate in this.

Before the war A. H. Laurie (1933) collected the data then available about the weights of Blue whales. A whale 77 feet 9 inches (23·72 m.) long was weighed piecemeal in Newfoundland in 1903 and was calculated to have a weight of 63 tons. Another 97 feet (29·5 m.) long, weighed piecemeal in South Georgia, was calculated, from the number of blubber, meat and bone boilers which it filled, to weigh 163·7 tons exclusive of blood. Laurie thought that its total weight was probably about 174 tons. In 1926 two other Blue whales were weighed piecemeal in South Georgia; one of 89 feet (27·18 m.) weighed 162·2 tons and another of 66 feet 7 inches (20·3 m.) weighed 49·9 tons, both being exclusive of blood.

From the growth curves which these figures gave, based on the three most accurate weighings (49·9, 126·2 and 63 tons), it is evident that D'Arcy Thompson's 90 feet Blue whale would weigh about 133·5

tons and his estimate of 184 tons, based on the weight–length relationship, was too high possibly owing to the fact that as the foetus grows
into a young whale and thence into an adult the bodily proportions
change enough to upset the calculation.

Since the war several large Blue whales have been weighed entire
on board the Japanese factory ship *Hashidate Maru* (G.H.Q., Far East
Command, 1948). The weights, including blood and stomach contents,
are as follows:

Length (ft.)	Weight (tons)
77	104·4
83	100·8
83	118·0
86	116·4
88	121·6
89	136·4

These figures fit in quite well with those of Laurie and fall within
the growth curve which he prepared.

The Problem of Size

Such an enormous weight as these figures show would be a very
serious handicap for an animal on land which would be faced with
problems arising from what is known as the 'principle of similitude'.
This lays down that for any shape the surface area is proportional to
the square of the linear dimensions while the volume, and thus the
weight, is proportional to the cube of the linear dimensions. The
most significant linear dimension for an animal is the length of the
body and for a man the height of the body. As the linear dimensions,
length, breadth and height, increase the surface area diminishes in
relation to the volume. A small animal with short linear dimensions
has a very large surface area in relation to its volume and a large
animal, with long linear dimensions, has a relatively very small surface
area.

A small animal, such as a mouse, continually loses heat from its
large surface area and must feed continuously in order to replace it.
A mouse, in fact, eats a quarter of its weight a day. This continuous
feeding means a high rate of oxidation, or metabolic rate, in other
words rate of living activity, in order to produce the necessary heat so
that a small animal lives in a state of constant movement, as do
mice, small birds and insects. It breeds prolifically and is short-lived,
soon, as it were, burning itself out. The pygmy shrew, the smallest

Above: Flensing a Blue whale on the plan deck of a factory ship

Below: Krill. Stomach contents of a Blue whale 72 ft. long on the deck of Fl. f. *Harvester*. The flensing knife is 5 ft. long.

of all mammals, weighing less than a sixpenny piece, lives only for a year.

Large animals, on the other hand, have the opposite problem. Their surface area is small in relation to their volume so that they have difficulty in getting rid of heat fast enough. For this reason they often love to wallow in water so as to keep cool, like the hippopotamus, the water buffalo and the elephant who enjoys squirting it over himself with his trunk. They move slowly, as a rule, breed slowly and are long-lived. The giant reptiles of the Tertiary era must have had to face these problems and the largest of them, Diplodocus and Brontosaurus, probably spent their lives wallowing in shallow water, browsing on vegetation.

Whales are able to avoid this problem of heat exchange by reason of their aquatic life. The cool marine environment conducts the heat away from the body's surface and, indeed, in the Antarctic the question is rather how to retain heat than how to lose it and this is solved by the increase in the thickness of the blubber which takes place when the southern migration occurs. Large size, in fact, is an advantage in polar regions because the relatively small surface area makes keeping warm easier. This is one of the reasons why there are no small mammals in the polar regions and the small birds, like Wilson's petrel in the Antarctic, are summer visitors.

There are other problems for large animals arising from the principle of similitude, and they apply also to human giants. While the volume, and therefore the weight, of an animal or man is proportional to the cube of the length (height in a man) yet the pull which the muscles can exert and the strength of the bones depend on their cross-sectional areas. In each individual muscle or bone the cross-sectional area is proportional to its length. Large animals must therefore have very thick bones to support their muscles and human giants are always weaklings with skeletons and muscles lacking the strength necessary for their long limbs. A giant ten times heavier than a normal man would break his leg every time he took a step unless his thigh bone were so thickened as to be too heavy for him to move it at all. If the story of Goliath is taken literally he was six cubits and a span in height, about $11\frac{1}{2}$ feet. He was thus about twice the average height of a man and should have weight $\times$ 2^3, that is eight times the normal weight of a man, about 96 stone or somewhat over half a ton (Comber, L. C., 1968). His muscles and bones, however, would have had a cross section of only $2^2 = 4$ times those of an average man, so he would have been a weakling with inadequate muscles and bones, and almost certainly no match for David who was a husky, normal-sized youth.

Another problem which giants and very large animals have to cope with is that of transporting blood to their tissues. The heart has to pump much harder than does that of a small animal in order to keep the tissues and organs supplied with the same amount of blood. Any extra work or exertion puts a great strain on the pump and human giants usually have weak hearts.

The whale, again, avoids this problem owing to its aquatic life. The dense medium supports its body in all directions and buoys it up so that it can make do with a relatively light and feeble skeleton. The same is true also of fish. Swimming through water calls for very much less effort than moving about on land, putting far less strain on the heart and circulation. When a whale has the misfortune to become stranded on a beach its weight suddenly becomes so enormous that it cannot move at all, even its tail or flippers, and certainly cannot attempt to get back into the sea. It dies of suffocation because of its own weight pressing upon its lungs, making breathing impossible. Stranded whales also often have broken backs, the comparatively frail backbone being unable to support the body when not in the water.

Age

The great size of the larger whales, together with their knobbly, encrusted appearance, gave rise to the idea that whales must live to a great age, but until recently no method of determining the age of a whale was known. It was realized thirty years ago, when the 'Discovery' work began, that it would be most desirable to find a method since it would help greatly in population analysis if the proportions of whales of different ages were known.

To a certain extent the length of the body is a rough guide to the age of a whale for large whales are obviously older than small ones, but it is of no value after growth in length ceases. In just the same way we can tell a boy of, say, fifteen from one of, say, eight by his height, but we cannot tell a man of forty from a man of twenty-five by height alone.

A possible clue to age was thought to lie in the skin scars of unknown origin that we saw on the plan. Since they were acquired during the whale's visits to warm waters it was thought that by counting the apparent ages of the scars it might be possible to judge how often the whale had visited the tropics, but the older scars proved to be very confused and it was always doubtful how many generations of them there were so this method had to be abandoned.

Another possible clue lay in the numbers of scars left in the ovaries by the shed eggs. Since every egg on being shed leaves a permanent scar it might be possible by counting the scars to tell how many breeding seasons the whale had experienced. On an average 2·8 scars are formed in the ovaries of a cow Fin whale every two years, and there was found to be a periodicity in the number of scars counted in the ovaries at South Georgia (Wheeler, J. F. G., 1930). By far the largest number of cows had only two scars. Next there was a group which had seven or eight, then one with between eleven and fourteen, and after that a rather indefinite group with sixteen or more. It was thought that these groups represented separate periods of egg shedding, breeding seasons in fact. As we saw, breeding seasons occur every other year in the life of a cow whale so it was thought that the separate groups of scars must represent two-year periods. Cows which had the first three groups of scars (2, 7-8, 11-14) did not, with few exceptions, have the bony discs fused in the backbone and were not, therefore, fully grown. Those with the fourth group (16 and more) almost always had the discs fused and were fully grown. If the groups represented two years in the cow's life then fully grown cows (16 scars and more) must reach full physical maturity at least six years after the attainment of sexual maturity. If we can assume that sexual maturity is reached at two years from birth we can judge the age of any cow Fin whale up to the attainment of physical maturity, which must occur at the age of eight years from birth.

This was a great step forward but there were two objections. One concerned the assumption that sexual maturity (puberty) was reached at an age of two years. As other methods of age determination were discovered it seemed that this was an under-estimate and that a period of three to seven years (average five) seemed more probable. The other objection was that the method gave no clue to the age of whales after the attainment of physical maturity, nor did it give any clue to the age of bull whales.

We saw on the plan that the surfaces of the baleen plates showed transverse ridges due to variations in the thickness of the cortical layer surrounding the microscopic hollow tubes within the plates. Professor Johan Ruud (1940, 1945), who worked on the subject for some years, believed that these ridges, and the depressions between them, must represent periodic variations in the rate at which the cortical material is formed in the gum. The rate must depend on the whale's metabolism which would be higher during the summer months of feeding in the south than during the months of starvation and exhaustion in the tropics. He devised an instrument with a stylus which magnified these ridges and depressions and made tracings of them. These showed that the ridges and depressions were irregular in form but arranged in groups with steps between them from the base of the plate to its apex as though the laying down of cortical material in the gum proceeded in periodic bursts throughout the growth of the plate. Ruud thought that each of these groups must represent one year in the life of the plate and the steps between them must mark seasonal increases in the thickness of the cortical material, signifying an increase in the whale's metabolic rate. There were, however, several drawbacks to this method of judging a whale's age. In the first place, the baleen plates wear away by friction, as do finger and toe nails, renewing themselves about every seven years. No plate, therefore, carried indications of more than about five years' growth, dating from birth. Further, the ridges and depressions were often irregular and difficult to distinguish. An untrained, uninitiated observer, looking at Ruud's figures of his tracings, might be excused for thinking that his periodic steps in thickness had been somewhat arbitrarily drawn.

The most promising method of age determination lies in the horny plug of the ear. If it is cut longitudinally the interior cut surface of the plug can be seen to be striated by alternate light and dark bands like the rings in the trunk of a tree or in the ear bones of a fish. These, too, immediately suggest some kind of periodicity. The horny plug is laid down inside the ear passage by the skin which lines it, continuous with that on the outside of the body. Dr. Purves (1955), who first described these layers in the plug, thought that they must be due to annual periods of growth, during which horny matter was laid down in the ear, alternating with resting periods when little was laid down. He supposed that the growth periods corresponded with visits to the Antarctic and the resting periods with visits to the tropics. If this is so then one layer (one light plus one dark band) would represent one year in the life of the whale. Yet it might be that the bands represent north and south migrations, growth being arrested while the whale is on passage, in which case two layers (two light and two dark bands) would represent one year.

Until 1962 most writers, British, Australian (working on Humpbacks) and Japanese, believed that two light plus two dark layers, or 'laminae' as they are called, were formed per year in the ear plug and represented one year in the life of the whale. In 1962, however, evidence that only one layer or lamina (one light plus one dark) was laid down per year came from the new technique of whale marking.

Whale Marking

So far we have drawn a picture of the life of the great Antarctic Rorquals based largely on inference. By examining enough carcasses in the polar regions and at subtropical and tropical whaling stations it has been possible to gain enough evidence to infer that the Rorquals spend their lives migrating between the polar regions and the tropics or subtropics in both hemispheres. We have inferred that in the southern hemisphere they spend the summer feeding on krill in Antarctic waters because we found them in the south with full stomachs. There was no Antarctic whaling during the southern winter because there were no whales—so, by inference, they must have gone elsewhere. In the southern subtropics there is whaling during the winter but not during the summer when whales are scarce because they are presumed to be in the Antarctic. In the subtropics in winter the whales have empty stomachs and are obviously not feeding. Cow whales taken in the Antarctic in the summer are 50 per cent pregnant, with small foetuses in the spring, gradually becoming larger up to about birth size in March or April (autumn). In the spring small young whales are taken among the bigger ones while calves and nursing mothers are sometimes taken at this time by accident. In the subtropics in winter, on the other hand, pregnant cows are carrying minute foetuses. Some have no foetus but ovaries in a state of breeding activity while bulls show activity in the testes. From all this we infer, though we have no proof, that mating takes place in subtropical waters during the winter and birth roughly a year later when the mother is on her way north again, nursing her calf during the winter and weaning it in the spring. What was lacking was actual proof that whales do, in fact, migrate north and south as we believe.

A well-perfected technique in fisheries research consists of marking fish in order to trace their movements and migrations. A numbered label is attached to them and they are put back in the sea. In course of time these marked fish are caught again during fishing operations and the numbered labels give a clue not only to migrations but also, if enough fish have been marked and recovered, to mortality caused by fishing.

Obviously it has never been possible to catch a whale, mark it and put it back in the sea, but at the end of the last century Blue whales had been taken by Norwegians in the Barentz Sea with American-made harpoons embedded in them. This gave the 'Discovery' Committee in 1924 the idea that it might be possible to shoot some sort of numbered dart into a whale which could be retained in the blubber and found again during the course of whaling operations. A lead in the experiments was given by the late Sir Sidney Harmer, Director of the Natural History Museum, and Mr. (now Sir Alister) Hardy. At the same time the great Norwegian fishery scientist, Professor Johan Hjort, was experimenting along the same lines. The dart which was finally evolved on the British side was a large steel drawing pin about two inches in diameter and three inches in length (Fig. 11a). It had a barbed point and was fixed to the head of a slender wooden shaft about a foot long. This was muzzle-loaded into a cut down 12-bore shot gun, the shaft being fitted with felt rings to keep it in place in the barrel. When the dart hit the whale the stud remained embedded in the blubber and the shaft broke off. The Norwegians arrived at a barbed mark mounted on a metal shaft muzzle-loaded into a shoulder harpoon gun. The shaft carried out a line coiled in a metal container below the gun barrel. On making a hit the shaft came away from the head embedded in the blubber and could be hauled in by the line, or recovered by the line if it missed.

The British mark was light, handy and cheap. Round the disc of the stud were inscribed the words 'Reward for return to the Discovery Committee, Colonial Office, London'. All the whaling companies were circularized with accounts of the darts and instructions about what to do when they were found. During the late twenties hundreds of them were fired into whales, which did not seem to notice them when hit, mostly from the 'Discovery' Committee's second research ship *William Scoresby*, cruising off South Georgia. She had been built principally for this job. Nevertheless, the years went on and no marks were ever recovered so that it seemed that they must be rejected by the blubber, sloughed out in the same way as we saw parasites, such as the tassel-like *Penella*, being sloughed out in the Antarctic after becoming attached in the tropics.

In 1932 a new kind of mark was devised, large enough to penetrate through the blubber into the underlying muscles and so stick there, and also large enough not to be missed by the flensers during the stripping of the whale, yet not large enough to harm the whale. It consisted of a stainless steel tube $10\frac{1}{2}$ inches long and $\frac{3}{4}$ inch in diameter with a cone-shaped lead head (Fig. 11b). A cartridge was fitted on to the tail end of the tube and the dart was breech-loaded into a cut down 12–bore gun. The same inscription was engraved lengthwise along the tube.

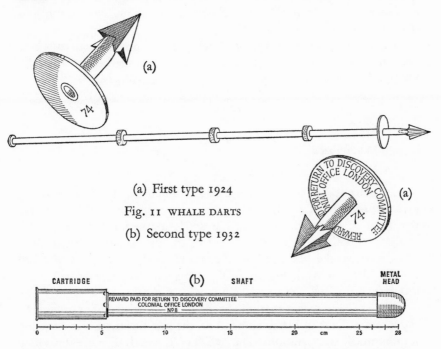

(a) First type 1924

Fig. 11 WHALE DARTS

(b) Second type 1932

This mark was first tried out during the 1932–33 season from a hired whale catcher off South Georgia, and proved a success. Hits were scored and the shaft was seen to penetrate the blubber. Accordingly a campaign of whale marking was embarked upon using the *William Scoresby* and hired whale catchers. Various members of the 'Discovery' staff undertook this arduous task and darts were recovered in numbers large enough for the results up to the outbreak of World War II to be summarized in a report by G. W. Rayner (1940) who played a leading part in the campaign. I myself never went on a whale marking cruise, but I know that it is a chilly though exciting form of sport, and no easy matter to hit the fleeting target presented by the whale's back from the fo'c'sle of a small pitching ship at a distance of

fifty yards. I have, of course, used a whale marking gun on many
occasions but I do not know that I have ever made a hit. Once in the
Bay of Whales I missed a sitting target from the poop of *Discovery II*
in full view of many of the crew. It was a Minke whale surfacing in
an ice pool under the ship's stern. I fired directly down on top of it.
An eloquent silence followed the shot, and then a burst of laughter.
On another occasion I fired at a Fin whale near Chagos Archipelago in
the Indian Ocean from the deck of our 30 foot fishing vessel. I missed
that one too, but excusably.

The outbreak of World War II temporarily put an end to whale
marking, but by then over 5,000 whales had been marked in Antarctic
waters. The numbers returned were (Rayner, G. W., 1940):

	No. marked	No. returned	Per cent.
Blue	668	33	4·9
Fin	3,915	118	3·0
Humpback	548	36	6·5

A few Right, Sei and Sperm whales were also marked.

The percentages of returns are small, much smaller than those of
tags returned from a fish marking campaign of comparable size, but
this is to be expected. Some of the whale marks were evidently still
being lost, perhaps by sloughing out of the tissues, or by penetrating
right through the blubber into the muscle and so being overlooked
on the plan, or by being so badly damaged that little of the shaft
was left.

After the war whale marking went more slowly, mainly owing to
the increased cost of hiring ships to do the job, but there was growing
international co-operation. The whalers themselves were provided
with guns and marks and amused themselves by potting at whales
from their catchers on the way to and from the whaling grounds or
before the start of whaling operations or after their closure.

The National Institute of Oceanography, which after the war
included the 'Discovery' organization, was obliged to give up special
whale marking cruises for reasons of expense but the Russians and
Japanese have been carrying on the work and in 1953 an international
whale marking expedition went south financed by Norwegian, British
and Dutch whaling interests. A whale catcher, the *Enern*, was specially
built for this and an improved kind of mark was used, fired from a
tube (Morris tube) inside the harpoon gun. The marks had coloured
nylon streamers inside the shaft which were ejected on impact so that

they hung outside the whale and were intended to help in spotting the presence of the marks and in recovering them if they went right through the blubber into the muscles. The marks were covered with penicillin so that they would not cause septic wounds which might slough them out or cause the whale to sicken and die. The *Enern* made two trips to the Antarctic, in 1953 when 110 whales were marked, and in 1954 when 243 were marked. So far, I think, none has been recovered in spite of modern refinements.

Up to the end of 1958 the numbers of marks fired and recovered were as follows (Brown, S. G., 1962):

| | | Marked | Recovered | | | Total | Per cent |
			1st season	*2nd season*	*3rd season*		
Pre-war	Blue	668	18			33	4·9
	Fin	3,915	34	21	13	118	3·0
Post-war	Blue	194	22	7		31	16·0
	Fin	903	53	20	17	95	10·5

Marks from pre-war years also came in fairly steadily throughout the post-war years, some from whales which had been marked many years ago. For instance, a Blue whale marked by a German expedition in 1938 between 50° and 60° S. to the southward of the Cape of Good Hope was recovered fourteen years later between 05° E. and 39° W. longitude. Among Fin whales no fewer than sixty marks were recovered after a lapse of fifteen years or more. Two marks fired in January and February 1935 off Enderby Land were recovered twenty-three years later in March 1958 in the same sector of the Antarctic. If we allow three years for these Fin whales to reach sexual maturity, and a suitable size to be fired at, they must have been at least twenty-six years old when killed.

Marking and Migration

The figures show that most of the marks fired near South Georgia were recovered in the same season in which they were fired (1st season) and were found far to the southward some weeks later, confirming what was always suspected, that Blue and Fin whales off South Georgia are on passage southward.

The evidence from recovered marks shows that Blue, Fin and Humpback whales tend to return year after year to the same sector of the Antarctic, though there is a certain amount of east–west dispersal, an average of fifty degrees of longitude for Fin whales and

ninety degrees for Blue (Brown, S. G., 1962). There is one record
of a Blue which covered 170° of longitude, half-way round the world
from 60° E. in the Indian Ocean to 125° W. in the Pacific in a little
over two years. Blue whales evidently disperse east and west along
the ice edge more freely than Fin and Brown believes that older Blue
whales arrive on the feeding grounds before the younger ones which
disperse more widely looking for unoccupied grounds.

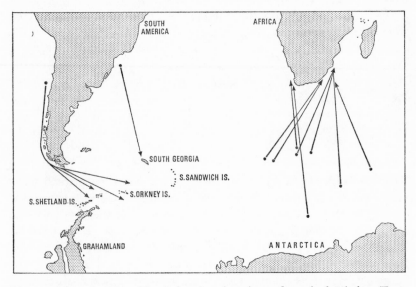

Fig. 12 Map showing North-South migration of marked whales (From
Hardy, A. C., 1967)

As we have already seen (Chapter 2) from Lund's work on iodine
numbers, there is reason to suppose that each area of the Antarctic
has its own population of whales which return to it year after year.
The results of whale marking have confirmed this, for Brown (1962)
writes: 'Although the records of movement of both Blue and Fin
whales between the different whaling areas are incomplete, they
suggest that most of the areas (see Chapter 10) have some reality and
that they reflect a division of both species on the Antarctic whaling
grounds into groups of whales, but the exact nature of these is not
clear.'

The evidence of a north–south migration of Blue and Fin whales
from the results of marking is at present rather meagre, but it is
accumulating (Fig. 12). Before the war a 69-ft. Fin cow was marked

in the Antarctic in 65° S. south of South Africa and its mark was recovered off Saldanha Bay, Cape Province, two and a half years later. In January 1949 a male Fin whale of 73 feet was captured off South Georgia with a mark which had been fired into it eleven years earlier in October 1937 off the coast of Brazil. Since then Brown (1962) has reported eight further instances of marks fired in the Antarctic south of South Africa which were recovered in South African waters, two at Saldanha Bay and six at Durban. Professor Hardy, in his book *Great Waters* (1967), mentions four others marked off the coast of Chile which were recovered in the South Shetland area of the Antarctic, so that some at least of the whales we saw at South Georgia had evidently come from the coast of South America. On the other hand a Fin whale marked at Bouvet Island, in 50° S. south of the Cape, was captured the following season at South Georgia, a shift to the westward of about 50 degrees of longitude.

Scanty though the evidence is at present it does provide a definite proof of migration from the Antarctic to subtropical waters for the Fin whale at any rate, and it must be only a matter of time before evidence for the migration of Blue whales comes to hand.

More definite proof of migration from Antarctic waters to the subtropics has been given by the results of marking Humpback whales since they follow well-defined migration routes along the eastern and western coasts of all the southern continents and New Zealand. Whaling statistics and sightings had led to the belief that Humpbacks move north to breed and produce their young in the southern winter, travelling back to their equally well-defined Antarctic feeding grounds in the summer. These are situated south of the coasts along which the Humpbacks migrate for breeding (Fig. 19). Whale marking results have confirmed this belief. Marks fired in Antarctic waters south of Australia have been recovered off the coasts of western and eastern Australia, and two marks fired south of South Africa in Antarctic waters have been recovered off the coast of Madagascar. There seems to be little east–west dispersal of Humpbacks from one feeding ground to another.

Whale Marking and the Age of Whales

Whale marking results have a bearing on the age of individual whales as indicated by the layers or laminae in the ear plugs. We have already noted that two marks were recovered which had been fired as long as twenty-three years previously, showing that the whales must have been at least twenty-six years old (Brown, S. G., 1962).

If some long-term marks such as these could be recovered and the number of layers in the ear plugs of the whales counted it would be possible to check positively how many laminae in the ear plug represent one year in the life of the whale. All that would be necessary would be to divide the number of laminae counted by the number of years since the mark was fired, plus something for the probable age of the whale when it was marked. This has, in fact, been done. Six marks fired into Fin whales by 'Discovery' scientists in the Antarctic were recovered by Japanese whaling ships twenty-five years later (Ohsumi, S., 1962). The laminae in the ear plugs of these whales were counted and it was found that in every case there were between 28 and 38 light and dark layers. The number of layers (one light plus one dark) per year is therefore between one and one and a half, or perhaps less since we do not know how old the whales were when they were marked. In a list of marks recovered by Japanese ships in the North Pacific (Ohsumi, S., 1964) there were three which had been fired three, five and nearly six years before recovery. The whales had respectively six, nine and ten layers in their ear plugs. If two layers represent a year in the life of a whale then the one with nine layers in its ear plugs was about $4\frac{1}{2}$ years old. But it had been already carrying a mark for five years so it must have been marked before it was born. This, as the Japanese author writes with truth, 'is not practical' and it is evident that one layer (one light plus one dark band) represents one year in the whale's life.

Further evidence that one layer represents a year in the life of a Fin whale, and so probably in that of other whalebone whales, has come from work carried out in the Whale Research Unit of the National Institute of Oceanography (Roe, H. S. J., 1967). The active layer-forming tissue at the basal surface of the ear plug was examined microscopically in 621 Fin whales taken in the Antarctic in the summer and at Durban in the winter. It was found that layers were formed continuously at the base of the plug and there was no plug in which either a new light or a new dark band was not being formed. The light bands were distinguished by a much higher fat content than the dark ones, but the dark bands were built up of much larger cells than the light ones.

If the whales were grouped into months throughout the year it was found that the percentage of them in which a light band was being actively formed at the base of the plug rose to a peak of 90 per cent at midsummer, while the percentage in which a dark band was being formed rose to a corresponding peak at mid-winter. Whatever it is that causes the formation of light bands is at a maximum in summer, and whatever it is that causes the formation of dark bands is at a corresponding maximum in winter. It may be that this is connected with nutrition, for the light bands with a high fat content are laid down when the whale is feeding on krill in Antarctic waters. The dark bands with their thick-walled cells are formed when the whale is fasting in the tropics and Roe quotes evidence that dogs fed on a fat-deficient diet develop large thick-walled cells in the skin.

Whatever the cause of layer formation it is clear from this work that one dark plus one light band represent one year in the life of a Fin whale and that scientists, after thirty years of patient and painstaking research, have arrived at a reliable guide to the age of individual whalebone whales. Unfortunately this result has been achieved too late to be of use for Blue and Humpback whales which are already on the verge of extermination but a reappraisal of all the evidence bearing on the age of Fin whales is now being undertaken for the International Whaling Commission.

It has been shown that physical maturity in Fin whales (fusion of the bony plates of the backbone) corresponds with 32 layers in the ear plug (Purves, P. E. and Mountford, M. D., 1959) and physical maturity must occur at an age of 32 years and not eight as was formerly supposed.

In his report Roe (1967) reproduces a photograph of a microscopic section of an ear plug of a Fin whale which had eighty layers. Here then, is proof of the longevity of Fin whales at least, for this individual must have been not less than eighty years of age when it was killed.

CHAPTER 9

On Board a Factory Ship

The whaling factory ship in which I spent the months of the phoney war as a whaling inspector belonged to the Leith firm of C. A. Salvesen & Co., one of the only two British firms engaged in whaling operations in the fateful year of 1939. On a fine day in October she was lying in the Tyne, the war being only a month old, and I was humping a number of heavy cases on to a lighter in order to take them aboard her. Among them were a couple of cases of not too expensive whisky which looked rather conspicuous beside my personal baggage and three cases of scientific equipment marked O.H.M.S.

Quite early in our stay at South Georgia we had all made the discovery that in the south among the whalers there was a special currency with which you could buy favours, preferential treatment or indulgences, or a man's labour and skill. It was whisky. The lowest coin in the currency was a tot, next highest was half a bottle and the largest denomination was a whole bottle, but that was paying dearly. Nobody worried very much about the quality, what mattered was the quantity, so we used to keep a supply of a less expensive brand while reserving the better for social occasions, for marks of special favour or signal honour.

The consumption of alcohol was nominally forbidden to all whaling personnel both on board ships and at shore stations, except for the upper crust, the manager and his staff, the ships' officers, gunners and so on. If this had not been the rule very little whaling would have got itself done either aboard ship or ashore, and the great Norwegian whaling industry would have ground to a standstill, for the perpetual craving for spirits is the northern weakness.

The prohibition was, of course, at least as much honoured in the breach as in the observance and gave rise to strange activities and to a good deal of smuggling. One heard frequently stories of cases of whisky being passed from ship to shore by lines under water at night, of bottles concealed behind panelling, between the hull frames or among stores being unloaded. In South Georgia illicit stills used to enjoy a brief existence from time to time, manufacturing gin from the company's potatoes and vegetables. But the fact that an infuriating liquid must be in circulation was usually betrayed sooner or later by one or more persons being obviously but unaccountably intoxicated while on duty. Towards the end of a long season some of the men apparently found the craving more than could be borne and resorted to desperate shifts to satisfy it. In one instance a whale catcher had to return to harbour because her compass had gone wrong. Some one had removed and drunk the alcohol from it. One old shellback, who had been out to South Georgia season after season for many years, bought all the brilliantine in the canteen and got beautifully drunk on it. Another, towards the end of the season when all other sources were exhausted, spread black boot polish on bread and made himself a sandwich. It has a kick of sorts, I believe.

As whaling inspector aboard the factory ship *Salvestria* I had extra duties. Those of inspector were not very onerous and not likely by themselves to occupy me for many hours a day, so I had been asked by the 'Discovery' Committee to carry out investigations on the carcasses of whales similar to those at South Georgia. Accordingly I foresaw that a supply of illegal tender would be a primary necessity, but I had to provide it myself at my own expense because I could hardly expect the government to recognize such goings on.

In the three cases marked O.H.M.S. which I was humping on board I had packed at the Natural History Museum what may conveniently be described as 'laboratory materials', jars for specimens, log books, dishes, formalin and even alcohol for preserving. I had some trepidation about the last and knew that I should have to keep a sharp eye on it. These and my personal baggage, with the two cases of whisky, went out in the lighter with me sitting among them to the big, grey, ungainly ship lying in the roads. She had come from Sandefjord where she had recruited the Norwegian part of her complement who now looked down at me from her decks with mild curiosity.

Salvestria

The *Salvestria* had once been a Cunarder, one of the less magnificent of the North Atlantic fleet, and she was already elderly when Salvesens bought her and converted her into a floating factory in the mid-thirties. She was a vessel of about 12,000 tons with oil-burning steam engines and a single midships funnel. Now she looked more like a great fortress than a ship riding in the smoky Tyne, top-heavy in appearance and painted battleship grey. She had been converted for whaling by adding another deck flush with her raised fo'c'sle head and poop, covering over with a steel roof her forward and after well decks. A wide rectangular hole in her stern gave upon a sloping steel slipway which slanted from the water line to the wide clear after top deck which was the flensing plan. The blubber boilers were underneath this after deck where once the after well deck had been. It had been partly cut away to make room for them. In the midships superstructure were the cabin accommodation, saloon and navigating bridge, and the squat single funnel rose from the middle of it. Forward of the super-structure were the meat and bone plans with the boilers below where once had been the forward well deck. In modern factory ships the plan deck is one vast continuous expanse from the stern slipway to the bows. The engines are right aft with twin screws and twin funnels, one on each side of the slipway. The *Salvestria* had twin screws but no way had been found of getting rid of the superstructure amidships. This had certain disadvantages when the factory was operating for it meant that each carcass, after the blubber had been removed, had to be hauled along the side deck past the superstructure, past all the cabin accommodation and ship's offices, in order to reach the meat and bone plan forward. The boat deck, one up from the plan deck and carried on gantries above it, made a sort of tunnel through which the carcasses had to pass. Large ones often got stuck in this, their flippers fouling the steel supports and sometimes bending them quite badly, but appearances were of no more importance in the Antarctic than they were in the old whaling days when Richard Dana was so shocked at the untidy look of a whaling ship.

The officers' accommodation was amidships and the saloon, where we all ate and mainly lived for six months, was beneath the plan deck level. It was the original dining saloon of the Cunarder and its windows had once looked out over the fore well deck. Now they looked into the meat cookery, a cavernous gloomy place lit by single electric bulbs and flanked by the gleaming bellies of the meat boilers. No daylight could penetrate into the saloon and we ate and lived by artificial light.

My cabin was near the saloon on the same level and was quite spacious and comfortable with a writing desk in it and the solid varnished teak furniture found in British ships built before World War I. Over the door, which gave on to a thwartships alleyway, was the word *Inspektør*. At the other end of the alleyway was the doctor's surgery with the word *Laege* (Leech) over the door. The whalers were a pretty tough lot, I think, and seldom suffered from anything worse than a hangover—they were never given the opportunity to acquire any worse complaint—so that the doctor did not have much to do other than bind up a few cuts, sprains and bruises. Occasional rather horrid and gory accidents occurred on the plan, hands caught between a wire and a winch drum, limbs broken by flicking hawsers, gashes from flensing knives. But these did not tax medical skill very highly and almost any morning the Leech could be seen in his consulting-room, a large, florid, immensely good-humoured young man newly graduated from Edinburgh, leaning back in his swivel chair, his feet on his desk, his hands clasped behind his head. 'Thus the great battle against disease goes on,' he would say cheerfully. 'Let's go and have a drink.'

The ship's company was a mixture of Norwegians, Shetlanders and Scots. There were a number of Geordies also but I was the only representative from south of the Tyne. The whalers themselves were mostly Norwegians and we carried the five gunners with their crews for the *Salvestria*'s whale catchers laid up at South Georgia. The Captain and his officers and the seamen were all Shetlanders.

Most factory ships have a Captain, who runs and navigates the ship, and a Manager who looks after the factory and the business side of the expedition, but in the *Salvestria* the two offices of Captain and Manager were combined in the jovial person of one individual. He was a round-bellied, round-faced genial man with a fuzz of white hair like a tonsure round his bald crown, a clear ruddy complexion and twinkling blue eyes. He was a friendly and loquacious soul with an endless, or so it seemed, repertoire of rude stories with which he regaled anyone who could be found to listen, whether the moment were opportune or not. He and his Chief Radio Officer used to have competitions to see who could tell the most and conversation at meal times was apt to consist of dialogues divided into sections each beginning 'D'you know the one about . . .?' But 'Cappie' was a popular captain with his officers who put up with his stories because they liked him and knew that he was both competent and fair. Anyhow some of the stories were quite funny. The engineers, as usual, were

12

Scots and I remember with especial affection the Chief Engineer from Dundee. He surrounded himself with an air of gloom and pessimism illumined by a humorous twinkle in his eye and by a smile that was always about to break on his granite-like features.

I think most of the administrative work of the factory was done by the Norwegian secretary, and the senior representative of the Norwegian contingent was the Number One gunner, a large talkative man who spoke very little English but a great deal of Norwegian.

On Passage

We sailed on a blustery October day, escorted by a single destroyer which danced and flashed its signal lights around us and sometimes shot ahead throwing up fans of spray. The weather was even more blustery going down the Channel and I saw with sympathy a sad little group of 'peggies' (galley and pantry boys, the youngest members of the crew), at sea and among strangers for the first time in their lives, huddled together on the plan deck, their faces wan, collars turned up and shoulders hunched, their hands thrust deep in their trouser pockets. They looked like a group of distressed, half-drowned birds. There was one other ship with us in the convoy, a Frenchman, and on the way down the Channel a small armed merchant cruiser joined us. Some way out beyond Ushant the next morning our naval escort and the Frenchman left us and we felt very lonely indeed. Before us lay the heaving Atlantic under shafts of sunlight.

A circular platform straddling the whale slipway in the stern carried a 3-inch gun. This was served by a D.E.M.S. crew of four sailors—a leading and three ordinary seamen. The letters D.E.M.S. in those days stood for 'Defensively Equipped Merchant Ships' and every British or allied merchant ship was similarly armed and carried a small unit of this corps of brave but now almost forgotten men. Their lives at sea consisted of long days of boredom punctuated by moments of extreme danger and the risk of sudden death. Yet this was a voluntary branch of the naval service which never lacked recruits. The men were on their own and, of course, the pay was higher than for the same rank in the service itself, but the chief inducement, I think, was freedom from what sailors call 'flannel' or, more expressively, 'being buggered about' which all sailors hope to achieve somewhere during their service but very few do. Being isolated from any larger unit, with no superior officers to give them orders, D.E.M.S. crews had only their own resources of morale and courage to rely on. I never heard that they failed and often wondered if any other nation could have employed small officerless units of this sort with the same success. Our gun carried out a shooting practice one day in the latitude of the Azores and fired four shots which fell into the sea about a mile away making four little white columns of spray. It gave us all confidence, this display of fire power, and greatly added to the prestige of the gun crew. But the enemy did not appear.

The sun shone and the sea looked blue and fair, stippled with white horses in the north-east trades, and it was hard to believe in the war. The 'peggies' cheered up and one of them signalized his return to health and spirits by emptying a tray full of saloon glass and cutlery into the Atlantic Ocean.

'It's a recht skelpin' yon loon's needin',' said the Chief Engineer, interrupting the ineffectual rage of the Chief Steward.

We all met four times daily for meals in the saloon. There were two long tables, one on each side of the room, but only one was used for meals. The other was usually occupied by bridge fours or poker games which went on more or less continuously throughout the trip. The Captain sat at the head of the table and the Senior Gunner at the foot. I sat on the Captain's left and must have listened to a million stories before we reached the Antarctic, while the Chief Mate, another Shetlander, sat on his right. The company at table was divided fairly evenly into Shetlanders and Scots (I made one lone Englishman) at the Captain's end and Norwegians at the other. The latter conversed in their own sing-song Norsk tongue among themselves but most, though not all, of them spoke English well enough. They called me *Inspektør* and occasionally shot questions at me, especially the youngest of the five gunners, a big young man whose handsome features were losing their outline in fat.

'*Inspektør*, you find some nice girls in Newcastle?'

'I didn't have time to look, Olaf.'

'When we get back we will go ashore together and find some, yes?'

Fate, however, decreed otherwise.

Our only stop before South Georgia was at the oil island of Aruba near Curaçao in the Dutch West Indies and I should think it must be one of the most dreadful places on earth. The island seems to be entirely occupied by an enormous oil refinery sprouting like a metal fungal growth on a barren waste of sand. The climate is oppressively hot and humid and a choking stench of fuel oil fills the air before the ship enters the harbour. The refinery looks like something from a particularly horrifying and nonsensical science fiction film. One sees a large number of giant silver tennis balls and a tangle of silver pipes that seem to writhe like snakes. Some of them raised their heads above the others and opened their mouths to spit acrid smoke by day and flames by night. We found a club with an immense bar where the Leech and I joined numbers of Americans drowning their sorrows.

During the long passage south through the Atlantic tropics and the south-east trades there was nothing for me to do, but plenty for the whalers and the crew. A false deck of planks was laid down over the plan deck from bow to stern. All windows and scuttles looking out on the plan deck were boarded over and barricades of planks were placed around all projections and corners at deck level. Winches and steam saws were overhauled and made ready with new steel hawsers where necessary. Rope fenders of every conceivable size and shape were made. Harpoon lines and stores were got ready for the catchers awaiting us at South Georgia.

In the tropics the men amused themselves after work in a way that seemed unusual aboard ship. In addition to rigging a canvas swimming bath on the after plan deck, which was filled with shouting, splashing bodies until a late hour, they held a wrestling tournament on the after plan deck. The Inspector, however, was not expected to indulge in the indignity of wrestling, fortunately perhaps, and the swimming bath was only for the crew, so I mostly sat reading on the boat deck under the stars. But the hot days did not last long and soon the sky clouded. Albatrosses appeared, ever poised above the fore or main truck, swooping down to the sea and dropping astern, only to reappear at their stations above the masts without apparent effort. Soon the sea took on a more familiar aspect, grey with winking flecks of white, and there came the sudden drop in temperature that marks the passage over the Antarctic convergence.

The Antarctic Convergence

The Antarctic convergence (Fig. 13) is the northern boundary of cold surface water drifting northwards, cooled and diluted by the melting of pack ice around the Antarctic continent. It meets warmer subtropical water and, since it is colder and therefore heavier, sinks beneath it along a line which encircles the southern hemisphere. This line, the Antarctic convergence, is met with fairly constantly in about latitude 50° S. in the Atlantic and Indian Oceans but considerably more to the southward, in about 60° S., in the Pacific Ocean. The

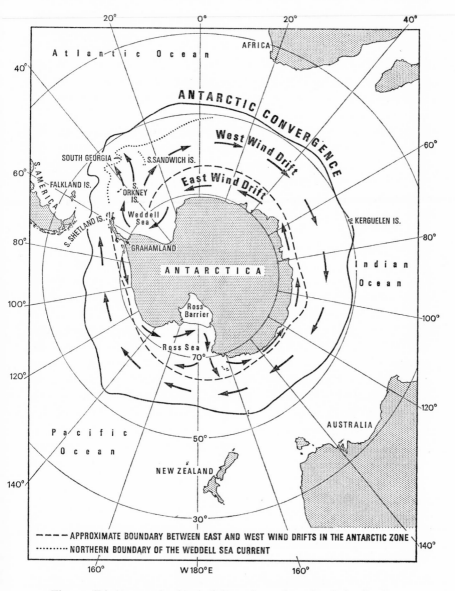

Fig. 13 Diagrammatic chart of Oceanic surface circulation in the
Southern Ocean and Antarctic waters

position of the line does not differ much with the seasons and is marked on passage by a sudden drop in the temperature of the sea, more pronounced in some parts of the hemisphere than others, especially so in the South Atlantic over which we were travelling southwards. There is a correspondingly sharp drop in the air temperature also and fur-lined caps appear soon after the line has been crossed. The sudden drop in the temperature of the sea is marked by an abrupt change in the inhabitants of the sea itself, of the plant and animal plankton, and, as a visible sign of the change, of the birds also. For this reason the Antarctic convergence is looked upon really as the northern boundary of the Antarctic region both from the oceanographical and biological points of view. It is a more definite and significant line of demarcation than the Antarctic Circle which is a purely arbitrary line drawn along latitude 66° 30' S.

Now the sea took on the green turbid look often seen in the English Channel and North Sea which is due to the dense clouds of unicellular plants (diatoms) with siliceous skeletons which crowd into the surface fifty fathoms illuminated by daylight. Spring in these southern seas south of the Antarctic convergence produces an abundant flowering of this vast ocean meadow which extends southwards to the edge of the pack ice. The spring outburst of plant life is succeeded by the growth of the multitudinous animal plankton, making of these seas, to the eye so desolate and barren, fields of inexhaustible richness, among the most fertile in the world.

The Plankton

The time of the vernal outbursts of the plant plankton, as well as that of the animal plankton which succeeds it, depends on the temperature of the sea, and for this reason it takes place first in the more northerly waters just south of the convergence, spreading slowly south throughout the summer as the ice retreats. It may be said to begin in the warmer waters just south of the convergence in September, moving south to South Georgia in October or November, but the position of the pack ice is the governing factor and this varies from year to year, but the maximum proliferation occurs around South Georgia about Christmas time. At the end of the summer the plankton, both plant and animal, dies down again, beginning to diminish around South Georgia in February and sinking to a mid-winter minimum in May or June.

The reason for the extraordinary richness of the sea in the northern part of the Antarctic zone is in part its low temperature. Diatoms, like all green plants, contain chlorophyll by means of which they build up organic compounds with the aid of sunlight and carbon dioxide. They need oxygen for respiration just as do all living things. Both carbon dioxide and oxygen are more soluble in cold water than in warm, and are therefore more available for plant life in circumpolar than in tropical waters. Plants also need what are known as the 'nutrient salts' of the sea. These are the phosphate, nitrate, nitrite and sulphate salts which circulate in the oceans under the influence of currents. They are largely derived from the processes of decay, decomposition and solution which go on ceaselessly in the sea. Antarctic waters are especially rich in them.

Now we had really crossed into the Antarctic region and, as if to mark the occasion, a school of pilot whales (blackfish) went porpoising through the waves, butting into them with their round, black noses. As each one arched through the water we could see its blowholes open to shoot out a little spout of wind-blown spray with a short, sharp puff. The birds, too, were now familiar to us old hands, as I felt myself to be with my battered fur-lined cap in contrast to the shiny new ones of many of the crew. I pointed out the birds to the new hands, like the doctor, and hoped I was right. He would never know anyway. There were whale birds hurrying low over the waves purposefully in formation. Silver-grey fulmar petrels accompanied us and so did black and white speckled cape pigeons, often gathering on the water in groups astern to chatter and quarrel over fragments of galley waste, and then hurrying on after the ship. The wandering albatrosses kept station on motionless outstretched pinions, twelve feet across from tip to tip, snow white beneath and sooty black above, the most majestic and beautiful of all the birds of the ocean. There were many other smaller sorts of albatross, too, including the lovely smoky grey sooty albatross which nests on the steep slopes of South Georgia.

Leith Harbour, South Georgia

We arrived at South Georgia three weeks after leaving the Tyne and anchored in Leith Harbour, where the firm of C. A. Salvesen & Co. had a whaling station built in 1909, three years after C. A. Larsen built his at Grytviken. The steep mountain sides that overlooked the narrow anchorage showed black patches on their white flanks and were only just beginning to change to their summer dress of white patches on black. It was a lively scene, the beginning of a long and busy whaling season, and the smoke rose black from the tall chimneys of the station against the white slopes. The familiar rich, slightly acrid smell of a whaling station greeted us directly we dropped anchor.

The Leith Harbour station went on operating throughout the years of World War II and up to 1963 when it was leased to a Japanese firm who operated for a few weeks during the seasons 1963–64 and 1964–65. Since then it has been abandoned like all the other stations in South Georgia.

We dropped anchor in the forenoon and, after a convivial lunch at which we drank their healths and wished them luck, the five gunners left with their crews to join their catchers. These had left their winter moorings at the head of the bay and came to lie alongside the factory like a brood of ducklings alongside their mother. A small group of the ship's company stood at the head of the gangway and wished the crews '*God fangst*—Good hunting' as they went down the gangway, each man carrying a seabag on his shoulder. Here, too, we lost our four D.E.M.S. sailors who transferred themselves ashore to await a ship homeward bound to a more dangerous climate. Their gun was covered up until the voyage home, so far ahead as to seem astronomically far off. Then we took on fuel oil and, after a stay of three days during which there were one or two drunken fights, the *Salvestria* steamed out of the narrow harbour and turned her head southwards, followed by her five whale catchers in line ahead.

The Pack Ice

We were heading for the edge of the pack ice. It was here that Blue whales were to be found in greatest abundance and in that year, 1939, they still accounted for some 30–40 per cent of the catch in the Antarctic. Since they gave the highest oil yield the whalers tended to seek them out in preference to the less productive Fins and Humpbacks. The whaling fleet distributed itself along the edge of the ice, moving southwards with it as the season progressed and the ice retreated. After the decline of the Blue whale catches and, latterly, the total prohibition of the taking of Blue whales, the whalers followed the Fin whale herds which keep to waters somewhat distant from the pack ice edge.

It was not known how far south of South Georgia we should have to steam before we met the edge of the ice. Unlike the Antarctic convergence the position of the ice edge varies greatly from month to month and from season to season, retreating southwards during the summer and advancing northwards during the winter. It advances much farther north in some winters than in others and retreats farther south in some summers than in others, in some years opening up and clearing away from stretches of the continental coast but in others keeping the coast largely inaccessible. At the beginning of the whaling season, in the spring, the ice edge may lie far to the northward in the Southern Ocean, even to the north of South Georgia and encompassing Bouvet Island in latitude 50° S. As the summer goes on the ice retreats until in February or March parts of the coast of the Antarctic continent, usually south of the Indian Ocean, are more or less free of ice.

The Antarctic continent is shaped roughly like a figure of eight with two large bights in its coastline on opposite sides. One of these, on the Atlantic side, is the Weddell Sea (Fig. 13) and the other, on the Pacific side, the Ross Sea. Over the Southern Ocean south of the convergence a massive current, known as the West Wind Drift, flows slowly eastward clockwise round the hemisphere, but along the coast of the Antarctic continent a current known as the East Wind Drift flows in the opposite direction, anti-clockwise, westward, to enter the bight of the Weddell Sea. Here it is deflected northward by the long peninsula of Graham Land on the western side of the bight and flows out again north-eastwards to join the West Wind Drift. This current carries pack ice far northwards into the Southern Ocean and a great field of drift ice, hundreds of square miles in area, covers the South Atlantic Ocean in the spring and early summer between longitudes 30° W and 30° E.

A similar circulation also exists within the other bight, the Ross Sea (Fig. 13), but there is no long peninsula on the western side of it so that the outflow spills out around the Balleny Islands and does not carry the ice far to the northward.

Whaling Grounds

The ice-bearing current flowing out of the Weddell Sea constitutes the richest whaling ground in the world. By far the greatest abundance of krill is found in this sector of the Southern Ocean (Marr, J. W. S., 1962), between the South Shetland Islands and South Georgia on the west and longitude 30° E. (Fig. 14). This great whale feeding ground is uncovered gradually as the pack ice melts, like a cloth being slowly rolled back from over a rich repast. Here the great whalebone whales gorge themselves during the southern summer, moving south with the ice edge. In this area the majority of the whaling fleet used to congregate, the factories at the ice edge and their catchers ranging

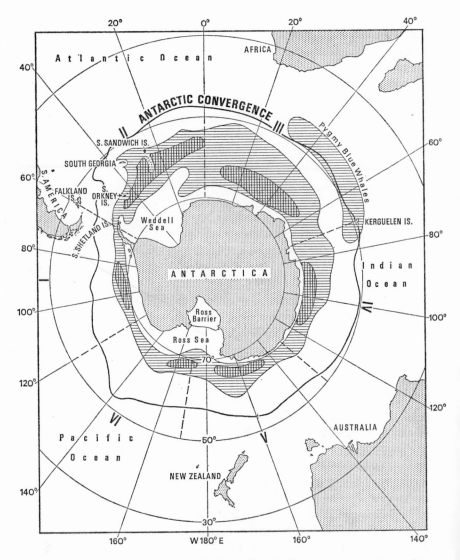

Fig. 14. Diagrammatic chart of Antarctic whaling grounds and whaling
areas. (From Mackintosh, N. A., 1965).
Shaded—Area of whaling activity in the last 35 years.
Dark—Area of maximum activity in the 1930's.

along it. Sometimes the catchers would penetrate into the ice itself but not more often or farther than was absolutely necessary.

For convenience in plotting the movements of whales and of factory ships the waters surrounding the Antarctic continent south of latitude 50° S. have been divided into six areas (Fig. 14) as follows:

Area	Longitude	Sector
I	120° W.–60° W.	Pacific Ocean
II	60° W.– 0°	Western South Atlantic including the Falkland Islands and Dependencies
III	0° – 70° E.	South of the Cape of Good Hope and the Indian Ocean as far east as Kerguelen Island
IV	70° E.–130° E.	Indian Ocean from Kerguelen Island to Western Australia
V	130° E.–170° W.	Australia, New Zealand and the western part of the Ross Sea
VI	170°W.–120°W.	Eastern part of the Ross Sea

By far the greatest concentration of Blue and Fin whales was always to be found in Areas II and III in waters influenced by the northern outflow from the Weddell Sea. Another lesser concentration was found along the ice edge south of the Indian Ocean between the longitudes of Kerguelen Island and Western Australia (Area IV). There is another area of abundance of krill here (Marr, J. W. S., 1962) corresponding with a slight deflection of the East Wind Drift current towards the north. Areas I and VI are almost barren of whales and are seldom visited by factory ships.

The *Salvestria* made the shortest passage she could to the pack ice edge, heading south-east because at that time of year, late November, the ice edge trends somewhat north-east to south-west. She did not have far to go. She had sailed from South Georgia soon after breakfast and by daylight next morning a white glare was visible in the sky to the southward. This white reflection of the ice against the grey clouds is known as 'ice blink' and gives warning of the nearness of the ice at a distance of an hour's steaming or more. Another sure sign that we were approaching the ice edge was the presence around the ship of white Antarctic petrels, snow-white birds with a hurried, busy flight rather like that of the cape pigeon. They are never seen more than fifty miles from the ice edge. Soon after sighting the 'blink' the sea became covered with fragments of drifting ice fretted and carved into fantastic shapes by the action of small waves, many resembling strange birds or other creatures with long necks or tails. Soon larger pieces of ice clothed the surface of the sea as far as the eye could travel, giving a kind of geography, a populated look, to its otherwise featureless expanse. These, too, were sculptured into strange shapes with towers and pinnacles, a silent, dead city of glass palaces driving past us. Not quite dead, for on some of the floes penguins were riding stiffly at attention and dived neatly into the water as the ship bore down upon them. The crew rushed up on deck, especially the 'peggies', and pointed a battery of box cameras at them. The waves were now damped down but long, low swells followed each other and the houses of the city rose up and down upon their backs. To the south-eastward a continuous hard line of white, under a glaring white sky, stood along the middle distance stretching away south-westward and north-east-ward. This was fairly heavy pack ice made up of large floes, so the *Salvestria* stopped. We had arrived.

The Factory at Work

Hunting began at midnight on 7th December, the following day (8th) being the date agreed for the first day of whaling in the season 1939–40 by the International Whaling Convention signed at the London conference of 1937. Limitation of the season by quotas of blue whale units was not introduced until 1944. The season was to continue until 7th March.

The catchers now dispersed along the pack ice edge which was here about a hundred miles south-east of South Georgia. Where we were situated the ice was light enough but the gunners were soon reporting on their radios heavier ice to the eastward. At breakfast on the 8th the Captain said, 'You'll soon be busy. Carlsen had three Blues at eight o'clock and Olaf has one Blue and one Fin. They'll be in about nine-thirty.' The radio room had been talking to the catchers who reported plenty of whales about and good weather.

The first whale came up the slipway about ten o'clock that morning, and thereafter work on the plan continued day and night until midnight on 7th March 1940, except for a break on Christmas Day and one or two intervals when there were no whales owing to bad weather during which everyone was plunged into the deepest gloom. Whalers are permanently pessimistic like fishermen and farmers.

I leaned over the rail alongside the slipway and watched the first whale, a big Blue cow, come up. The catchers dropped their carcasses at the stern of the factory and then either came alongside for fuel or else spun round and headed out into the ice-strewn sea once more.

Whenever a catcher came alongside for fuel the gunner came on board and had one, maybe two, tots in the saloon. He usually told us that there were very few whales about and the weather was the worst for the time of year he could ever remember. Each carcass, as it was dropped, was made fast to the stern of the factory by a steel strop which could be shackled to a winch wire. This brought the tail of the carcass into position at the bottom of the slipway. Then a heavy steel claw on the end of the hawser from the main hauling winch was lowered on to the tail by means of wires. The claw had two fingers which gripped the tail in front of the flukes on either side of the caudal peduncle. Then the hawser began to pull and as soon as the weight came on it the steel fingers tightened their grip. Slowly the huge, grooved, slate-blue carcass inched its way up the slope on to the after deck. Since it was quite fresh and had not been lying in fouled water it was shining and clean and gave off the curious sweet rubbery smell that fresh whales have. But it was not long before the fore and after decks became scenes of carnage, wreathed in clouds of steam and running with blood that trickled, and sometimes spouted, down the sides of the ship into the sea. Hordes of birds gathered from Heaven knew where to gorge themselves on the filth that spread around the factory as she lay in her pool among the ice. Soon the new planking which had been laid down on the voyage south was splintered and gory and covered with grease so that it was impossible to stand on it without spiked boots.

My duties on board the factory divided themselves into those of whaling inspector and those of biologist which I had to carry out for the 'Discovery' Committee. Work on the plan, as is usual on board all factory ships, went on continuously day and night with alternating day and night shifts who changed over at six o'clock. At South Georgia it had been our aim to examine every whale which arrived at the station during the season, and it was our boast that we did so. Obviously, with continuous working, I could not hope to do this on board the *Salvestria* either as inspector or biologist, so I worked with the day shift from six in the morning to six in the evening. As inspector I had to note the species, length, sex and sexual condition (whether pregnant, resting or immature) of every whale and also the length and sex of every foetus. I had to report to the management (Cappie) any infringement of the regulations that came to my notice, any undersized whales taken, any cows which were nursing (milk flowing) and had therefore obviously been shot when running with a calf. But of course I could not see those that came up at night so that if the regulations were broken then they remained broken. I think this very rarely happened. Under the regulations every part of the carcass had to be used, but if there were many whales waiting at the stern and things got a bit rushed it was not unknown for gut, tongue, and even meat to be tipped over the side and to hell with the regulations. This did not happen in the daytime when the inspector was about but little birds sometimes told me that it did happen at night. But not having seen it and not having any proof, I did nothing about it. If I did see any breach of the rules I had to go up on the bridge and report the transgressions to Cappie who was supposed to strike that particular undersized whale or nursing cow off the log. That meant that everyone on board from the Captain-Manager and the gunners down to the youngest 'peggy' would lose his share of the bonus on that whale, for all hands, both in factory ships and at shore stations, were on the 'lay' system. Cappie put on a serious face and so did I, but what other action, if any, was taken I never knew and it wasn't my job to ask. Usually, in these cases, I had to listen to a long explanation by the gunner when he next came on board the factory. Sometimes he came alongside and visited me specially to tell me about it. It had been dark or foggy. He did not see the calf. I smiled and felt like an indulgent schoolmaster and reached for the Red Label Johnnie Walker. At the end of the season, when whaling operations were finished and the factory was on her way back to South Georgia, Cappie called me up to the bridge and told me he had been talking on the radio to the other factories, three of them, working for Salvesens along the ice edge that season. He said, rather reproachfully, that the *Salvestria*'s inspector had condemned three times the number of whales which had been condemned in the other three ships together. He winked, and so did I. The trouble was that my biological duties on the plan deck compelled my constant presence there during daylight hours. Nothing escaped my vigilance for I was always around like an unpleasant smell. On other factory ships the inspectors spent varying amounts of time on the plan deck according to the view they took of their duties. Some of them, I believe, had very elastic ideas about this and did not visit the plan very often.

I soon saw that my biological job would be rather different on board the *Salvestria* from what it was at South Georgia. There had been three of us then but now I was alone. However, I found that the work went rather more slowly on board ship than at a whaling station because of the lack of space and the difficulty of handling a big carcass on a comparatively narrow deck, so I was able to get around by myself fairly successfully. After the blubber had been stripped off there was always a slightly anxious interval during which the stripped *skrott* was passed through the side passage beneath the boat deck to reach the foredeck plan where the lemmers were waiting for it. Sometimes this process, accompanied by a lot of shouting and signalling with up-raised arms, took as much as a quarter of an hour and often the flippers got jammed and bent the stanchion posts. Sometimes the carcass was so big it seemed doubtful if it would go through at all.

I found an ally in the plan foreman, a genial giant with a red spade beard which he had been growing since Aruba. He thought me a great joke and held the other end of my measuring tape for me, and even sometimes delayed the work for a minute or two for my con-venience. But I had a lot of hurrying to and fro to do in my spiked boots between the fore and after plan. On the foredeck plan space was very cramped and a good deal of mountaineering was necessary over mounds of red flesh and piles of bones, and skilful dodging over taut and criss-crossing steel hawsers to the accompaniment of the usual warning shouts. An additional hazard was added by the boiler tops which were simply holes flush with the deck, covered over by square wooden hatches when not in use. When the plan was working they were gaping mouths swallowing gobbets of flesh and joints of bone. It was easy to see how a whole mass of slithery tissue, such as the tongue, might slide down into them.

The plan workers were a racial mixture. On the after plan the flensers, and the blubber boys who dragged the cut blocks of blubber to the aperture in the port side of the deck to feed the cutter beneath, were Norwegians, as was the bearded foreman. But on the fore plan two of the three lemmers were Shetlanders and some of the meat haulers were Shetlanders also. There were also a few Scots and I remember one from Leith who wore a red and white polka dot scarf round his neck which, he said, brought him luck.

The Shetlanders were a fine lot and on the whole worked amicably with the Norwegians with whom they shared a weakness for strong refreshments. They were mostly big chaps with ruddy complexions and dark hair. In this they resembled the Norwegians for it is wrong to think of the Norsemen as a race of stolid, flaxen-haired giants. Many of them were small of stature and dark-haired. Moreover they were not at all stolid but excitable and volatile.

At the height of the season the factory usually got through ten or fifteen whales per twelve-hour shift, according to their size. This was fewer than at South Georgia but quite enough for me. The work was more strenuous than at South Georgia because of the amount of climbing and scrambling about I had to do, and because very often the great old tub was rolling slightly all the time. Usually, when whales were being 'worked up', as it was called, the factory lay near the pack ice edge or in an open lead, but, being a steel ship, she could not penetrate into the ice. Often it is necessary to go some miles into the ice before the ocean swell, riding through the pack, is lost. You see the floes rise and fall together as the swells follow one another and the ice looks like a blanket under which a slow breathing is perceptible, a giant asleep. The floes clink and knock against one another, but there are dangers there for a steel ship because seven-eighths of an ice floe or iceberg are invisible under the surface. Often when we were at work the swells ran in round and smooth and the *Salvestria* rose and fell with them gently as I tottered about the deck in my spiked boots. I was never sorry when the hooter blew at six o'clock.

The weather was, on the whole, a good deal more inclement and just as changeable as at South Georgia. There at midsummer many blue, still days occur which are like a fine day in early March in England. In February it is often dark and wet with heavy grey clouds low on the mountain sides. At the pack ice edge violent blizzards with driving snow are interspersed with a few, but only a very few, blue and white days so still that you can hear the ice floes clinking against one another from a long way off. Penguins play around, plopping in and out of the water, and seals, lying on the floes, scratch themselves in the sun. There are days of fog, too, when all the white and grey world looks as though seen through gauze. But these pauses never last for long and soon the snow is whirling and flying once more. It is never very cold at sea far from the land but temperatures round about freezing were usual.

My comfortable cabin was directly underneath the fore-plan deck winches. They thundered and rumbled over my head all night, making the bunk vibrate, yet after a few nights I slept soundly in spite of the racket which mingled with my dreams. More trying than the noise or the vibration was the stench, almost tangible, which occasionally invaded my privacy. Like the thunder in *Alice Through the Looking Glass* it rolled about the room in great lumps and knocked over the tables and chairs. It originated in the meat and bone cookery next door, the main entrance of which was just round the corner forward of my cabin. The sudden attacks of choking stench, like gas attacks, may have been due to changes in the lie of the ship's head. When the wind was dead ahead it blew into my cabin through the cookery bearing on its wings the odour of very old and very dirty, sweaty socks. It woke me up far more effectively than any amount of noise or vibration. An alternative smell was like very highly concentrated but ancient roast beef. I think these sudden overwhelming stinks may have come from the process of making guano or fertilizer from the bone and meat residues which were dried by blasts of hot air in a rotating cylinder housed in the meat cookery. Or they may have been caused by the process of steam cleaning the meat boilers after the residues had been emptied out. From time to time thin trickles of blood from the plan deck above ran down the white painted bulkheads of my cabin, but I was pretty well used to blood, and it was as nothing compared with the stench which sometimes drove me out altogether.

As headquarters for my biological work Cappie gave me another cabin down aft on the starboard side off the blubber cookery. Near it was a door from the cookery opening on to the poop deck from which one could look down the stern slipway. It was a small two-berth cabin with a settee, but otherwise quite empty, lit by a single bare electric bulb. Here I unpacked my cases of scientific gear—log-books, dishes, screw-topped jars, glass tubes, formalin and alcohol—and made a small laboratory. Luckily the door had a reliable lock or I should not have kept my two Winchester quart bottles of absolute alcohol very long. As a precaution I poured the alcohol into bottles labelled 'Formaldehyde 40%—Poison'. After my work on the plan was done, and I had had a wash and supper, I retired to my laboratory and wrote up my logs, examined the ovaries I had taken and placed in formalin or alcohol any specimens I had taken during the day. All this gave me a good excuse to keep clear of the interminable bridge and poker that went on in the saloon. Working quietly alone while the winches of the blubber plan rumbled overhead and the blubber cutter thrashed on the other side of the cookery I found soothing to the nerves, though I was often so tired that it was hard not to fall asleep. However, I was not left alone for long. The space on the poop deck alongside the slipway, or just inside the cookery door if the weather was bad, was a meeting place for members of the crew off duty. The 'peggies' came here to talk and argue and skylark, in broad accents of the Tyne and Clydeside. They soon spotted me each evening going into the cabin and locking the door in a conspiratorial manner. The chatter stopped for a moment as I passed and then resumed after my door was closed. One of them, bolder than the rest, a red-headed boy from Edinburgh, one evening plucked up courage.

'Excuse me, sir. D'ye min' me askin'? What d'ye dae in yon wee cabin?'

'Come in and see,' I said.

That was fatal. At first they came in one at a time, a different one each evening, and I overheard muffled disputes about whose turn it was next. Each gazed around at my improvised arrangements with as much awe as one might feel looking round a laboratory for nuclear physics for the first time. Writing in my printed log-books, slicing away at ovaries or pickling obscure-looking objects taken from whales I was aware that I had suddenly acquired all the glamour of a magician in his cave. Only skulls and retorts were needed to complete the picture. Soon my little cubby-hole became as much a meeting place as the alleyway outside or the poop deck. All sorts of people drifted in. There was a settee and it was warm and dry, and there was the half comic figure of the Inspector burrowing away at something vaguely known as Science. One evening the Captain came in to see how I was getting on, to tell me another story or to finish one that had been interrupted at supper time. I had six visitors in the cabin of various ages and sizes all arguing furiously about football. They vanished like driven snow when the 'Old Man' appeared, melting into the bulkheads.

'Do these chaps worry you?' he asked, evidently rather astonished to find them there. 'Kick them out if they do.'

'They don't,' I told him, and when he had finished the story and I had laughed and thought of a counterblast, he said 'Good night' and left. Then one by one my visitors returned. But there were times when I had to say—'Look, I'm very busy this evening. Hop it now and come back in an hour's time.' And they always went without a word.

Slowly the ice edge moved south from the position where we had met it, a hundred miles south-east of South Georgia, at the beginning of December and the factory moved south-west along the ice edge until just before Christmas we were working within sight of Elephant Island from which in 1916 Shackleton and his companions made their famous boat journey to South Georgia six hundred miles to the north-east. It is a barren, forbidding spot with only sea elephants and penguins on its beaches. Then the factory turned eastwards and on New Year's Day we were half-way between the South Orkneys and the southernmost of the South Sandwich Islands.

Christmas Day was the first in over seven weeks on which the winches were silent and there was no work on the plan. Instead the men shaved and put on clean clothes and walked up and down the plan deck, wishing each other '*God Jul*—Merry Christmas'. The catchers were all alongside and the gunners came on board wearing smart clothes. In the evening there was a great dinner in the saloon with a Christmas tree. We punished my two cases of whisky and my cabin was full of flensers and lemmers, the plan foreman with the beard and many other people with Norwegian, Tyneside and Scots voices. We all swore we were the best people we had ever met. The gunners said they had met many whaling inspectors but I was the first one who—something or other, but I have forgotten what.

Next day the winches were rattling away as hard as ever. The factory moved on eastwards and now the character of the catch began to change. Blue whales had predominated before Christmas but now Fin whales were taken in greater numbers. Soon after Christmas a tanker came alongside the factory as she lay at the ice edge and took off a load of whale oil for the United Kingdom.

Meanwhile we did not forget that a war of sorts was going on at home. Though the factory kept radio silence we received news bulletins and so heard about the Battle of the River Plate and the gallant actions of the armed merchant cruisers *Jervis Bay* and *Rawalpindi*. The lurking apprehension that any day a German commerce raider might appear over the dark northern horizon was always present, but in this we were lucky for nothing happened. After that season there was practically no pelagic whaling until 1945, but by then twenty-eight of the forty-one factory ships which were scattered along the ice edge in 1940 had been sunk, including the *Salvestria*, while working as tankers.

We began to look forward to 7th March when whaling would close down. The men were getting tired and the weather was worsening. Towards the end of January howling gales with slanting snow were the rule and in February we had thick fog. By then we were some distance from the ice edge, hence the larger number of Fin whales in the catch. By the end of that month we were east of the southern South Sandwich Islands at the entrance of the Weddell Sea in the cold current flowing out of it. The catchers often reported themselves fog-bound and unable to see anything. Gloom descended on everyone as always happens when there is the least pause in the stream of whales which mean money. I especially remember one of these gloomy mornings of despair and pessimism because the sea was like glass with ice floes stuck in it apparently immobile. Not the least movement disturbed the surface of the sea around them and the world was like the inside of one of those glass spheres which you shake to make snow. Snowflakes wandered down as though uncertain whether to settle or not and in the water did not immediately dissolve. The Chief Engineer and I gazed from the alleyway door at this ghostly prospect and decided that all was lost and there was no shred of hope. But, as usual, this did not last long for Olaf brought in a Fin whale and by noon we were working on it head down in the driving snow.

By 7th March we had taken about 400 Blue whales, 630 Fin and 60 Sperm. Humpbacks were prohibited in that year south of latitude 40° S. We had a total yield of about 82,000 barrels of oil.

Homeward Bound

Everyone was in fine spirits as we turned north west and headed for South Georgia. The Norwegians especially talked of bonuses and good times to come. They little knew what was in store for them. The rest of us were already wondering, perhaps, what was awaiting us at the end of our long homeward journey.

The factory stayed at South Georgia for four days, time enough to lay up the catchers once again alongside the whaling station and to take on fuel oil, time enough for a few drunks and fights. Then we slipped out again past the black and white mountains, already beginning to gather their winter snow, and the tussock slopes where the sea elephants were assembling to rest and moult. The majestic processes of nature took no account of man's wars. I have never seen those mountains since and never will again in this life.

We made an uneventful passage up the blue Atlantic and stopped at Freetown, Sierra Leone, on a day in early April in order to await convoy and escort. We lay there for ten days in a heat like a Turkish bath with the ship blacked out and battened down all night. No one was allowed ashore or on deck after dark. Over endless games of bridge, pontoon, poker and darts we sweated and cursed.

Every evening we gathered in the Captain's cabin to listen to the news bulletins which we had been following anxiously, especially those about the campaign in Finland which came to an end in March.

It was during these sessions in Cappie's cabin in Freetown that we heard of the German invasion of Norway, and the assault on and occupation of Oslo. It was distressing and moving to see the grief of our Norwegian shipmates who had been looking forward eagerly to meeting their wives and families. Now they knew their homes were in danger. I cannot say that their reaction to this dreadful news was very impressive. I remember no fever to get home and drive the enemy from the sacred soil. Chiefly there was a kind of stunned dismay and some tears, and a good deal of querulous blaming of the British.

We left Freetown thankfully, so far as I was concerned, in a large convoy escorted by a single small armed merchant cruiser. Off the Azores there was a scare when the convoy zig-zagged and our escort did a lot of signal flashing. Off Ushant we were joined by two destroyers.

I said goodbye to the great grey hulk at Portland and Cappie told me positively the last story at the head of the gangway before I went down into the waiting motor-launch. It was a most beautiful day in early May of that perfect spring of 1940 and the English country-side had never looked so lovely, and certainly never will again. I never again saw any of my friends of the last six months and the *Salvestria* was sunk by an acoustic mine in the Firth of Forth in July of that same summer. It was the one that got away that bumped her for the channel had been carefully swept just before the convoy moved up the Firth. Evidently this stray one had the old ship's name on it. I heard, and believed for many years after the war, a rumour that nearly all hands were lost, but I saw with great relief only quite recently an old newspaper cutting which reported that there were only twelve casualties, but I believe Cappie was one of them.

CHAPTER 10

Krill

The Food of Whales

The 'krill', the sole food of whalebone whales in Antarctic waters, is a small shrimp-like crustacean about 2½ inches in length when fully grown (Fig. 15). It belongs to the order Euphausiacea the members of which differ from those of the order Decapoda (crabs, crayfish, lobsters, shrimps, prawns) in having forked legs under the fore-part of the body or thorax while the Decapoda have simple jointed unforked legs.

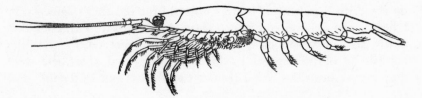

Fig. 15 The adult krill

In the northern hemisphere the diet of whalebone whales is much less restricted. Blue and Fin whales in the North Atlantic mainly feed on a much smaller member of the same order as the Antarctic krill, which likewise occurs in dense swarms, and it was probably to this rather than to the southern whale food that the name 'krill' was originally applied. Fin whales, however, may go for small herring off the Norwegian coast and are for that reason often known as 'herring' whales while the Sei whale with its silky baleen bristles, and the Greenland Right whale, feed on swarms of 'brit', the *Calanus* copepod which is the food of herrings. In the southern hemisphere

198

also there are a few exceptions to the general monotonous diet of krill. Off the Patagonian coast Sei whales eat the surface-swarming larvae of a rock lobster, called 'lobster krill' on account of the two long claws they carry. Off the coast of South Africa Bryde's whale is said to feed on small sardine-like fish.

In the Antarctic the krill occupies a position of basic importance in the marine economy for not only is it the staple food of the great whales but it is also the main, and in some cases the sole, food of a great number of other inhabitants of the region, of seals, penguins, albatrosses and a vast multitude of other birds. It is an extraordinary fact that this host of living creatures, including the enormous whale-bone whale with its prodigious rate of growth, should depend for existence on this one frail but multitudinous animal of the plankton.

The krill is also preyed upon at all stages of its life history by other animals of the plankton, many of which are voracious predators. The krill is, in fact, the central link in a number of food chains. It is itself a voracious feeder on the planktonic plant life (mainly diatoms) so that the energy of sunlight, which is responsible for life processes in the plants, becomes converted into whale flesh in three stages—plants, krill, whales. On this energy turns the whole whaling industry and the many human activities and processes which derive from it.

Obviously where the whales' food is there we may expect the whales to be found, and their migrations and distribution are likely to be governed by changes in the abundance of krill. For this reason a knowledge of the life history of this important and incredibly abundant member of the plankton was one of the primary objectives of the research carried out by the 'Discovery' Investigations.

The Swarming of Krill

The individual krill (*Euphausia superba*) is a creature of remarkable beauty, glassily red and blush-pink with a bright green area in the thorax which is the stomach filled with green plant food. The black eyes are held forward like headlamps and its feathery legs are in busy ceaseless motion. It paddles forwards with its legs working like wheels but shoots backwards with a stroke of its tail if its antennae give it warning. In front of our laboratory at Grytviken the tide came into the cove in a clockwise swirl from the open sea round the headland, near but out of sight. Certain tides used to bring shoals of krill up to the shelving beach of pebbles where we had a wooden jetty built out over the water. Here on these rare occasions some of us have watched the whale food moving in a massed swarm around the wooden piles of the jetty. They would remain in a tight, compact mass which constantly changed its shape and moved in the same way as a shoal of fish or a flight of starlings, turning and wheeling together but with no apparent leadership or purpose. If you lowered a bucket among them they fled from it momentarily in all directions but swiftly closed up again directly you lifted it out. If you threw a stone it passed through the mass leaving a momentary hole which was soon obliterated. The swarm bore a resemblance to an amoeba for it seemed to have a sort of life of its own as though the swarm collectively transcended the individuals which composed it. It had little depth and nowhere seemed to be more than a few individuals thick. They all seemed exactly alike in size and colour and I do not remember being able to distinguish the two sexes among them so they were probably not yet fully adult.

I watched one particular swarm with the late Rolfe Gunther, a member of the 'Discovery' staff who was killed in World War II. He was in for a few days' rest from a whale marking cruise. Marr (1962) quotes from the rough notes which Gunther made on this occasion (p. 155): 'The tide was ebbing at the rate of about a third of a knot (about 30 ft. per min.) southwards under the jetty. In spite of the current the swarm as a whole showed no tendency to drift towards or under the jetty, but, heading upstream for several hours, maintained its position where first seen in the full glare of the sun. Indeed the krill seemed to have a definite preference for the sunlight, for there were none directly under the jetty or in the shadow it cast upon the water.'

Out in the open sea what we may call the staple whale food, the adult or almost adult krill, form swarms miles in extent which behave, so far as one can see, exactly like those we had watched from our jetty. They consist of individuals in the same stage of development so that we must assume that each swarm comes from a cloud of eggs all hatched at the same time. This is true also of the krill in whales' stomachs. Two distinct sizes have been found in the stomachs of whales at South Georgia but segregated inside the stomach as though the whale had engulfed two separate swarms (Mackintosh, N. A. and Wheeler, J. F. G., 1929).

So dense are the swarms at sea that they often give the water a reddish colour but they are always broken up into patches, usually of the same approximate size but of very different, irregular and constantly changing shapes. They tend to concentrate at or just below the surface for nets towed by the *Discovery II* at the surface, especially at night, caught a far greater number of krill than those towed at deeper levels (Marr, J. W. S., 1962).

This irregular patchiness seems to be common to all plankton animals that drift about in huge aggregates, like the *Calanus* or 'brit'. Nets towed continuously astern of the ship have demonstrated this many times, taking now heavy and now much sparser catches both by day and by night.

The small separate patches into which the larger masses are broken up may well be due to the mechanical action of waves. A continuous sheet of ice on the surface or of leaves on a pond becomes soon broken up into separate patches by small waves. Larger waves cause them to coalesce so as to form floes or big aggregations. Waves might well act in a similar way on a continuous sheet of plankton. The patches continually change their shape because of the limited power of movement of the individual animals, although the aggregate mass of them may be drifting helplessly. Larger, more widespread variations in the distribution of krill and plankton generally are due to fundamental causes such as currents and temperature.

Swarms of krill at sea, like those we watched from the jetty, have an area out of all proportion to their depth which is seldom more than 15–30 feet (5–10 m.). The swarms, in fact, tend to form rafts spread out over wide areas of the surface. In this they differ from shoals of fish which tend to be ellipsoid or globular in shape, behaving like a drop of immiscible liquid with a higher surface tension than that of the surrounding liquid. In shallow water a shoal of fish spreads out into a thin layer as a globule of oil would. Shoals of krill, in fact, seem to act like a liquid with a lower surface tension than the surrounding medium and are more or less permanently extended as a layer or film irrespective of the depth of the medium.

It has been shown (Shaw, E., 1960) that fishes in a shoal are held together by a powerful visual attraction between individuals. If one moves away from its neighbour the attraction tends to pull it back, but if it approaches its neighbour to within a certain distance the attraction becomes a repulsion and tends to widen the distance between the two. All shoaling fishes have large prominent eyes with a wide lateral field of vision and one may suspect that a similar visual attraction holds together shoals of krill whose prominent eyes with an almost all round field of vision would seem ideally suited for this purpose.

How do Whales find the Krill?

How do whales know where the krill is and come upon it in the murk of opaque southern seas and often at night? In the waters where it occurs the krill is more or less everywhere during the summer months but it becomes obvious from an examination of whales' stomachs that it is the dense swarms that they go for, engulfing huge quantities of them. These swarms form isolated masses in the ocean, though in some cases square miles in area and always broken up into many subsidiary patches. The whales are known from experience to congregate in numbers where the krill is, so they must have some mechanism for locating the swarms. The eyes are hardly likely to provide the mechanism. There seems to be a good deal of doubt how far and how accurately whalebone whales can see, but it is certain that they have only lateral vision and therefore no perspective, and they cannot turn their heads. In addition the water is always to a certain extent opaque, around midsummer densely so, as a result of the plankton growth it contains. At night the inky blackness of the sea is lit only by pale and evanescent fires from the phosphorescence of plankton animals. The krill carries a row of luminous organs down each side which give out a wan bluish light when the animal is stimulated. Hardy (1956) has suggested that these myriad tiny points of light, like the windows of a vast fleet of air liners, may light up the swarms and guide the whales to them so that they find their repast 'lit up like a restaurant', but Marr (1962, p. 241) disagrees, pointing out that the lights are not normally switched on, only flashing momentarily on stimulation, and the shoals do not appear to exhibit mass phosphorescence at night. Marr believed that the whale's acute and sensitive ear with its accurate directional sense can locate the swarms of krill, possibly, though not certainly, with visual aid. 'It may be, too,' he wrote (p. 241), 'that the incessant movement of the limbs . . . of the concentrated myriads of a swimming and feeding swarm creates a vibrational disturbance in the water to which the whales are acutely sensitive.'

It is a fact that shoals of small fishes make noises as they move through the water, caused by the friction of the muscles, skeletal parts and scales of the individual fishes, and by the water flowing over the surfaces of their bodies. These sounds are similar to the hydrodynamic noises made by a ship's hull moving through the water, and in fairly large shoals they can be recorded by instruments. At

Bermuda the noises made by the fry of a small anchovy have been recorded (Moulton, J. M., 1960). There seems no reason to doubt that a swarm of krill, especially a large one, would make very appreciable hydrodynamic noises which could easily be picked up by the ear of a whale at a considerable distance.

In addition whales are now known to have an echo-locating system which operates in the head. Toothed whales are believed to have a fairly accurate short wave transmission with which they can locate their prey while whalebone whales are thought to have a low frequency long wave transmission, but nothing is known about its capabilities for echo-location.

Life History of Krill

In spite of collecting at sea on a quite unprecedented scale, and years of painstaking research, there are still gaps in our knowledge of the life history of the Antarctic krill and points which remain to be explained.

In order to understand what we do know one must keep in mind a picture of the circulation of the currents in Antarctic waters (Fig. 16). The West Wind Drift, propelled by the prevailing westerlies, occupies a comparatively thin layer of surface water, perhaps 500 feet deep, cooled and diluted by the melting of pack ice. At the Antarctic convergence this layer sinks beneath warmer water because it is colder and denser. South of about latitude 60° S. the opposite East Wind Drift, under the influence of prevailing easterlies, flows westwards, enters the Weddell Sea and then flows out north-east into the South Atlantic.

Beneath the cold surface water of the West Wind Drift a much more massive slow current of comparatively warmer water (1°–2° C.) moves southwards and eastwards from the three great oceans. It forms a layer about 4,000 feet thick where it enters the Antarctic and is known as the Warm Deep Current. In due course it comes up against the Antarctic continental shelf where part of it rises upwards to join the East Wind Drift and a much larger part sinks as a cold dense mass of water (0°–1° C.) which creeps north along the ocean floor and forms an underlying layer about 5,000 feet thick where it leaves the Antarctic. This is called the Antarctic Bottom or Cold Deep Current.

So we have a cold shallow layer at the surface and a massive cold layer at the bottom both moving north and east, while a thick layer of warmer water in between moves south to replace them, and this is true all round the Antarctic continent where there is enough depth.

As the covering of pack ice retreats from Antarctic seas with the advance of spring and summer a great outburst of unicellular plant life (mainly diatoms) fills the upper layer. So great is the proliferation that even the coarse canvas nets with which we fished at the surface for whale food came up clogged with a thick, slimy green porridge. This outburst begins as soon as the ice melts and allows the sunlight to penetrate the surface water and this happens earlier around South Georgia than farther south around the colder South Shetlands, and there again earlier than in the cold Weddell Sea. The growth of the

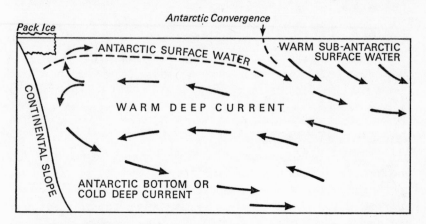

Fig. 16 Diagram of the vertical circulation in Antarctic waters

plants is followed by that of the animal plankton. In a few weeks the animals of the plankton spawn and shed eggs and soon the surface of the open sea is filled with clouds of larvae and young forms. The animals graze upon the plants like sheep upon a pasture and at the same time prey upon and devour each other. They themselves are fed upon by sea birds. Many of the plankton animals form dense swarms and the krill is only one of the many plankton animals that do so, though it is perhaps the most prolific and certainly the most important for mankind.

By the end of the summer huge quantities of krill and other plankton animals have been eaten by whales, seals and birds and devoured by each other. Others die off after spawning during the summer in the normal course of their lives, but a remnant remains in the surface water to sink down into the southward-moving Warm Deep Current and so spend the winter drifting back towards the south. This has been shown to be true of many of the larger plankton animals (Mackintosh, N. A., 1937 and Foxton, P., 1956) but not, as yet, of the krill. In this way the plankton population of Antarctic waters maintains itself in position and replenishes itself, for if all the animals remained in the surface water throughout the winter they would eventually drift northwards out of their environment and perish, emptying the Antarctic seas of life. In the spring the animals, a much diminished host compared with their summer abundance, rise to the surface again as the pack ice melts and the plant bloom begins. Soon they fill the northward-flowing surface water once more with a cloud of young forms.

No evidence has been found that the krill takes part in this general winter descent into the Warm Deep water. Marr (1962) found no evidence of it in the many hauls taken in the autumn and winter months by the ship's plankton nets. Yet this descent must surely take place and the reason why it has not been spotted might be that it happens after the pack ice has once more covered the sea.

During the summer the krill is spread out all round the Antarctic in waters of the East Wind Drift (Marr, J. W. S., 1962) but is concentrated in enormous richness in the cold surface current flowing out of the Weddell Sea (Fig. 13). This is evidently a reservoir of krill which continually replenishes itself throughout the summer.

The krill has a two-year life cycle so that two sizes of individuals appear in the Weddell Sea current, adolescents about $\frac{1}{2}$ inch long and young adults between $1\frac{1}{2}$ and $1\frac{3}{4}$ inches long. The former belong to the hatching of the previous summer and the latter to the hatching of the summer before that. Hence the appearance of two sizes in the stomachs of many whales on the plan. In the spring the small ones are found in the Weddell Sea current but later in the summer they are found right up against the coast of the continent far to the southward. The large adult krill, up to $2\frac{1}{2}$ inches in length, are found during the summer first in the cold Weddell Sea water and later farther south and in the East Wind Drift. As the larger krill spawn and die off in the summer, or are devoured, the smaller grow up to replace them, but will not spawn until the following year, only reaching adolescent size ($1\frac{3}{4}$ in.) by the onset of winter. Thus a continuous oncoming of krill goes on in the southern seas through the summer with older adults spawning and dying off and the adolescents, from progressively later hatchings as the pack ice retreats, growing up to replace them.

Breeding

In the final full grown stage, $2\frac{1}{2}$ inches long, the male and female krill can be distinguished easily enough. In the earlier stages it is difficult to tell the male from the female except that the male is slightly larger than the female, but at maturity she catches up and both sexes are the same size though somewhat different in appearance. The most distinctive feature of the male is that the inner branch of each of his first pair of forked swimming limbs (on the first segment of the segmented 'tail' behind the carapace) is modified into a complicated kind of grasping organ. It is really a kind of hand, or instrument, for passing the male cells to the female.

The spermatozoa of the krill are oval and, like those of many other Crustacea, non-motile. The male stores them in club-shaped packets called 'spermatophores' (sperm bearers), and by means of the hand on his first swimming limb transfers a pair of them, sometimes more, to a pouch under the genital aperture of the female. For this purpose the sexes copulate, swimming with their under-surfaces together. When the female's eggs are ripe they pass into her pouch where they come into contact with the sperm which the male has placed there and are fertilized. The female full of ripe eggs ready to be fertilized and shed has a very swollen appearance and is said to be 'gravid'. Dr. Bargmann (1937) counted over 11,000 eggs in a gravid female, each $\frac{1}{2}$ mm. in diameter. One day off South Georgia in 1930 the *Discovery II* caught a quantity of gravid female krill and they were placed in an aquarium tank. They all shed their eggs overnight but none developed, probably because conditions in the tank were not just right for them. Developing eggs are exceedingly delicate and will not develop unless conditions are precisely right.

Like many marine invertebrates, insects and lower vertebrates (frogs, toads, newts) the krill begins its life in the form of a larva, a youthful form which is totally unlike the adult it will eventually become in appearance, structure and habits. Examples of larvae most immediately familiar are the caterpillar and the tadpole, both of which are respectively totally unlike the butterfly and the frog they will become. There are many examples among marine invertebrates of larvae which were known for a long time before any connection with the adult was discovered, so that they were thought to be distinct species. The larva of the fresh water eel is one, a glassy, transparent ribbon-like creature that lives in the sea. It was named *Leptocephalus* (flat head) until its metamorphosis into the eel was discovered in 1896 by two Italians. It had previously been believed that eels were spontaneously generated out of mud.

All the Crustacea and insects, since they have a hard external skeleton, can only grow by casting their skins and growing new ones. Development from the egg to the adult proceeds by means of a series of jumps, each cast of skin marked by a growth in size and a progressive development of structure, each stage being more like the adult than the preceding one. At length, after a greater or lesser number of stages, the adult form is reached. The Antarctic krill goes through no fewer than twelve different larval stages from the egg to the adolescent, small krill form.

This progressive larval development has been worked out in great detail from collections made around South Georgia and farther south (Fraser, F. C., 1936). The young krill reach a length of somewhat less than $\frac{1}{2}$ inch by the time the winter sets in and they are then in a late larval stage. At the end of summer there are thus, again, two sizes of krill in the surface waters—these young ones hatched that summer and the small adolescents from the previous summer, $1\frac{3}{4}$ inches in length. During the cold dark winter months growth is slowed down so that the young krill appear among the plankton at the ice edge next spring as young adolescents about $\frac{1}{2}$ inch in length (Bargmann, H., 1945). They are the small krill of the spring, while those $1\frac{3}{4}$ inches long at the end of summer appear in the spring about 2 inches long and will spawn and die off that year.

The question remains, when and where does all this story, with its delicate transfer of sperm packets and the progress from egg to adult, take place?

The signs that spawning has recently taken place in an area of sea are the appearance in the nets of gravid and 'spent' females (empty of eggs, thin and flaccid from having recently shed them), of both sexes carrying spermatophores and of recently shed eggs. Marr (1962) found these, except the eggs, from mid- to late summer in the waters of the East Wind Drift and in the cold current flowing out of the Weddell Sea, especially to the east of South Georgia.

The mystery is that comparatively few eggs were found in all the thousands of net hauls which Marr examined. He found very few in the South Georgia area or in the Weddell Sea current and for that reason concluded that no spawning, and certainly no hatching, took place in these waters in spite of finding gravid and spent females there.

Nevertheless, although eggs were not found it does not follow that they were not there. Those that were found were taken in the cold northward-moving Antarctic Bottom Current. But most of the nets did not go as deep as this so that the cold bottom current was only sampled in fairly shallow water close up against the continental coast. This possibly gives a false impression that the krill only hatch in the very far south in the cold bottom current. Perhaps if this current had been sampled more widely away from the continental shelf in the open ocean in depths of perhaps 500 fathoms or more, hatching krill eggs would have been found dispersed over the area of the East Wind Drift and Weddell Sea current where Marr found the other signs of spawning, the individuals carrying sperm packets and the gravid and spent females. Thus the spawning probably takes place where Marr found the signs of it but in very deep water and proceeds progressively farther south later in the year with the retreat of the pack ice. We may suppose the eggs sink after shedding to hatch in the northward-flowing cold bottom current. This seems likely from the fact that they have no oil globule to keep them afloat and are heavier than sea water, sinking more rapidly in cold water with sub-zero temperatures than in warmer water. Fish eggs, which develop floating at the surface, have an oil globule which gives them buoyancy.

The early larval stages of the krill go through their development during what Marr has called 'the development ascent'. As soon as the little first stage, the 'nauplius'—not very different from the first stage of other Crustacea, though larger—is hatched out and has some power of movement of its own it begins its long slow journey towards the surface from several hundred fathoms. The earliest stages rise out of the cold bottom water into the Warm Deep Current which is moving southwards (Fig. 16). In the Weddell Sea current they appear in this water during December and by about mid-January the later stages have reached the surface water. Here they spread eastwards in vast numbers as the final larval stages, reaching as far as longitude 20° E., travelling, Marr thinks, at a speed of eight to fourteen miles a day. In the East Wind Drift the developmental ascent takes place somewhat later, on account of the later withdrawal of the pack ice, so that the early larvae do not appear deep down until January with the first appearance at the surface in mid-February.

All Marr's charts (1962) of the distribution of adult whale food, adolescents and larvae show an enormous mass of them crowding the surface waters of the current flowing out of the Weddell Sea (Fig. 13), moving eastwards throughout the summer as far as longitude 20° E. south of South Africa. Not many observations were made to the east of this longitude and this perhaps might be the reason why the charts seem to show the procession of eastward-drifting krill coming to a stop at this line. There seems to be no dispersal eastward of it into the Indian Ocean. If this is indeed true then something must happen to the krill in this area. Sir Alister Hardy (*Great Waters*, 1967) thinks there must be a sinking of the surface water here carrying the krill down into the Warm Deep Current and so carrying them southwards. Japanese workers have in fact found indications of something of the sort farther east. Yet no such sinking of surface water here could possibly be on a large enough scale to return this vast multitude of krill southwards even if it were proved that such a localized sinking exists, so it seems that we must leave this point as something at present unexplained to be cleared up one day by further research.

The whole question, in fact, of how this teeming population of whale food maintains itself in Antarctic waters is at present unanswered. I think it will one day be found that adolescent and adult krill do descend into the Warm Deep Current, as do other members of the plankton community, and so spend the winter moving south, maintaining the population in position. It may be that they sink down after the surface has been covered by the returning pack ice in the early winter months. If this is so the nets of the *Discovery II* would not have sampled them. As soon as the covering of pack ice is removed in the spring and summer the krill probably come up to the surface again, progressively farther south and later as the ice disappears.

In the nature of things it was inevitable that the *Discovery II* had to work largely blind, as it were, collecting at random without knowing just what and where to collect. An expensive ship with a highly specialized personnel cannot be held up for months, or perhaps years, while scientists examine the results of previous cruises and decide what points ought to be cleared up next. The development of the young stages of krill (Fraser, F. C., 1936) was not published until the ship was already on her fourth two-year cruise in polar waters, while Marr's immensely detailed report did not appear until 1962 nearly ten years after the ship's last Antarctic voyage. Now it is evident that more work is needed, in the Cold Deep Current in search of krill eggs, in longitude 20°–30° E. south of South Africa in order to find out what happens to the eastward stream of krill in this area. Lastly, towing deep nets under the pack ice is needed in order to find out if

14

the krill do descend in the winter into the Warm Deep Current and rise to the surface in the spring, but this would call for altogether new techniques.

Marr calculated that between 1933 and 1939, during the whaling boom, the krill were being grazed down by whalebone whales alone at a rate of about 38 million tons per year, or 47 million million individuals. One of the results of the present decline of the whale population must be an enormous surplus of krill in polar seas. A Russian expedition has gone to the Antarctic to investigate the effects of this on the bionomics of the sea and to study the question of utilizing the krill for human food. We started this in a small way in *Discovery II* by frying some krill for tea, but I must confess it was not pleasant. Perhaps the Russians will have better luck and invent new processing techniques.

The Sperm Whale

Durban

In the southern winter of 1930 Alec Laurie and I went to Durban,
Natal, in order to supplement the work which Mackintosh and Wheeler
(1929) had done at Saldanha Bay, Cape Province, in 1926. The whaling
season at Durban lasted from March to October and we worked
on the plan of one of the two whaling stations there from early June
until mid-September, when the *Discovery II* arrived and took us back to
South Georgia for another summer season.

In those days Durban had not yet become the roaring metropolis
that it is now. It was a fairly small seaside resort with a still lingering
colonial air about it. The inhabitants were worried because the Zulus
had lately, after some controversy, acquired the right to walk on the
pavements in the main streets of the town, and did not always step
off when a white man approached. One wondered what the world was
coming to.

The lovely landlocked harbour has a very narrow entrance into
which the big Union Castle liners slide almost, it seems, touching the
jetties on either side. On one side of the harbour lies the town with
its jacarandas and avenues of flame trees with white Dutch-style houses,
while on the other, the southern side, there is a long low promontory
called the Bluff. In those days it was covered with scrub in which
there were monkeys and snakes but today, I believe, it is covered
with modern houses and streets with daylight lamps. Southward of
the Bluff a long straight stretch of sand goes on for miles, where the
Indian ocean rollers come crashing in and skinny Indians fish in the
surf with long rods supported in leather sockets on their groins. On
this long sandy stretch Durban's two whaling stations were situated,

and I believe they are still there, though no longer operating. One, that of the Union Whaling Company, was about a mile along the beach from the harbour mouth and the tip of the Bluff headland with its lighthouse, while the other, that of the Premier Whaling Company, was about half a mile farther on. The inhabitants of Durban never ceased complaining about the smell from the two whaling stations and swore that it was particularly offensive when the wind was from the south, but I must say I never noticed it, though I dare say I was pretty well hardened to smells by that time.

The unique feature of the whaling stations at Durban was the manner in which the whales arrived for their last rites. They came by train. A single-track railway of wobbly appearance ran from the harbour mouth round the headland behind the lighthouse and then along the mile and a half of loose driven sand to the whaling stations, both of which had the plan built alongside the track like a railway station platform. The catchers dropped their whales at the harbour entrance overnight and a harbour tug hauled them up to a slipway where they were in due course winched up on to specially built, low-slung bogey trucks. They were then trundled off to their obsequies by a tank engine with a cow catcher and a huge square headlamp on the front. The harbour authorities were very strict because of the complaints about the smell, so that no carcass was allowed to lie at the slipway for more than a few hours. If it had not been trundled away within the stipulated time the harbour tug towed it remorselessly out to sea. Owing to the wobbliness of the track, and the fact that it was often buried by wind-blown sand, the train with its monstrous cargo often got stuck or the trucks came off the rails. It then had to wait, with the engine hissing indignantly, until a breakdown crane was brought.

Laurie and I stayed in the town near the sea front in a hotel which had a convenient back entrance so that we could steal in and out unseen, and unsmelt, in the very old and malodorous clothes that we kept for our work. In the cool early morning, before the stars had quite disappeared, we took the first tram and ferry to the Bluff with the Indian fishermen and their rods. On one of the very first of those chill delightful journeys we sat on the top of the tram at the back and as we swayed past we watched the lights growing dim in the ships that lay at the quayside. We noticed, without paying much attention, that a crowd of black boys, dock labourers, were bunched uncomfortably in the back of the car behind us while all the seats in front of us were empty. Presently the conductor asked us to move forward so that the other passengers could sit down. The blacks were not allowed to sit in front of us, but that was forty years ago.

For three and a half months we worked on the plan of the Union Whaling Company's factory, the nearer of the two along the railway line, and every morning we walked there along the sandy track with the sunrise shining green through the rollers and flashing on their streaming hair, or along the pathway up and over the Bluff where the little grey monkeys rattled the glaucous foliage and vanished as we approached.

Work went on day and night on the plan because the carcasses had to be hauled up and got rid of as soon as they arrived. Accordingly there was a day and a night shift, so we worked with the day shift, timing our arrival for some time just before seven o'clock in the morning when the day shift came on. The day shift went off again at six-thirty in the evening and, if there were whales to be completed, we usually stayed until then.

The European staff of the station, the Manager, Secretary, Chief Engineer and two plan foremen were Norwegians. They lived in quarters on the station and seldom went into town, leading that strange remote, detached existence peculiar to Norwegian whalers everywhere. They do not seem to notice whether they are surrounded by the stony wastes and snows of South Georgia, the grim inferno of Deception Island, the thorny hot wilderness of a remote bay in Cape Province or a beach within sight of the beckoning lights of Durban. It is all the same to them. They gave Laurie and me a small room with a table in it behind the office building and there we unpacked our gear and wrote up our log books. We met the Norwegians for breakfast, luncheon and afternoon coffee but we found them dour, silent men with little to say except 'Plenty whales today', or 'Bad weather—no whales!'

The labour force, on the other hand, was anything but dour. It was made up mainly of Zulus but there was a proportion of boys from farther up country. The Zulus were coal-black and shining and had splendid white teeth, but there were several men of paler shades of brown, bronze and dull gold. They danced and pirouetted round the whale carcasses as though round a sacrificial victim, brandishing and twirling their flensing knives in the air so that the sun glinted on the blood-stained blades as on the assegais of Chaka's impis. Above the rattle of the winches and the hiss of steam echoed the wild shrieks and laughter of the blubber boys and the meat hauliers wielding their hooks. The flensers chanted as the crackling strips of blubber peeled back and sometimes danced around on their bare feet in the muck and slime holding their knives aloft like spears. Some took the long white chains of tape worms from the intestines of the whale and decorated themselves with loops of them over their shoulders and chests, over their arms and like girdles round their waists, and thus attired did their war dance, throwing back their heads and whirling their arms aloft, twirling their knives.

As we arrived we heard the half past six hooter go and saw the night shift streaming away to the wash place behind the plan where there were rows of showers. Here the Africans washed naked, looking like a bronze frieze. At seven the day shift came on, prancing and chanting with their knives at the ready, and with some of them we became familiar. The Chief Flenser was a very big Zulu whose wide face opened like a melon showing his white teeth on many occasions when he saw us grubbing in faeces or hauling out ovaries or testes. I do not think we lost any face over these activities, but they caused great amusement and even more astonishment. Future experience in Africa and the East was to convince me that one did not lose either face or dignity by visibly doing a job of work alongside the people themselves, even though they did not themselves understand what one was doing. Face and dignity were much more likely to be lost by standing about in immaculate white clothes pointing and shouting.

At six-thirty in the evening the hooter on the meat shed blew for knocking off. Away streamed the Zulus of the day shift, still singing, whistling and shouting, to the showers to wash away the grime, sweat and blood of a hot day's toil. Very often this meant leaving one or more whales unopened, or opened but uncompleted, on the plan for the night shift to finish off. We often waited for them to do so and this sometimes meant that we were still on the plan at eight or eight-thirty, by which time it was dark and the swaying arc-lamps were lit above the glistening expanse of the plan. But we did not always wait for the night shift, for after twelve hours in the heat, noise and stench we were usually dog-tired. When darkness fell, if you walked to the edge of the plan and leaned forward over the sandy railway tracks, looking down the diminishing rails to the left, you could see in the distance a row of lights glittering and shimmering across the bay. This was Durban in the July Handicap season, so we did not always wait.

The Catch at Durban

The catch of the Durban whaling stations in 1930 consisted of Blue,

Fin, Humpback and Sperm whales. The Blue and Fin whales were mostly young, possibly visiting tropical waters for the first time after being weaned in the south the previous spring, but there was also a number of large whales in an active breeding condition, the cows on heat or carrying very small foetuses recently conceived, the bulls with testes running with white spermatic fluid. We searched every full grown cow thoroughly and found a number of very small foetuses, I myself finding the smallest on record. It was that of a Blue whale 1·8 cm. (slightly over ½ in.) in length.

The chief interest of the Durban catch was the large number of Sperm whales which it contained. The Blue and Fins came mostly in June and July and then declined in numbers. In August and September Sperm whales predominated. Unfortunately the *Discovery II* arrived in the middle of September and took us away, so that our work at Durban came to an end in the middle of the glut of Sperms which seems to occur in these two months every year. It may be artificial and illusory, because the whalers did not take Sperm whales when they could get the much more valuable Rorquals, so it is possible that Sperms were really present off the Natal coast all the time although ignored by the whalers until the Rorquals departed.

The Sperm Whale

Forty years ago Sperm whales were not often taken by the whalers and the total world catch of Sperms was probably less than a thousand whales. They were unpopular because their oil, which is a wax, does not mix with whalebone whale oil. When a Sperm was reported captured there were groans. A boiler had to be emptied and cleaned to take the Sperm oil and a special tank was usually set aside to store it. After the carcass had been disposed of the whole plan had to be washed down. Further, the flensers and lemmers seemed to find the work of dismembering a Sperm much harder than a Rorqual. But after World War II, with the growing scarcity of whalebone whales, the numbers of Sperms taken each year has fairly steadily risen until in 1964, after Blues and Humpbacks had been declared protected, the total world catch of Sperm stood somewhere near 30,000 (Mackintosh, N. A., 1965) and the Antarctic catch near 5,000 (Fig. 1b).

In 1930 the two Durban whaling stations were among the few where Sperm whales were regularly taken. There were also one or two stations on the west coast of South America and one in Portuguese West Africa (Gabon) which regularly took them.

At South Georgia and in Antarctic waters generally the Sperm whales taken are always bulls, usually between 50 and 60 feet in length, old looking and with much white about them and many teeth in the lower jaw, but Durban regularly took the females as well as the males. The cows are smaller than the bulls, not more than 30 feet long, and it seemed a shame to kill them. They presented us with a personal problem in logistics because they were usually hauled up on the plan six or eight at a time so that we had to hop about frantically in order to get all the measurements and notes on all of them at the same time. However, we examined only 13 cow Sperm whales in the three months we were at Durban and 20 bulls. Of the cows six were examined all at once on one day in late August and five on a day in early September. It was trying work, because often we would hang about waiting for whales all day in the sand and hot sun, knowing there were several at the slipway. Then at half past six we would decide to give it up and go back to the town. At that moment the telephone would ring in the Manager's office.

'Whales coming now,' he would say, hanging up.

The Sperm whale is the largest of the toothed whales, the bull being far larger than the cow. At puberty the bull is between 37 and 41 feet in length (11·5 and 12·5 m.) and the cow is between 29 feet 6 inches and 31 feet 2 inches (9·0 and 9·5 m.) (Matthews, L. H., 1938). The largest bull among 67 specimens measured on various occasions by 'Discovery' scientists had a length of 57 feet 5 inches (17·5 m.) (Matthews, L. H., 1938). The largest cow out of 14 specimens measured had a length of 37 feet 1 inch. A bull of 59 feet weighed piecemeal had a weight of 54 tons and a second of 44 feet weighed 23 tons not including blood (Budker, P., 1958). A cow Sperm of 37 feet weighs 13 tons (Slijper, E. J., 1962).

After the war the International Whaling Commission fixed a minimum length for Sperm whales at 38 feet for factory ships and 35 feet for land stations, so that the Sperm became virtually entirely protected, because very few cows exceed these lengths and the catch was restricted to bulls. Unfortunately there is reason to believe that the rule is widely disregarded by the whalers.

The Sperm whale is a very strange-looking animal (Fig. 5a), so bizarre in its appearance indeed that it seems even more impersonal and unlike a once living creature when you see it on the plan than does a Rorqual. It is so different in appearance, in some points of structure and in its habits, from a whalebone whale that it is doubtful whether the two types are very closely related and they are thought to have had a different ancestry.

The colour of the monster is a uniform slate-grey or dark bluish-grey, but when wet it appears almost black. There is usually a certain amount of white on the under-surface and on the snout. It has been suggested (Beale, T., 1839) that much white pigmentation is a sign of old age and white pigmented whales were called 'grey heads' by the old-time whalers. The lone bulls of the Antarctic usually have a very hoary look with a lot of white about them and Herman Melville's 'Moby Dick' was evidently one of these. He was, in fact, almost an albino with 'a peculiar snow white wrinkled forehead and a high pyramidal white hump . . . The rest of his body was so streaked and spotted and marked with the same shrouded hue that in the end he gained his distinctive appellation of the "White Whale".' Exactly how long he was Melville does not say except that he was 'of uncommon bulk' and had a deformed, sickle-shaped lower jaw. The description reads as though Moby Dick was not a complete albino but had an exceptional amount of white about him.

This very white pigmentation and the deformed lower jaw are not uncommon among Sperm whales and are quite often seen in the Antarctic. Neither are albinos unknown among both whalebone and Sperm whales. The French explorer Alain Bombard had an encounter with an albino Fin whale in the Mediterranean (Budker, P., 1958) and in 1951 the factory ship *Anglo-Norse* captured an albino Sperm whale 55 feet long off the coast of Peru. It, too, had a deformed lower jaw.

Matthews (1938) does not believe that white pigmentation necessarily denotes old age and points out that hardly any of the hoary 'grey heads' of Antarctic waters are actually full grown on the evidence of the state of their backbones and the fusion of their discs.

A good deal of work has been done recently, largely by the Whale Research Unit of the National Institute of Oceanography (Gambell, R. and Grzegorzewska, C., 1967), on a method of telling the age of Sperm whales by examining very thin sections of their teeth. These, especially of the first teeth of the lower jaw, etched in formic acid, show a ringed structure with layers comparable to those found in the ear plugs of whalebone whales, but there is again some doubt whether one or two rings or layers in the tooth may represent a year's growth of the whale. At its nineteenth meeting (1969) the International Whaling Commission decided that there is at present not enough evidence on this point.

In its internal structure the Sperm whale is different in many ways from a whalebone whale. In the first place the barrel head contains a reservoir, known as 'the case', which holds the spermaceti, not floating about in the reservoir as a liquid, like water in a tank, but held by large numbers of fat cells in connective tissue. On board factory ships and at South Georgia the head was always cut off, as it was in the old whaling days when it was known as the 'junk piece', and a slit was cut in the upper surface so that the waxy fluid ran out into the top of one of the boilers specially prepared for it or, at a land station, into special receptacles. The liquid, very soft and said to be healing to the skin, congealed almost instantly like candle grease on contact with the air.

There is no doubt that 'the case' is a buoyancy chamber and that it profoundly affects the centre of gravity of the body. Accordingly, the shape of the skull beneath it and the layout of the nasal passages are drastically adapted to accommodate it.

In all whales, both toothed and whalebone, the facial bones of the skull have been produced forward and spread backwards (Fig. 17). The nose bones (nasals) have been moved upwards and backwards so as to bring the nostrils to the top of the head and similarly the jaw bones (maxillaries) have been extended upwards and backwards so as to separate the two cranial bones (parietals) from one another. This process is called the 'telescoping' of the skull.

In whalebone whales the nose bones are much reduced and situated right on top of the skull (Fig. 17B) while the upper jaw bones are prolonged forwards into a long beak. Behind they envelop the brain case. When the animal comes up to breathe the top of the head, where the nostrils (blowholes) are, breaks surface first and the whole of the top of the head becomes visible at once.

In the Sperm whale the bones of the front of the skull have been compressed and the nose bones greatly reduced (Fig. 17C), but they are still on top of the skull as in whalebone whales. But the front of the skull is concave in order to accommodate the 'case' (Fig. 17D), the presence of which so alters the position of the centre of gravity of the body that when the whale comes up to breathe the point of the snout (the front of the boiler-like head) breaks surface first. This is where the blowhole must therefore be, even though the nasal apertures of the skull are far back on the top of the cranium. For this reason two long nasal passages have been developed running obliquely from the nasal apertures of the skull, far back on the cranium beneath the 'case', to the single blowhole far forward on the tip of the snout (Fig. 17D). They

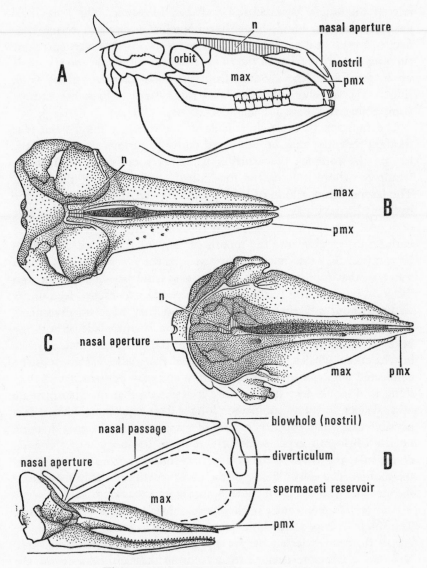

Fig. 17 DIAGRAMS OF SKULL AND HEAD OF

A Horse (side view)
B Whalebone whale (dorsal view)
C Sperm whale (dorsal view)
D „   „   (side view showing nasal passage)
max Maxillary, pmx Premaxillary, n Nasal bone.

join at the single asymmetrical S-shaped blowhole. The long nasal passages give off blind, finger-like branches encased in elastic connective tissue. In the Sperm whale there are two such 'diverticula', one running down the front of the snout from the blowhole and the other up to the top of the cranium from the nasal aperture of the skull. (Fig. 17D). In other toothed whales this system of branches is more complicated and there are lateral off-shoots.

The function of these diverticula is not certainly known but it is thought that they may be connected with the curious structure of the larynx, the complex of cartilages which surrounds the head of the windpipe where it joins the food canal at the back of the throat. The larynx forms a kind of beak projecting across the gullet into the back of the nasal passage so that the food canal passes on either side of it. Air can therefore pass from the lungs into the nasal passages without ever going into the mouth or into the food pipe. It used to be thought that this must be an arrangement for swallowing under water so that food could not get into the nasal passage, nor air into the food pipe, during feeding. But whalebone whales also feed under water without any such arrangement, and they have no diverticula along the nasal passage. The presence in the Sperm whale of both the beak on the larynx and the diverticula in the nose, and their absence in whalebone whales, has led to the belief that these features must be connected with one another in function and may perhaps have something to do with deep diving, since it is known that the Sperm whale dives deeper and stays submerged longer than whalebone whales. It is possible that when sudden changes of pressure arise during a dive the Sperm whale can expel some of the air in its lungs into the nasal diverticula, the beak of the larynx preventing it from escaping into the mouth. The elastic lining of the diverticula might help to squeeze the air back into the nasal passage during an exhalation.

Another strange feature of the Sperm whale's head is its asymmetry. The single S-shaped blowhole lying off centre to the left of the middle line of the head reflects a deeper asymmetry of the bones of the skull. Not only are they telescoped so as to bring the nasal bones on to the top of the head (Fig. 17C), but all of them on the right-hand side of the face, or what we must call the face, the upper jaw bones (maxillaries and premaxillaries), the nasals and the forehead bones (frontals) are considerably larger than the corresponding ones on the left-hand side. As a result the sutures between them, normally marking the middle line of the skull, are pushed well over to the left and the whole skull of the Sperm whale is lop-sided with the right hand side of its facial aspect larger than the left. This is not the case in whalebone whales whose skulls, though compressed and telescoped, are quite symmetrical about the middle line (Fig. 17B).

Naturally there has been a lot of speculation about the origin of this asymmetry. The first suggestion (Lahille, F., 1908) was that the ancestors of the Sperm whale must have sustained an injury to the skull which their descendants inherited. Another suggestion was that the tail flukes are unequally developed (Kükenthal, W., 1908) as, indeed, in the womb they are, the left one upturned and smaller than the right, which is downturned. The result of this would be that when the whale moved forward the head would tend to turn towards the left and so there would develop an asymmetry of the muscles used for pulling the head back to the right and a corresponding asymmetry of their bony attachments.

In fact an asymmetry exists within the thorax of all land mammals (Slijper, E. J., 1936). The heart is larger on the left side than on the right so that the left lung is smaller than the right one. Slijper found that in the domestic cat 60 per cent of the liver is on the right hand side. In whales, however, this asymmetry in the thorax does not exist, the organs being symmetrical about the middle line and therefore the centre of gravity of the body is in the median plane, giving stability in water.

Slijper suggested that during the ancestral history of toothed whales there must have been a period when the internal organs of the thorax were asymmetrical like those of modern land mammals. This produced an instability in the ancestral whale, the greater buoyancy coming on the right-hand side of the body and the greater weight on the left. The animal therefore tended to turn towards the left when swimming and in order to counteract this, the muscles became more developed on the right side of the head than on the left. Correspondingly there was a greater expansion of the bones to which these muscles were attached.

Except for the left-hand position of the single blowhole none of this asymmetry is visible externally though one writer (Guldberg, G. A., 1896—quoted by Slijper, E. J., 1936) claimed to have found the left eye to be smaller than the right, but no other observer has noticed anything of the sort. What strikes one about the Sperm whale is the greasiness of all the muscles and their very dark colour, much darker than those of a whalebone whale. This is due to the larger quantities of myohaemoglobin (oxygen-absorbing substance) which they carry. One also notices the length and comparatively narrow bore of the intestine. That of a 55 feet Sperm whale is calculated to be about 1,200 feet (Slijper, E. J., 1962). Allowing for post-mortem stretching to three or four times its length in life this gives the Sperm whale an intestine 400 to 500 feet long. It was always carefully searched under the watchful eye of the plan foreman for the coveted lumps of ambergris, but no true ambergris was found during our time at Durban.

Natural History

The Sperm whale is an inhabitant of warm seas, tropical and temperate, on both sides of the Equator, though lone bulls are found in polar regions both Arctic and Antarctic. It is polygamous, the cows roaming the tropical oceans in 'harem bands' in charge of one or more proprietor bulls or 'schoolmasters', as the old whalers called them.

The habits and natural history of the Sperm whale were studied by Dr. Robert Clarke (1954, 1956) of the 'Discovery' staff, who paid a visit to the whaling stations in the Azores where the Sperm is still hunted with open boats in a manner almost exactly similar to the method used by the nineteenth-century American whalers, many of whom were Portuguese. Only slight changes have been introduced during the passage of years. For instance, the harpooner and steersman do not make the perilous change of places after the whale has been struck so that the harpooner both makes fast to the whale and also finally lances it. There are certain modern adjuncts, of course, such as motor towing boats and radio-telephones from the look-out on the cliff, but in essentials Dr. Clarke found a surviving relic industry very similar to the bay whaling of the early nineteenth century.

It used to be thought that at the beginning of each summer breeding season the bulls, by competition or actual combat, gained the mastery of a harem of cows, variable in number, which they lorded over until the end of the breeding season (Beale, T., 1839). The lone bulls found in cold, temperate and polar seas were thought to be the unsuccessful ones which, on account of age or lack of prowess or for some other reason, had failed to win harems for themselves. Now it is thought that this picturesque idea may not be quite correct.

Clarke found that the cows were always in schools with one, two or three proprietors or 'schoolmasters', but there were also schools of pregnant or nursing cows without any bulls. The number of cows in the harem bands seems to be very variable though schools of about twenty cows were seen around the Azores.

The bulls may also be either in bachelor schools or they may be solitary, but it is believed that one solitary bull indicates others within a mile or two. In the tropics mixed schools of juveniles of both sexes are quite common.

Most accounts agree that there may be only one or as many as four 'schoolmasters' with the harem bands of cows. They usually withdraw some distance from the main body of the cows, sometimes in the van and sometimes at the side. Bullen in *The Cruise of the Cachalot* noted one or two bulls lying to windward. But wherever they are they seem to play a guardian role to the school.

Off the coast of California three kinds of association have been observed (Rice, Dale W., 1963), large, often dense schools of from twelve to fifty cows both young and adult, some pregnant and some nursing, accompanied by young and adult bulls up to 35 feet in length; next loose companies of young adult bulls 30 to 45 feet long, moving about as a unit but not formed up together; lastly solitary old bulls from 40 to 56 feet long. Off the coast of Natal, where travelling Sperm whales have been watched from aircraft, big bulls have been seen to be mostly solitary or in ones and twos with smaller bulls, the latter usually in groups of up to six (Gambell, R., 1967).

The Sperm whale is extremely gregarious and often travels in huge companies of fifty to several hundred. These the old whalers called 'herds', while smaller companies of twenty to fifty were called 'schools' and those of less than twenty were called 'gams'.

The lone bulls of polar regions certainly look old with a great deal of white about them, many teeth and the scars of battle around their jaws and heads, but as Matthews (1938) pointed out, few of them are fully grown and are therefore not yet past their sexual prime. It seems that in the middle of the breeding season, which is the summer in both hemispheres, a certain proportion of mature bulls make off alone for polar waters where there are no cows. The reason for this is still not known. It may be that these are bulls which, while they have not actually been driven out of the harems, have nevertheless for some reason or other failed to acquire one (Clarke, R., 1956). Presumably the bachelor bulls acquire harems afresh each year, as seals do. It is believed that the sexes are about equal in numbers, but a proportion of the cows in any mating season are either pregnant or not in a breeding condition (resting) so that the eligible bulls probably heavily outnumber the available breeding cows. Competition among them must therefore be keen and a certain proportion will every year fail to make the grade or pass whatever the test may be that wins you, if you are a bull Sperm whale, a company of little wives.

Clarke says that Sperm whales gather in herds in order to migrate, but little is known about the actual routes they take. Their migrations are in any case far less well defined and less extensive than those of whalebone whales. An American writer (Townsend, C. W., 1935) has drawn up charts showing the position and date of capture of all the Sperm whales taken by the American whaling fleet between the years 1761 and 1920. Nearly 37,000 entries recording the capture of Sperm whales were extracted from the logs of American whaling ships. They showed that Sperm whales may be taken anywhere in tropical waters all the year round but during the northern summer many more were taken north of the Equator than south of it. Conversely, during the southern summer many more were taken south of the Equator than north of it. This points to a movement towards the Equator during the winter in each hemisphere. Clarke points out that, according to Townsend's charts, the old whaling ships took many Sperm at the Cape Verde Islands in winter but few at the Azores much farther north. In summer, on the other hand, they took few at the Cape Verde Islands but many at the Azores.

Aircraft spotting at Durban has shown that Sperm whales travel north and south along the Natal coast but are much more widespread than the catch figures suggest, far beyond the range of the stations' catchers. The cows are most abundant in the autumn until mid-winter (Feb. to June), moving northwards. They then decline in numbers but pick up again in the spring (Sept.) until mid-summer (Dec.) moving southwards. Big breeding bulls are travelling northwards all the winter (Feb. to Sept.) but are most plentiful about mid-winter (Gambell,. R., 1967).

Sperm whales seem to have a liking for oceanic islands where the coast descends steeply into deep water and this may be because the squid on which they feed are plentiful in such localities. The famous Sperm whaling grounds of the old days were regions where cold water rises to the surface from below so as to produce a crop of rich plankton on which the squids feed, as, for example, off the coasts of Chile and Peru and the west coast of Africa. Similar favourable conditions exist where currents meet and move in opposite directions, as in the Atlantic and Pacific Equatorial zones where the famous 'Line Grounds' were located. Island grounds well known to the American whalers were around the Azores, Canaries, Madeira and the Cape Verde Islands. In the Indian Ocean the neighbourhood of the Seychelles and the Comoro Islands, north of Madagascar, was a much frequented ground although in all our fishing voyages in this area in 1948–49 I do not remember seeing a single Sperm whale. The Galapagos Islands and the coast of Japan were two other much frequented grounds on opposite sides of the Pacific, the former believed to be an area where the cows went to bear their young. Today the largest catches of Sperm whales are taken in the northern Pacific Ocean, the south-east Pacific off the west coast of South America, and the Antarctic (bulls only).

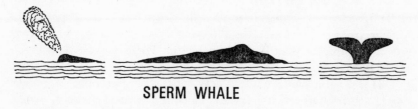

SPERM WHALE

Fig. 18

The Sperm whale is the most easily identifiable of all whales at sea because it throws a single spout, about the same length as that of a Fin but directed forwards from the single blowhole at an angle of about 45° (Fig. 18). Occasionally when it sounds, though not every time, it throws up its tail flukes clear of the water and their characteristic shape is unmistakable, blunt and rounder than those of the Humpback or Right whale, while the trailing edge has a rounded curve, not S-shaped (see phot. p. 144). It travels leisurely, almost lazily, through the blue tropic seas at a speed of about four knots when not disturbed or alarmed, but it can accelerate up to twelve knots, averaging about ten. When chased it can achieve bursts of sixteen to twenty knots and Dr. Robert Clarke in the Azores estimated that light whale boats were towed for short periods at twenty knots.

Sperm and Bottle-nosed whales are believed to dive much deeper than Rorquals and to remain submerged for much longer. When travelling undisturbed the Sperm whale sounds for any length of time up to half an hour (Clarke, R., 1954) and occasionally longer. Clarke timed one in the Azores which sounded for an hour and a quarter. On returning from the sound it blows many times at the surface, the actual number depending on the size of the whale and the duration

15

of the dive. Slijper (1962) gives an average of six breaths a minute for ten minutes—sixty blows—before sounding again. As to the depth reached in a sounding dive there is only indirect evidence. Fourteen instances have been recorded of Sperms becoming entangled in submarine cables (Budker, P., 1958). Five of these were at depths of 500 fathoms and one at 620 fathoms, but it does not follow that the whales died at the depths at which they were found. It has also been argued that some of the squid whose remains have been found in Sperm and Bottle-nosed whales' stomachs live at great depths, and could only have been found there by the whales, but this is a doubtful argument for little is known about the distribution of squid in the ocean.

Many observers have seen Sperm whales idling, lying almost stationary and horizontal on the surface, 'on the deep stretched like a promontory sleeps or swims and seems a moving land'. It is probable that they are indeed sleeping thus, basking in the sun. There have been occasions when ships have been damaged by ramming them while dozing like this. It is a habit which made it easy for the old whalers to approach them in their boats and it was often when the monster suddenly awoke that it threw up its tail in alarm, sending the whaleboat up with it.

There has been a lot of discussion about whether whales really do sleep. Nearly all animals do more or less, though in many cases it is more of a doze than a sleep. Horses and cows may sleep standing up but, again, this is really a doze. Fish also go into a state of suspended animation as any angler knows. There seems to be no doubt that Bottle-nosed dolphins and Pilot whales in the Marineland Seaquarium do doze, usually by day. All reports of dozing Sperm whales and of ships ramming them come from the tropics and I do not think anyone has seen whalebone whales dozing in polar waters. One of the South Georgia Customs officers, who used to visit the South Orkney Islands in the floating factory *Anglo-Norse* in the early days of pelagic whaling, told me that Fin whales were always found in the shallow waters over the shelf to the south of the islands. The whalers said they seemed to be curiously easy to approach and firmly believed that these whales were sleeping there.

The Sperm whale in its schools and herds shows what the Americans call 'social facilitation' in a high degree. This is defined as 'activity by an individual which stimulates the performance of the same activity by its neighbours' (Caldwell, David K. *et al.*, 1965). This we call, rather more simply, 'follow-my-leader'. Thus members of a herd of Sperm whales tend to dive and surface together, and may be seen swimming in ranks or in line ahead. This has often led to stranding when the leader of the herd or school makes a mistake in navigation. The members of the herd pick up sounds—probably clicks or creaking noises—by means of their sensitive ears and thus communicate with each other. At any rate it seems certain that an alarm can spread swiftly through a herd so that all the members give an almost simultaneous alarm reaction. The commonest is for all to dive at once but another has been seen which consisted of the herd crowding together at the surface 'still and trembling' (Bennett, F. D., 1840). A similar reaction has been seen among Californian Grey whales which crowd together when attacked by Killers. One feels a slight doubt whether anyone could really have observed Sperm whales trembling.

Both frolicsome and aggressive behaviour have been noted by many travellers who have watched Sperm whales gambolling on their way through the ocean, and there have also been many accounts of fierce and aggressive action by bulls (Caldwell, David K. *et al.*, 1965). Old bulls seem to be especially savage and some travellers have said that old cows may be dangerous too.

According to most accounts the gambols take two forms, 'breaching' and 'lobtailing'. 'Breaching' consists of rearing the boiler-like head and trunk far up out of the water, and then falling sideways or backwards with a fine resounding smack which can be heard a long way off. The body has been seen to leave the water altogether in these leaps (Beale, T., 1839) and one observer said he saw the setting sun beneath it. Most accounts agree, however, that the tail does not usually leave the water. 'Lobtailing' consists of standing head down more or less vertically in the water and waving the tail from side to side. A whole school has been seen following the leader, all doing this together. It does not seem to be certain whether these ponderous gambols result from sheer lightness of heart or have the less joyful purpose of ridding the body of its irritating parasites, its whale lice and barnacles.

As for aggressive action there were accounts in the old whaling days of ships being attacked and rammed head on by charging bulls and of whaleboats bitten clean in two. Alternately, the tail may be used as a weapon of offence. Bennett (1840) stated that when the flukes are thus used 'they are turned contrary to the direction of the object aimed at and the blow inflicted by the force of the recoil'. One would think this most improbable.

A Russian observer (Zenkovich, B. A., 1962) gave an account of bull Sperm whales fighting. A bull and a cow with an injured calf tried to join a herd protected by a number of old bulls. One of these went into action against the intruder. Most observers agree that the bull turns over on his side to attack belly upwards, or charges with the belly underneath but with the head reared up, the jaws widely agape and snapping. They may become interlocked and broken and it is not unusual to see bulls on the flensing plan with broken jaws. The Soviet scientist writes of chunks of flesh being torn from the head of both antagonists.

Feeding

Sperm whales feed on squids (Cephalopoda) which have ten arms, eight short and two long ones. They find them everywhere, both in the tropics and in the polar regions, and their stomachs are seldom empty. Usually the partly digested remains of past meals are found together with the horny beaks which the squid carries in its head. But even if the remains of the squids are absent the beaks are still there, in many cases great numbers of them. They are not easily digestible, or perhaps never digested at all, and are found in the fore-stomach where they apparently remain for a long time. They probably serve to grind up the soft food just as do the quantities of stones which seals swallow for that purpose. In Antarctic waters the 'grey heads' often bear around the mouth and upper jaw the scars of the many suckers with which the squids' tentacles are armed, bearing witness to hard-won and painful meals, but in tropical waters these battle scars are not so often seen. The scarred and scratched appearance of lone Antarctic bulls has been responsible for many quite imaginary accounts of Sperm whales engaging in lonely and desperate battles with their gigantic prey. In *The Cruise of the Cachalot* (Bullen, F., 1898) there is a description of a tussle between a Sperm whale and a giant squid at the surface of the sea but, like a good deal of that fine book of travel and adventure, it should surely be taken with a grain of salt.

Although Sperm whales are known to devour very large squids it is rather unusual to find their remains in the stomachs. By convention squids are measured from the tip of the fusiform body to the tips of the short arms, giving the 'standard length'. In the Azores Clarke found that the range of size of the squid in the stomachs of the whales he examined was from 2 to 8 feet, while about 3 feet was the average in the tropics and $4\frac{1}{4}$ feet in the Antarctic. At Durban the largest we found was a little over 5 feet (153 cms.) but Clarke saw a specimen of the giant *Architeuthis*, taken from a whale at Horta, Azores, which measured 16 feet 3 inches in standard length and 34 feet in total length from the tip of the body to the tips of the long arms. It weighed 400 lbs. He believes that these giants are swallowed more often than their rarity in the stomachs indicates and thinks that the whales often vomit on being struck by the harpoon, bringing up any large squids they may have swallowed. He actually saw a whale bring one up after being harpooned.

Squids must be very difficult to catch, for they are very agile and alert and can dart out of the way of the largest and fastest net with amazing speed. Nevertheless Sperm whales seem to be capable of devouring them in great quantities, judging by the numbers found in their stomachs, though it is still something of a mystery how they do it. The rod-like lower jaw with its battery of blunt teeth and the small recessed mouth do not seem to be a very efficient apparatus for capturing so elusive a prey. The jaw is essentially designed for seizing, and could hardly do much chewing. Further, the teeth do not show any signs of hard usage. In old whales they get somewhat worn down but barnacles, both sessile and stalked, grow quite happily on and between them and their large size often seems to indicate that they have been growing there for a long time. In addition, bent, broken or deformed lower jaws are often seen which could not possibly be of any use either for seizing or biting, but the whales that possess them seem to be perfectly healthy and well nourished and often have squids, or their beaks, in the stomach. One suggestion (Beale, T., 1839) is that Sperm whales do not go after their prey but wait for their prey to come to them, remaining stationary or idling slowly with the mouth open, exposing the white lining. Squids are very inquisitive and are attracted by anything white or shining in the water. When the inquisitive squid comes close enough the whale snaps the jaw closed suddenly before the prey has time to dart away. It would certainly have to snap with extraordinary speed.

It is known that Bottle-nosed dolphins, at any rate, have an echo-location system involving the ear and probably the larynx. Experiments have shown that this enables them to locate and seize small fishes with ease and accuracy and it is probable that Sperm whales also have something of the same sort.

Some idea of the depths at which feeding takes place can be gained by a study of the kinds of animals, and occasionally inanimate objects, which find their way into the stomachs in addition to the normal diet of squid. Spiny lobsters, crabs, sponges and gorgonians have all been found, together with stones and sand, all of which point to feeding on the bottom in shallow water. Glass buoys and pieces of fishing tackle have also occasionally been found, suggesting that the whales take fish from nets or lines, possibly in mid-water but not at great depths.

Breeding

According to Matthews (1938) and Clarke (1956) mating takes place in the spring and early summer on both sides of the Equator, in the north (Azores) from January to July with a maximum period in April, and in the south (Durban) from August to December with a maximum period in October.

The cow is pregnant for sixteen months, at least four months longer than a Rorqual, and birth is usually, though not always, followed by a resting period during which the cow is in a state of sexual inactivity and her ovary sheds no eggs. This is not always the case for some have been found to be pregnant while still nursing. Clarke estimated the nursing period to last about thirteen months, so that pregnancy must occur every third year and not every second like that of a Rorqual. This, again, would tend to make for keen competition among the bulls. The heat period is a long one, five to seven months (January to July or August to December), and it is not certain how many eggs are shed during it. The bull also has a long heat period and Matthews concluded that bulls must be sexually active even in the polar regions where there are no cows.

After its sixteen months' gestation the baby Sperm whale is born late in the summer or autumn with a maximum number of births in August in the north and February in the south, and its length at birth is about 13 feet. During the thirteen months of nursing the calf is believed to suckle by taking the mother's teat in the corner of its mouth, there being no tongue such as Rorquals have, while the mother lies on her side with one teat above the surface. The teeth of the calf do not break through the skin of the lower jaw until long after weaning when it has grown to a length of about 28 feet and is nearing puberty. Some of the cows in the school or herd which are not nursing are believed to act as 'aunts', giving help to a mother with a calf. If the calf is wounded or in difficulties the mother and several other cows will remain near it, supporting it until it either dies or recovers. Among whales the Bottle-nosed dolphin also has 'aunts' which act in this way, and so among land mammals do elephants and lions. Many observers have spoken of the care and devotion of the mother Sperm whale for her calf, no larger, it has been said, than a small porpoise.

In both sexes the calf is weaned at a length of about 22 feet, the young bulls reaching puberty at a length of 31 feet (Clarke, R., 1956) and the cow at 29 feet, so that the two sexes probably reach puberty at different ages, the bull at two years and the cow at fifteen months. The bull becomes fully grown, physically mature, at a length of about 60 feet and the cow at about 40 feet, both probably at an age of 8 or 9 years, though this may require revision in the light of work lately done on ageing. Clarke believes, on the evidence of harpoons recovered after a lapse of years, that the bull may live for as long as 32 years and the cow 22 years.

I myself have had little experience of Sperm whales for they were not often taken in my day, perhaps half a dozen in a season. I saw a few old bulls at South Georgia and on board the *Salvestria* and a few younger ones of both sexes at Durban. I often spotted the single forward blow at sea but never saw them in large herds or performing any of the gambols that have been so often described.

CHAPTER 12

Humpback and Sei Whales

The Humpback Whale

The Humpback is surely the unluckiest of all the commercial whales since it falls a victim to the hunters not only along the Antarctic ice edge, where it feeds on krill during the southern summer, but also off the tropical coasts along which it migrates in order to mate and bring forth its young during the southern winter months. It is thus subjected to an almost continuous persecution, hunted by catchers from factory ships in the summer and by those from shore whaling stations on subtropical or tropical coasts in the winter.

This misfortune does not befall the other commercial species. The majority of Rorquals keep far out to sea during their breeding migration to warm waters beyond the range of shore-based catchers, while factory ships are not allowed to operate north of latitude 40° S. As for the Sperm whale the grounds frequented by the old-time whalers are likewise inaccessible to shore-based catchers and the length limitations imposed by international agreement protect the cows.

The Humpback is a very slow swimmer, the slowest of all the Rorquals, travelling at not more than five knots in large schools, with bursts of up to ten knots when pressed or alarmed. For this reason it is easy to approach and kill, even for the slow, old-fashioned coal-burning catchers used at the beginning of the century when whaling first began in the Antarctic. Further its carcass floats when dead, as does that of a Right whale, while those of the Blue, Fin and Sei all sink. Some air, however, is usually pumped into it for safety. In addition it is primarily a coastal creature, especially during its breeding migration when it tends to follow the coasts of southern continents. It loves to cruise along close inshore where there are rocks, and this

232

makes it accessible from land stations and even possible to catch with nets. It has also made it one of the most studied and observed of all the whalebone whales. The Australians especially, under Dr. R. G. Chittleborough, have watched it in its natural environment, largely from the air, and observed its migrations along the coast of Western Australia, while the New Zealanders have observed it passing along the coasts of the two islands and through Cook Strait between them.

Northern Humpbacks

In the northern hemisphere Humpback whales were hunted long before whaling began in the south. In the autumn they were seen migrating from the coast of northern Norway down the west coast of Ireland to breeding grounds off the Cape Verde Islands and the north-west coast of Africa (Dawbin, W. H., 1965). In the western Atlantic they were sighted passing from Newfoundland down the east coast of the United States, but there was also a Humpback industry at Bermuda and whale boats used to hunt them in the eastern Caribbean. On the American west coast they travelled from Alaska as far south as the Gulf of California. In the Sea of Japan they are hunted to this day, in the Ryukyu Islands and formerly in the Marianas. In the northern winter they are seen off Hawaii. In the spring the Humpbacks return along the same routes to their northern feeding grounds along the Arctic ice edge.

Southern Humpbacks

In the southern hemisphere whale marking experiments along the Antarctic ice edge and off the coasts of the southern continents have shown that there are, broadly, five areas in the Antarctic where Humpback whales assemble for feeding (Fig. 19), though this is not to say that they are entirely absent between these areas. One of them lies in the South Atlantic to the eastward and slightly to the southward of South Georgia and a second lies in about the same latitude (between 50° and 60° S.) south of the Cape. Two more lie respectively south of Western Australia and of Tasmania and New Zealand. A fifth lies in the south-eastern Pacific south of the coast of Chile. From these five almost isolated feeding areas the Humpbacks go north along the same migration routes at the end of every summer to the coasts of the corresponding southern continents. Thus the South Atlantic group goes north both to the coast of Brazil and of West Africa. The group south of Africa migrates mainly up the east coast to Madagascar and

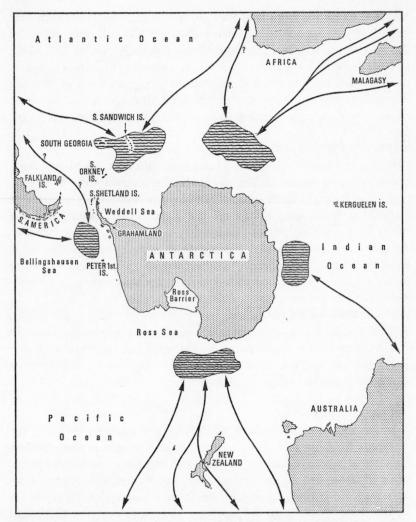

Fig. 19 Diagrammatic chart of Antarctic feeding areas and migration routes
of Humpback Whales (From Hardy, A. C., 1967)

the Mozambique Channel, but it is believed that some may also go
up the west coast to Angola. The two groups south of Australia and
of Tasmania and New Zealand go north to the coast of Western
Australia on the west and to New South Wales on the east, but also
along the New Zealand coast and through Cook Strait to breeding
grounds among the oceanic islands, perhaps off Tonga and New
Caledonia. South-east Pacific Humpbacks travel up the coasts of Chile

and Peru as far as the Galapagos Islands, but one marked at Tonga was recaptured in the Antarctic south-west of Cape Horn (Brown, S.G., 1957). Humpbacks in the Antarctic thus remain to a considerable extent segregated into separate populations though there may be a good deal of mingling between the South Atlantic and South African groups. Apart from this there seems to be little dispersal east and west between the five feeding grounds, but later arrivals at the ice edge probably fan out in search of unoccupied areas.

Humpbacks are found in the greatest numbers during January on their Antarctic grounds where they feed on the swarms of krill at the ice edge as do the other Rorquals. After that month they become less numerous as the northward migration begins. Off the coast of Western Australia they are present in the greatest numbers in August and seem to seek coastal waters with a temperature of 25° C. for their breeding grounds (Dawbin, W. H., 1965). The routes they take to get to these grounds bear no relationship to any conditions they may encounter in passing. They are not deterred or deflected by colder or warmer belts of water, by currents or river outflows. The schools travel northward at a speed of about four knots but gradually slow up and dawdle about as they near their destination. In the southern part of their route off the south-west coast of Australia or the southern coast of the South Island of New Zealand they cover about 220 nautical miles or three degrees of latitude per week (Dawbin, W. H., 1965) but farther north, around Norfolk Island or Cook Strait, marked whales have been captured as much as nine days after marking still in the same locality.

The procession of Humpback whales moving north and south along the coast of Western Australia has been watched from the air by Australian scientists using helicopters (Chittleborough, R. G., 1953), and New Zealanders have watched them passing through Cook Strait (Dawbin, W. H. and Falla, R. A., 1953; Dawbin, W. H., 1965). It could be seen that the migrating whales are to some extent separated into categories on their journey. For instance, the northward procession is headed by nursing cows with large calves and it is presumed that these are cows which mated very late in the breeding season and so could not get through the nursing period and wean their calves before the urge to move northward became too strong to resist. Then come grown cows in the resting non-breeding state—since they are un-accompanied by calves—and grown bulls together with young of both sexes. Lastly come cows in late pregnancy—swimming more slowly than the rest (Dawbin, W. H., 1960). The southward movement from the end of August onwards is led by cows which have recently mated and by young whales. Grown bulls and mothers with very young calves bring up the rear. The calves, small and very white, were seen from the air in the clear blue water swimming close behind their mothers' dorsal fin or beneath one of her flippers. It is believed that some of the cows in the Humpback schools, which do not have calves of their own, may act as 'aunts' as cow Sperm whales may do, help-ing the calves along and shielding them with their bodies if enemies such as Killer whales should be around. The mothers allow the 'aunts' to approach their calves but shield them from other inter-lopers. On one occasion a helicopter pilot saw four or five Killer whales attacking a school consisting of two adult Humpbacks and a calf. One adult, presumably the cow, kept the calf very close while the other, presumably the bull, went for the Killers and drove them off with swipes of his tail flukes (Chittleborough, R. G., 1953).

The Humpback is easily spotted at sea even at a considerable distance because of its habit of breaching the surface at frequent intervals (Fig. 9d). It is then that the great T-shaped tail is upraised for a second as in a derisive gesture before sliding down into the depths. The spout is pear-shaped but not very high, less than half the height of that of a Blue or Fin.

When whaling moved into Antarctic waters at the end of the nineteenth century it was the Humpback and Black Right whales that were its first victims. In those early days around South Georgia until the outbreak of World War I these two species were by far the most important. The Humpback alone far exceeded in numbers in the catches the Blue, Fin and Sei whales together (Fig. 1b), but it must be remembered that the total Antarctic catch, and that means principally South Georgia, was far smaller than it later became in the thirties.

At first Humpback whales used to be taken close inshore around South Georgia, even in the entrances to the harbours, but as whaling continued they moved offshore and by the outbreak of World War I the numbers caught around the island had seriously diminished while those of Blue and Fin whales fairly steadily increased. They are very timid creatures and soon learn to avoid danger. It may be that they were not so much killed off as frightened away. After World War I they continued to be taken sporadically in the Antarctic but the numbers were small and they made up only a tiny fraction of the total which consisted mainly of Blues and Fins (Fig. 1b). During the thirties there was a sudden spurt in the world catch of Humpbacks due partly to the decline of Blues and partly to the depredations of shore whaling stations on tropical coasts along the migration routes during the winter months. These made inroads upon populations already depleted by whaling along the ice edge during the summer.

By 1937 Humpbacks were becoming scarce on some of the regular feeding grounds in the Antarctic. Accordingly in that year a minimum length of 35 feet was set for Humpbacks by the First International Whaling Conference, but since the cow is larger than the bull this gave no protection to breeding cows as it did in the case of the Sperm whales. The following year the Whaling Conference prohibited the taking of Humpbacks altogether in the Antarctic and this prohibiton stood until 1949 when the International Whaling Commission, formed in 1946, decided to allow a numerical total of 1,245 Humpbacks to be taken in the Antarctic each whaling season, but there proved to be practical difficulties about operating a numerical limit for one particular species and it was later found easier to restrict the catch by time rather than by numbers. Catching Humpbacks was therefore limited to only four days in the year and this did actually result in an annual total catch of about 1,245 whales (Mackintosh, N. A., 1965). In 1963 the Humpback became a totally prohibited whale and it was forbidden to catch it through the southern hemisphere.

I myself examined 21 Humpbacks at South Georgia and 10 at Durban, and also a few on board the *Salvestria*. They are good whales, though small, with fine, white, thick blubber in the south during the summer. Most of the cows were about 40 feet in length and never exceeded 50 feet. Proportionately their blubber was thicker than that of large Blue whales.

Breeding

The Humpback breeds every two years, as do the Blue and Fin, although two pregnancies in three years may occur if a cow happens to become pregnant early in the breeding season. Pairing takes place in tropical waters from June to November in the southern hemisphere with a maximum in August off the coast of Western Australia but in July off Durban. In the northern hemisphere it breeds at the southern end of its range in the spring and early summer. Since the Humpback carries on its private affairs so close inshore it has been observed at its love-making by curious human eyes more than any other whale, but in spite of this there seems to be considerable difference of opinion as to exactly what occurs. This is hardly surprising in view of the creature's timidity and the flurry and splashing that go on in the water. Mr. H. F. Cook, a whaler of many years' experience off the coast of New Zealand, told me that he had often seen Humpbacks copulating and that they lie together in the water obliquely, belly to belly, at an angle of 45° to the horizontal with only their heads protruding above the surface. The bull has the upper position, embracing the cow with his long knobbly flippers. On the other hand two Japanese authors (Nishiwaki, M. and Hayashi, K., 1950) reported that the whales take up a vertical position and published sketches which they made on the spot showing them doing so, and many other observers have confirmed this. Scammon (1874) described them lying on the surface belly to belly horizontally, and this too has been confirmed by other observers. No doubt all three versions are true and we may assume that Humpback whales are as versatile in this respect as other more exalted mammals.

Pregnancy lasts for about eleven months, the cow giving birth during her next visit to the tropics after mating. The nursing period is about five months, as is that of the Fin whale, and the calf, born in tropical waters at a length of 15–16 feet, is weaned in most cases on arrival on the Antarctic feeding grounds at a length of 25–26 feet. Most calves reach puberty at an age of four or five years (Chittleborough, R. G., 1960) and are fully grown (physically mature) at the age of ten years (Matthews, L. H., 1937).

Humpback Whaling in New Zealand

In 1932 the *Discovery II* visited New Zealand and refitted at the lovely city of Auckland. While there I became interested in the whaling for Humpbacks which was being carried on in a small way at two stations, one in the North Island and one in the South. I wrote an account of this in 'Discovery' Reports (1933) from which the following is largely taken.

The station in North Island was situated at a place called Whangamumu in the Bay of Islands on the eastern coast of the long finger-like peninsula at the northern extremity of the island (Fig. 20). The very name of the place made me want to go there but unfortunately the station was not operating that year. It had closed down the year before and, I think, never reopened but I met and talked with the owner, Mr. H. F. Cook, in Auckland. He was a quiet spoken elderly man and must

be dead now some years. He had shipped to New Bedford, Massachusetts, and back to New Zealand in one of the last of the Yankee Sperm
whaling ships to visit New Zealand. On his return from this voyage
he built his station at Whangamumu for the capture of Humpback
whales which came close inshore around there during their migration
along the coast.

The method of capture which Mr. Cook used was a very ancient
one, with open boats and hand harpoons. A rope cable was stretched
between a certain rock and the shore across a channel about 50 yards
wide through which the whales always passed. In other places where
the whales could be intercepted the cable was slung between buoys
in a line 50 to 100 yards long seawards from the shore. Sections of
netting were hung from the cable and the whales became entangled
in them and, in their struggles to free themselves, carried away sections
of the net which made it so difficult for them to swim that they fell
an easy prey to the harpooners waiting in a rowing boat nearby.
At first rope nets were used but later one-inch meshes of wire shackled
together were found to be more satisfactory. This was almost exactly
the same method as that used by the Japanese for capturing Right
whales and Humpbacks at the end of the seventeenth century except
that they employed hundreds of men whereas Mr. Cook employed
only a dozen Maoris. The station at Whangamumu caught the Humpbacks on both their northern and southern migration, passing northward from late May or early June until August and southward in the
spring from early October to late November. The catches, however,
were very small when the nets were used, the largest annual bag being
19 whales.

In 1910 a steam whale catcher was built for the station and the
nets were abandoned. The station went on operating with the catcher
until 1931 taking an average of 48 whales a season, the largest catch
being 74 in 1927 (Dawbin, W. H. and Falla, R. A., 1953).

The other New Zealand whaling station was on the north coast of
South Island close to Cook Strait which separates the two islands,
North and South, from one another (Fig. 20). This is a beautiful part
of the country where long narrow parallel fjords run into the land
separated by narrow ridges of grass-covered hills like the green clothed
legs of a half-submerged giant. The fjords are drowned valleys where
quite recent subsidence has let in the sea. The hills slope gently down
to the water on either side of the fjords at the heads of which lie sleepy
little towns such as Picton.

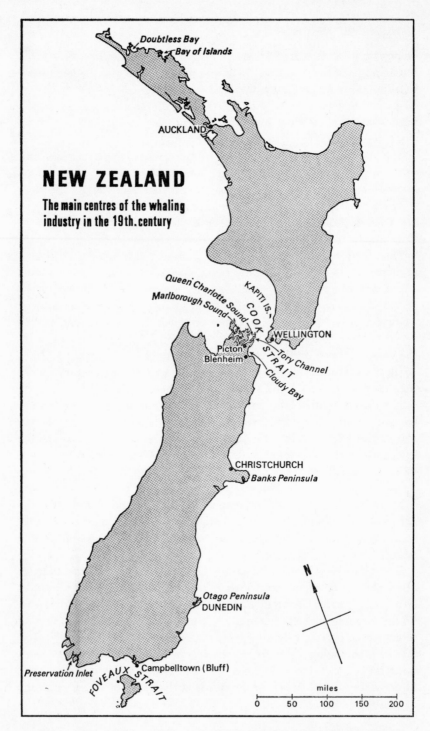

NEW ZEALAND

The main centres of the whaling industry in the 19th. century

Doubtless Bay
Bay of Islands
AUCKLAND

Queen Charlotte Sound
Marlborough Sound
KAPITI IS.
COOK STRAIT
WELLINGTON
Picton
Tory Channel
Blenheim
Cloudy Bay

CHRISTCHURCH
Banks Peninsula

N

Otago Peninsula
DUNEDIN

Preservation Inlet
FOVEAUX STRAIT
Campbelltown (Bluff)

miles
0   50   100   150   200

Fig. 20 Map of New Zealand showing location of whaling stations

During the bay whaling days in the nineteenth century when the Right whale was abundant around the coast there were several shore whaling establishments in this area.

One of the fjords, Queen Charlotte Sound, is connected with Cook Strait by a narrow strip of water named Tory Channel. Here, in an open bay named Te-Awaiti, which had a shelving beach, a certain Captain John Guard had built a whaling station as long ago as 1827 after taking shelter there during a sealing expedition. He built himself a house and, as seals became scarce in the locality, took to the pursuit of the Right whale. Other whalers followed and, when bay whaling was at its height, as many as twenty whale boats used to go out from Tory Channel. The Maoris also hunted whales, selling them to the whalers for £20 each. But the Right whales declined in numbers and about 1840 all these activities came to an end. There was then no further whaling in Tory Channel until an Italian immigrant fisherman, Joseph Perano, built a station at Te-Awaiti in 1909 in order to hunt the Humpback whale in Cook Strait. The station operated only during the winter season, June, July and August, when the whales were passing northward through the strait, for there is no second appearance of Humpbacks there and they do not pass through the strait on their way southward in the spring.

I met Joseph Perano, a dark-skinned, wiry man, and his two sons who were like him, and they showed me their station. The plant was tiny and primitive by Antarctic standards with only two pressure boilers and all the work was done by Perano, father and sons, assisted by a few Maori labourers. He told me that the whales appeared on the flood tides and were nearly all bulls. In this connection it seems that there is always an excess of males over females in tropical waters among Humpbacks while in the Antarctic there is always an excess of cows. This may be due to the fact that the cows always leave the tropics at once directly they have either mated or given birth while the bulls tend to remain on the breeding ground and dawdle about and so are more easily and more often captured (Matthews, L. H., 1937). Some of the bulls, indeed, may remain in tropical waters throughout the summer and not go south at all, or perhaps not so far south as the cows on the southward migration (Mackintosh, N. A., 1942). Perano said that a few cows occasionally turned up at his station carrying large young about 14 feet long and just about to give birth.

Perano knew nothing of Norwegian methods of whaling and had

16

no experience of them at all when he started up. He and his sons had evolved their method of hunting entirely on their own and it was in many respects unique. They used three fast motor-boats, 34 feet long, capable of speeds of over 20 knots and extremely manœuvrable, able to stop and turn almost in their own length. Unfortunately the station was not in operation when I paid it a visit in late August and the season was over but they took me out in one of the roaring motor-launches and put it through its paces, ploughing along at full throttle and then whirling round, throwing up a wall of spray. In the bow was mounted a light harpoon gun of $1\frac{1}{4}$ inch bore on a pillar about three feet high, turning on a swivel pivot. The harpoon was much lighter than that used by the Norwegians and had three slightly curved slender barbs while the explosive grenade was triangular in cross section and had a very home-made, rough and ready look about it. The harpoon line, also much ligher than the Norwegian one, was kept coiled down in the stern and paid out from that position when the shot was fired. The explosion of the grenade inside the whale stunned but did not kill it and, after the shot, the launch was brought alongside the stunned but floating body which was then inflated with air by means of a lance injector just as the Norwegians do it, except that the whale was still alive though stunned. After inflation it was finally despatched by inserting into the upturned underside of the thorax a long lance with a hollow cast iron head filled with gelignite. It held a pound and a half of explosive, touched off inside the thorax by an electric detonator. This was the tricky part because sometimes the charge went off before the lance was properly inserted in the whale's body, and several serious accidents resulted from this. The inflation operation was not without hazards too because the whale was apt to come to in the middle of it.

During the winter season Perano and his sons used to encamp on a headland overlooking Cook Strait and, directly they saw the spout of a whale, put out in their launches anchored in the bay below. When the station first began there was a rival establishment on the opposite side of the channel and Perano told me of nerve-tingling races between boats from the rival stations for the same whale. These seem to have been highly dangerous, carried out with great dash and regardless of consequences, often resulting in collisions and serious damage. The fact that the opposition station belonged to Perano's brother made the rivalry all the keener.

The catches at the Te-Awaiti station averaged 50 whales a season but in 1938 improvements were introduced into the catching methods which increased the average to 94 whales a season (Dawbin, W. H. and Falla, R. A., 1953). Only the blubber was used, sold in Australia where it took part in the manufacture of hemp rope.

Small individual whaling industries such as this survived for a long time in some parts of the world though I think very few exist today. The methods they used were independently evolved but were often similar to those used elsewhere on the other side of the globe or to those used centuries ago. While Mr. Cook was catching his Humpbacks with nets in New Zealand, very much as the Japanese did in the seventeenth century, Russian whalers were using exactly the same method in Kamchatka. Perano used an up-to-date version of methods used for bay whaling in New Zealand in the eighteenth century. Dr. Robert Clarke found a relic Sperm whaling industry in the Azores using methods similar to those of the Yankee Sperm whalers. Perhaps the strangest method of whaling was that used in a fjord near Bergen, Norway, at the beginning of this century. Here Fin and Sei whales were driven into a narrow fjord the entrance to which was closed by means of a net drawn across it so as to entrap the whale. It was then assailed with lances which had been dipped in the putrefying flesh of previously killed whales. In a few days the victim died in the fjord from gangrene—a barbarous way of killing an animal for commerce.

The Sei Whale

Antarctic whaling began at the beginning of the twentieth century with the Humpback and Right whale predominant in the catches but soon sinking to an insignificant fraction of the total, the Right whale fading out altogether in the twenties. Blue whales predominated between the wars but after World War II they declined and their dominant position was taken by Fin whales (Fig. 1a). Whaling in the south ends with the Sei whale predominant in the catches after representing only a small fraction of it for sixty years.

The small Sei whale, less than 50 feet long, was ignored by the whalers as long as the larger and better Blue or Fin whales were available, for it is on the whole a poor yielding whale and in the calculation of the 'Blue whale unit' of production one Blue whale is the equivalent of six Sei. But as the larger Rorquals declined the small Sei became more popular. It began to increase in the catches in the fifties and rose rapidly to about 20,000 in the season 1964–65. Now a decline of this, the last of the commercial whalebone whales in the Antarctic, has set in (Fig. 1a).

In 1929–31 only a few Sei were taken each year at South Georgia and they always appeared at the end of the season in February and March. When the catchers began to bring them in it was generally held that the season was over. There would be no more Blues or Fins and it was time to go home. It was at first thought that this appearance of Sei whales at the end of the season between January and May at South Georgia, with a maximum in March, might be due to the absence of Blues and Fins which had passed on their way southward by February (Matthews, L. H., 1938). But during the seasons 1963–64 and 1964–65 there were no Blue or Fin whales available at all, yet the Sei whales still appeared after Christmas and not before, so they must represent an influx from the north (Gambell, R., 1968). In those years the maximum was in January whereas it was in March during the thirties when Blues and Fins were available. It may be that the absence of these has somehow altered the migration pattern of the surviving Seis which now appear earlier at South Georgia than they formerly did.

The strange feature of the Sei whale population at South Georgia is that it includes no young whales. Pregnant cows arrive first, carrying mid-term foetuses, and later non-breeding (resting) cows arrive which have possibly just weaned their calves. Grown bulls are present also. Presumably these adult whales are part of a population to be found somewhere else among which there must be a proportion of young ones. The Sei is a warm water whale and the adults come south to the more northerly Antarctic waters when the temperature of the sea is at its highest (about $2\frac{1}{4}°$ C.), but the young evidently do not venture as far south as this. No Sei whales are ever seen at the South Shetlands or far south along the ice edge and it seems that South Georgia is their southerly limit.

The Sei has always been irregular and sporadic in its appearances, abundant in some years, scarce in others, particularly at South African stations. It was not taken at all at South Georgia before 1913–14 (Matthews, L. H., 1938) though this may have been due to the abundance of other whales, especially Humpbacks and Rights which were so much easier to take until they declined in 1913. In the northern hemisphere Sei whales made a sudden appearance off the Hebrides and Shetlands in 1909 but this may be explained by the removal of the 40-mile hunting limit which formerly existed for catchers working from those islands.

Feeding

In the Antarctic the Sei feeds exclusively on krill so that the fluctuations in its appearance have nothing to do with the abundance or scarcity of its food. Some at least of the Sei whales taken at South Georgia come from the coast of Patagonia where their food is the 'lobster krill' while in the northern hemisphere it is often the *Calanus* or 'brit'. At Saldanha Bay the much digested fragments of small crus-taceans were sometimes found in Sei whales' stomachs but so seldom that it is evident that Sei whales feed very little in tropical waters.

Migrations

The migration pattern of the Sei resembles that of other whalebone whales in the southern hemisphere, a movement into warm waters to mate and calve in the winter and a southerly movement in the summer for feeding. The movements seem to be more limited than those of the Blue, Fin or Humpback in that they do not extend so far south, but the Sei travels as far north as the Congo and Ecuador.

At South African stations the Sei catches are quite different from those at South Georgia. At Saldanha Bay, Cape Province, there are two periods of greatest abundance during the year, one in the autumn (April and May) and a second in spring (August–October), the first being the northbound migration and the second the return southbound. More than half the northbound stream is made up of young whales of both sexes, near puberty or only just past it, but the southbound stream consists of older whales. At Durban, about 600 miles farther north, the numbers of Sei whales are small in the autumn (March–May) but increase suddenly in June, climbing to a high maximum in spring (September) (Gambell, R., 1968). After this peak in September it is believed the numbers fall off rapidly at Durban but there has been no whaling there in October since 1963. During the autumn and early winter at Durban the Seis are mostly young of both sexes, older whales arriving later with a high proportion of bulls. It has been seen from the air that most of them are moving north-east along the coast in May and June while in July there does not seem to be any particular direction. In the spring (August and September) a general southward drift sets in and soon becomes a definite southerly movement (Bannister, J. L. and Gambell, R., 1965). Thus there is only a single maximum at Durban, during the spring, instead of two as at Saldanha Bay, which seems to indicate that the locality of Durban is about the northerly limit of the breeding migration along the coast of East Africa. At Angola there is also only a single maximum (Matthews, L. H., 1938) so that this is probably the northern limit on the west coast.

Breeding

The breeding cycle of the Sei resembles that of the Fin whale. Mating off the coast of Africa takes place in winter between April and August with a maximum in June. The cycle occupies two years with a twelve months' pregnancy and six months' nursing followed by a resting period before the next pregnancy. Unlike the Fin the bull Sei shows no special 'heat' period, the testis being fully active and running with sperm at all times of the year. The calf is about 15 feet long at birth and 26–30 feet at weaning during the mother's second southward voyage after mating. The cow reaches puberty at 46 feet and the bull at 45 feet, both at an age of about eighteen months. Matthews (1938) believes that growth is completed (physical maturity) at an age of ten to eleven years and the oldest whale out of 220 examined by 'Discovery' scientists was about fifteen years of age, but there is little doubt that Sei whales live much longer than that.

CHAPTER 13

High and Dry

Caa'ing the Whale

For hundreds of years the people of the Orkney and Shetland Islands and the Faroes have hunted the Blackfish or Pilot whale for its oil, which has provided these remote islands with fuel for the winter. The Blackfish is a rather small toothed whale which reaches a length of about 28 feet and is quite black all over with a round, globular forehead bulging over the upper jaw. It occurs mainly in northern waters though in the *Discovery II* we often saw Blackfish in the more northerly subantarctic region, but they may not have been identical with those of the North Atlantic.

The Blackfish is very gregarious and travels in herds numbering hundreds, leaping blithely through the waves and blowing in short, sharp puffs like a steam engine. During the summer months it comes close inshore into the bays around our northern islands, following the herring. The islanders watch for the herds of Blackfish from the shore and from the cliffs, and when they see them entering certain bays the hunters, armed with lances, put out in their boats. With them go hundreds of other boats with every available man and boy carrying kerosene drums, cans, tins, boxes, rattles or anything that will make a noise. The hunters, followed by this uproarious armada, then manœuvre themselves between the whale herd and the open sea and, with their followers making as much din as they can, they drive the whales towards the shore. When the whales are close enough to the beach a few of the leading ones are lanced by the hunters. Maddened by pain and fear the poor beasts panic and rush up the beach where they become stranded. The rest of the herd, already terrified by the noise, then obey their 'follow-my-leader' instinct and likewise rush ashore until the whole herd, maybe a hundred or so whales, is lying helpless in the shallows, unable to move and scarcely to breathe. The bays where these hunts take place all have shelving beaches of sand or small stones. In the very shallow water the weight of the whales' ribs becomes so great that the rib muscles cannot lift them, while the tail becomes so heavy that the back muscles cannot move it. The whales suffocate while the whalers carve them up with flensing knives still alive. They can make no movement to help themselves in the edge of the harbour reddened with their blood.

In the Scottish islands this kind of whale hunting used to be known as 'Caa'ing the whale', for which reason the Blackfish or Pilot whale is often called the Caa'ing whale. There has been no caa'ing the whale in the Orkneys or Shetlands for some years but it was carried out in the Faroes during World War II.

Stranding

The explanation of the Blackfish running ashore like this seems to be simple enough. The whales that are lanced are maddened by pain and fear and, one may suppose, lose their sense of direction. They cannot turn round and face the terrifying din behind them so they charge blindly ahead on to the beach whither the rest of the herd automatically follow them. This is the explanation which fits this particular case, but the fact is that whales of many species often become stranded on beaches, sometimes singly or in small groups but sometimes also as whole large herds, without being driven there at all. They apparently just charge ashore into the shallows and there, unable to move, die of suffocation. Stranger still, there have been reports that well-meaning bystanders have tried, with considerable effort and even at some risk to themselves, to lift or tow the stranded whales out into deep water, whereupon the silly creatures have promptly turned round and headed back to the shore and to their deaths.

This phenomenon of the stranding of whales has been a great puzzle for a long time, and many different explanations of it have been offered, some more and some less plausible. A kind of racial urge to commit suicide is one explanation and another is that some whales suffer from a disease of the brain causing madness. One writer, discussing a mass stranding of 200–300 False Killer whales in Cape Province, South Africa, thought that the herd must have been looking for a lost channel from the Atlantic to the Indian Ocean which their kind was accustomed to use in a bygone geological age and of which the whales had a kind of racial memory. Others have tried to associate the stranding of whales with high winds and have suggested that gales drive the whales' food, usually squid, close inshore so that the whales follow it blindly into the shallows, or that the gales stir up the sandy bottom so that the sand gets into the whales' eyes and either blinds them or drives them crazy with pain. But the fact is that whales frequently strand in flat calm weather and not even always on sandy beaches.

It is easy enough to understand that once the leaders of a herd have run ashore the rest may follow in obedience to their 'follow-my-leader' instinct, but the puzzle is—what makes the leaders run ashore in the first place?

This problem interested a distinguished Dutch scientist, Mr. W. H. Dudok van Heel, on the staff of the Netherlands Institute for Sea Research at Den Helder, Holland, and much of the information that follows is taken from his report on experiments which he carried out on the directional hearing of porpoises (Dudok van Heel, W. H., 1962).

Echo-location

Whales make sounds which they use in echo-location. The smaller whales give out whistles, howls, grunts and squeaks which can be picked up by recording instruments but are not audible to the human ear. Sperm whales are known to give out clicks and whalebone whales low frequency moans and screams. All these, too, are of a frequency above the hearing range of the human ear, but can be perceived by the sensitive auditory apparatus of whales and they are used in the same way as 'sonar' or 'asdic'.

'Sonar' is the term used by the U.S. Navy for echo-location (Sound Navigation and Ranging) while the British term 'Asdic' (Anti-submarine Detection Investigation Committee) was used earlier when anti-submarine devices first came into use during the war. Both make use of sound waves in water. Air is a poor conductor of sound waves compared with water (about a quarter as good) so that for echo-location in air radio waves are used instead of sound. 'Radar' (Radio Detection and Ranging) is the term for echo-location using radio-magnetic waves.

The principle of echo-location is simple enough. Sound, or electro-magnetic waves, are sent out as a series of pulses, in Asdic and Sonar under water and in Radar through air, by means of an instrument called a 'transducer'. When the waves hit a solid object, a cliff, a rock, a ship, an aircraft, or even a small fish, they are reflected back as an echo which is picked up by the same or another instrument.

This is the principle of the echo-sounder. The speed of sound waves in water is known so that the depth of the water at any point can be calculated from the time which elapses between the moment when the transducer emits a pulse and the moment when it or another transducer near it picks up the echo of that pulse. In modern echo-sounders this time interval is automatically converted into fathoms or metres and recorded as such by a stylus moving over a roll of graduated paper.

An Asdic set is really an echo-sounder turned horizontally. There is one instrument or transducer which both sends out the pulses and receives the echo. It protrudes (or can be protruded and withdrawn) from the ship's bottom and can be turned in any direction or rotated so as to direct the sound waves at will. They travel away from the transducer as a beam. Long waves of low frequency are sent out in a long, wide beam but give poor definition and indistinct echoes. Short waves of high frequency are sent out in a short, narrow beam and give good definition but have a limited range. The navy, using Asdic for detecting submarines, uses long, low frequency waves because the farther away the enemy is spotted the better and exact definition does not matter very much. Fishing vessels, using Asdic for fish detection, use short, high frequency waves with a short, narrow beam. Their definition is very precise and fish detectors are now so accurate that the species of fish can actually be identified from the type of echo they produce.

Whales and dolphins seem to be able to alter the frequencies of the pulses they send out. This is called 'frequency modulation' and it is believed that they use long waves of low frequency when in the open sea but modulate, or switch, to short waves of high frequency when near the shore or hunting prey (Dudok van Heel, W. H., 1965).

As might be expected hard, compact surfaces, cliffs, rocks or ships' hulls, even the bodies of fishes, give better defined and clearer echoes than soft, yielding surfaces like mud or sand, which often give very vague, ill-defined echoes or even none at all. Rough turbulent water has a very confusing effect on the echo pattern.

Records of Strandings

In 1911 the British Museum (Natural History), under the late Sir Sidney Harmer, started to keep a record of all whales stranded around the coasts of the British Isles, noting the species and numbers of the whales and the circumstances at the time. This has been continued under Dr. F. C. Fraser and the records now add up to a large number of strandings. Dudok van Heel (1962) compiled a list, which included the British Museum records, of all the whale strandings of which he could find evidence since the end of the sixteenth century with notes on the circumstances (weather and so on) and the nature of the beach. His list comprises notes of 133 strandings but it cannot represent anything like the actual number which have occurred in the time but only those of which records could be found. For instance, there are only seven from the whole of the vast coastline of the U.S.A., which has never had a system of records comparable with that of the British Museum, and probably could hardly be expected to do so with such an enormous length of coast.

According to these records the whale which appears to get stranded far more often than any others is the Blackfish or Pilot whale of which 39 instances are listed, though some of them may have actually been Killer whales or False Killers which in New Zealand, where some of the strandings occurred, are lumped together with Blackfish.

Since Blackfish travel in huge herds they often get stranded in large numbers. For instance, more than 300 ran ashore at Port Welshpool, Tasmania, in 1957.

The whale next most often stranded is the False Killer which also travels in large herds. There are 19 instances listed and several hundred ran ashore at Chatham Island, in the Pacific Ocean, in 1906. Forty-one ran ashore on Barrie Sands, near Carnoustie, Angus, in 1935. Third in frequency of stranding comes the Sperm whale with 18 instances. Thirty-seven ran ashore in Tasmania in 1911 and thirteen in New Zealand in 1958.

Only five strandings of whalebone whales are recorded, one a Piked whale at Buddon Ness, Angus, at the entrance to the Firth of Tay in 1926.

All these misfortunes happened on gently sloping beaches, the great majority of sand or mud. Only eight were on rocky shores and the rocks were either mixed with sand or very gently sloping. The evidence anyhow is enough to show that whales only run ashore on wide, shallow, gently sloping beaches, usually of sand or mud. They do not strand on steep rocky coasts though carcasses have been known to arrive there adventitiously and whales which have been harpooned have been known to get washed on to rocks.

The Asdic Beam of Whales

Experiments have been carried out designed to define the shape of the asdic beam emitted by whales (Norris *et al.*, 1961). A Bottle-nosed dolphin (common porpoise in America) was blindfolded and fragments of fish were floated into the water all round it. Although the animal could not see it snapped at and accurately seized without the slightest hesitation all the fragments immediately in front of and above its snout. Those below the level of its snout and eye it missed altogether while those above but behind the snout it missed at the first try but took at a second pass. From this it was evident that the dolphin was emitting a beam which did not extend below the horizontal plane of the snout and eyes and was directed only upwards. Its accuracy in seizing the fragments of fish was such that it must have been using a very high frequency wave and was evidently using a narrow beam because it found it necessary to make scanning movements from side to side with its head while approaching the target.

In addition to the beam being directed solely above the horizontal it is probable that the directional sense of the ear is poor in the vertical plane. We have already seen (Chapter 7) that the directional sense of the ear is due to the time interval in reception between the two sides. The wider apart the ears are the more acute the directional sense in the horizontal plane, but in the vertical plane the time interval between the two sides tends to diminish with height. Our own auditory directional sense is also poor in the vertical plane and we can pin-point a sound much more easily at ground level than above our heads. In his experiments with porpoises Dukok van Heel (1962) trained them to take fish from points at which a sound signal was given. He found that a porpoise could not perceive the direction of the sound if it were dead ahead or at less than an angle of seven degrees on either side of dead centre.

Now we can see how handicapped whales must be when approaching a sandy or muddy, gently shelving beach (Fig. 21). Their upwardly directed wave beam will give them no echo at all underneath. They will have no indication at all of the depth of the water and will probably not perceive the shelving sand or mud beneath them. Surf or wind-blown waves will make any echoes more confused. Scanning from side to side with their heads will give only confused echoes from sand or mud and, using a short high frequency beam, they will get no echo ahead and run aground believing themselves to be in safe water. Add to this the panic which spreads through the herd when the leader loses his way, so that in a very short time the whole herd has gone aground.

On occasion whales have run ashore on small sandy beaches between stretches of rock as though deliberately aiming at their doom. Dudok van Heel quotes the example of 32 Sperm whales which ran ashore in a smooth sandy cove on the rocky coast of Brittany as long ago as 1784. They must have been getting good echoes from the rocks on either side but none, or only confused, echoes from dead ahead. They ran aground, in fact, believing that they had a clear channel ahead.

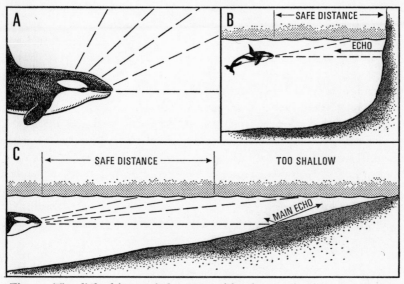

Fig. 21 The difficulties a whale meets with when navigating close inshore
(From Dudok van Heel, 1962)

Oceanic species of whale, the Blackfish, the False Killer or the Sperm, seem to be more liable to be confused by faint and ill-defined echoes than coastal ones such as the common dolphin or the common porpoise. One reason for this may be that oceanic whales tend to travel in large herds so that the great crowd of bodies must itself be often productive of false echoes. The 'follow-my-leader' instinct in a big herd is stronger than in a small school and the catastrophe all the greater when something goes wrong.

No mass, as opposed to isolated, strandings of whalebone whales have ever been recorded. The reason for this may be that, since they feed only on fish or swarms of plankton in the open ocean, they use only low frequency waves with a long, wide beam giving warning of the coast a long way off but no detail. The smaller toothed whales which feed on fish or squid close inshore use high frequency waves in a short, narrow beam and get shorter notice of approaching danger (Dudok van Heel, W. H., 1962).

Stories about bystanders helping stranded whales out to deep water only to see them turn and run ashore again are mostly suspect (Dudok van Heel, W. H., 1962). They seldom come from very reliable witnesses but there remains the possibility that a rescued whale, as soon as it finds itself back in deep water, would experience exactly the same confusion of echoes again and would be unable to get its bearings. Then the 'follow-my-leader' instinct would drive it ashore once more. In one well attested case in 1928 120 False Killer whales ran ashore on Cape Peninsula, South Africa, and several of them were rescued but drifted ashore again because they were too weak to swim, but this is not the same thing as deliberately running ashore.

Evidently, then, mass strandings of whales most probably result from navigational errors by the leaders of the herd and individual strandings of single whales or small numbers are due to the same cause. There are built-in deficiencies in the whale's echo-location apparatus which does not record below the horizontal plane of the head. Soft sandy bottoms give confused echoes and the confusion is increased if the water is rough owing to a surf or wind. Panic probably drives the main body of a herd ashore after the leaders have stranded.

CHAPTER 14

How Many Whales?

Population Dynamics

The exploitation by man of the various living populations of this planet in their natural environment, whether of fish, whales, game or any other creature, has given rise during the last ten years or so to the highly mathematical science of population dynamics by means of which the changes due to the impact of exploitation can be calculated and recorded and probable future ones predicted. Estimates can be made of the effects of future exploitation and forecasts made of the level at which it can be allowed to proceed without unduly restricting the natural growth of the population or causing a ruinous decline.

This is not the place in which to embark upon an exposition of this recondite subject, even if the author were qualified to do so which he certainly is not. In the final chapter of Dr. N. A. Mackintosh's book *The Stocks of Whales* (1965) the basic principles of the subject are set down with admirable clarity.

I shall content myself with attempting only the barest outline of what this is about. One may assume that a population of wild animals in its natural environment is in a state of balance with it. The number of young added to the population each year balances the number lost by death so that the population is static, or the number of young added each year may slightly exceed the number lost so that the population grows slowly. The number added to the population in a given time is called the 'rate of recruitment', while the number lost in the same time is called the 'rate of natural mortality'. Sometimes the balance may be upset and pushed in one or other of two directions. Something may happen to increase the rate of recruitment—a temporary excess of food, for instance, or the failure of a predatory enemy. If this happens the rate of mortality will, after a time lag, eventually go up too so as to bring about an adjustment back to the normal balance, for an excess of food or the failure of an enemy will in time produce more mouths to feed, keener competition and presently less food for all. On the other hand the balance may be pushed the other way and something may bring about an increase in the rate of mortality—a temporary food shortage, an epidemic disease or an increase in a predatory enemy—so that, again after a time lag, there will be an increase in the rate of recruitment.

When exploitation of the population begins the mortality rate is artificially increased and compensating mechanisms come into play which tend to restore the balance. There may be a lowering of the rate of mortality from natural causes, perhaps faster growth to puberty, more mating or changes in the sexual rhythm, all tending to increase the natural birth rate. This may overtake the rate of natural mortality, but not, as a rule, the rate of mortality due to man's activities, to exploitation, which is known as the 'rate of fishing or catching mortality', distinguished from the rate of natural mortality which is the death rate due to natural causes.

In wartime similar compensating mechanisms come into play among human populations. An increase in the birth rate may take place so that it exceeds the natural death rate, but not the death rate due to the war itself.

It is the aim of population dynamics to forecast the level to which fishing or catching should be adjusted in order that this surplus of the rate of recruitment over the natural death rate shall be almost but not quite absorbed by exploitation year after year, so that the population may remain stable or even slowly increase. The catch which ought to be taken each year with this end in view is called the 'sustainable yield' or 'optimum catch'. It is usually forecast between upper and lower limits, the upper one being called the 'maximum sustainable yield'.

Catch Statistics

The figures of the catches of all whaling expeditions are sent every year to the International Bureau of Whaling Statistics in Sandefjord, Norway, which records the numbers of each kind of whale taken in each of the six areas into which the Antarctic whaling grounds are divided (Chap. 9), together with details of sex, length and foetuses month by month. These are issued in an annual publication. International Whaling Statistics, and similar records are kept for the rest of the world outside the Antarctic.

These records give a picture of the catches from year to year. There are also details of the fishing capacities of all expeditions, numbers of catchers per factory with their horse-power, speed and so on.

In order to form a true picture of the impact of exploitation on the whale population certain adjustments to the catch figures must be made, for while the records may show increasing catches from year to year yet these may be due, in part at any rate, to increased fishing or catching power, such as improved catchers or new methods like the use of towing boats or tracking devices, or greater efficiency on board the factory itself, or more catchers per factory ship. Conversely smaller catches may be due to restrictions imposed by the International Whaling Commission, or to bad weather, or to catchers going out of service for repairs. A true gauge of the effect of whaling, as of fishing, on the population of whales or fish is the catch taken by each unit (man, ship, trawl, catcher or whatever is most suitable) in a given time. In whaling it is the daily catch per catcher that is used and called the 'catcher's day's work', but this is less simple than it sounds because whale catchers differ in tonnage, horse-power and speed, and these are increasing year by year. The weather, too, affects the efficiency of catchers and varies in time and locality. For these reasons it is necessary to separate days spent catching from the total time spent in the Antarctic, and in the calculation of catch per catcher's days' work all these factors are allowed for.

The catch per catcher's day's work, corrected as above, is used as an index for comparing the relative sizes of the whale population in different years or areas. The actual, as opposed to the relative, sizes of the populations ('stock sizes') can be calculated from the total catch and the rate of catching mortality, the fraction of the total which are killed each year by catching alone.

Stock Size and Sustainable Yield

In 1961 the International Whaling Commission appointed a committee of three distinguished scientists (later adding a fourth) to make a report on the condition of the whale stocks and to forecast, as far as possible, the probable effects of future whaling. The committee reported in 1963 to the fourteenth annual meeting of the Commission and made, as a result of their calculations, a number of forecasts.

With regard to Fin whales, at that time the most important Antarctic

17

species, the committee said that if whaling were to continue at the pace prevailing during the season 1962–63 the catch the following year (1963–64) would be 14,000 Fin whales. It was, in fact, 13,853. The committee also calculated that the total number of Fin whales available to be caught in the Antarctic, that is, the total catchable population or stock size, at the beginning of the season 1963–64 was about 40,000 Fin whales, having shrunk from 110,000 in 1955–56. They forecast that at the beginning of the season 1964–65 there would be 35,000–36,000 Fin whales waiting to be caught and the catch would be about 12,000. They estimated that the sustainable yield, the catch which could safely be taken without endangering the supply, was only between 4,000 and 5,000. Nevertheless, the whaling nations could not agree among themselves and caught nearly 8,000 Fin whales in that year with 20,380 Sei and 4,350 Sperm (International Whaling Statistics LX, 1968).

Meanwhile the Sei whale was rapidly gaining in importance in the Antarctic catch and more than 8,000 were caught in 1963–64 compared with about 5,500 in 1962–63. The committee estimated that in the former year there must have been about 20,000 Sei whales waiting to be caught in the Antarctic and recommended a catch of between 2,400 and 8,400, the upper and lower limits of the sustainable yield. The actual catch for 1963–64 was 8,695, slightly above the upper limit, indicating that the Sei whale population too was already on the downward path.

The great Blue whale, once the most eagerly sought and valuable of all and dominant in the catches before the war, had diminished to a position where it was declared a protected whale in 1963 in order to save it from total extinction. It was prohibited throughout the whole of the southern whaling area except for a comparatively small segment in the central south Indian Ocean which was said to be inhabited by Pygmy Blue whales.

In 1962–63 the sustainable yield of Blue whales had been estimated to be about 200. In 1963–64, the first season of prohibition, the only information available about the size of the Blue whale stock came from Norwegian factories and catchers who reported the numbers they had seen. Only eight were sighted during that season by 30 catchers operating from four factory ships, so low had the Blue whale population fallen. The committee thought that the sustainable yield of Blue whales could not be more than a few individuals, probably much fewer than 70 whales.

It is hoped that in due time, after a period of protection, the Blue whale population may recover to a point where a sustainable yield of 6,000 whales a year could be taken season after season. At a guess this might mean a population of 100,000 whales. Mackintosh (1965) thinks it may take the present remnant fifty years to recover to that level.

The Humpback whale was judged to be in grave danger of extinction during the 1962–63 season and, like the Blue, was declared to be a protected whale. The population in the areas IV and V, south of Australia and New Zealand, had shrunk to about 1,600 whales from 20,000 before the war (Mackintosh, N. A., 1965) and in 1962–63 the committee calculated the sustainable yield to be less than 100 whales.

Pre-war Stock Sizes and Species Ratios

The scientific committee of the International Whaling Commission had calculated the total populations of whalebone whales for each year back to the mid-fifties. In 1955–56 Fin whales numbered about 110,000. Attempts to estimate the pre-war populations have been made by a method entirely different from calculations involving catch per unit of effort used by the committee. Some idea of the sizes of pre-war whale populations is useful in judging the effects upon the whale stocks of exploitation continued over a long series of years.

The method used involved the actual counting of whales sighted at sea. The *Discovery II* was almost continuously in the Antarctic for ten years from 1929 to 1939. Her cruises covered the entire whaling area and totalled hundreds of thousands of miles. For six years, from 1933 to 1939, it was the practice, when the ship was on passage, to station a seaman in the masthead barrel look-out during daylight hours in order to keep a watch for spouting whales. Naturally he was only there if the weather was suitable and clear enough. When he sighted a whale or whales, or their spouts, he would shout down to the bridge and draw the attention of the Officer of the Watch who would then try to identify the whales from the spouts, estimate the number of them and, if possible, their direction of travel. At the end of his watch he would send down to the scientists in the laboratory a chit for each of the sightings giving date, time and position as well as the details above. All these were recorded in a special 'whale log'.

From these records attempts have been made to obtain an estimate of the ratio of the three species, Blue, Fin and Humpback, to one another (Mackintosh, N. A., 1942) and of the total populations (stock sizes) of each of the three species in the Antarctic month by month (Mackintosh, N. A. and Brown, S. G., 1956).

Only those observations from the ship were used in which the identification of the whales was absolutely certain. Identifying whales at sea is not at all easy but as the years went on the ship's officers and crew, especially those who had made more than one trip to the south in her, became practised at whale spotting so that there were more certain identifications during the 1937-39 cruise than during the two previous ones (1933-35 and 1935-37).

Of the 1,046 sightings kept for the record 735 or 70 per cent were 'certain' or 'almost certain' and 311 or 30 per cent were 'probable'. From these the ratios of the three species sighted during the three two-year cruises were—Blue 16·5 per cent, Fin 77·1 per cent and Humpback 6·4 per cent.

Now the question remains, to what extent do these percentages represent the proportions in which these three kinds of whalebone whales actually existed in Antarctic waters?

There are two independent means of checking the ratios. Firstly, between the years 1932 and 1938 the research ship *William Scoresby* made cruises along the ice edge for the sole purpose of marking whales, a job for which she had been specially designed. In addition 'Discovery' scientists made whale marking cruises around South Georgia in hired whale catchers. The actual shooting at the whales, both in the *William Scoresby* and in the hired catchers, was done by scientists who were experienced whale observers. Since they were within fifty yards of the whales they were firing at they could hardly fail to identify them accurately.

Mackintosh (1942) accordingly used the numbers of the three species either marked or fired at during these whale marking cruises as a check on the observations from *Discovery II*.

There were 5,131 records of whales either marked or fired at. The species proportions were—Blue 13 per cent, Fin 76·3 per cent and Humpback 10·7 per cent. The agreement with the *Discovery II* sightings is thus pretty good, especially with regard to Blue and Fin whales.

There was also a second way of checking the species ratio. This was to lump together the total catches for a number of Antarctic summer seasons and a number of southern winter seasons and see how the proportions of the three species emerge from the process. The ratios for five summer and five winter seasons from 1933 to

1938 were—Blue 44 per cent, Fin 41 per cent and Humpback 14 per cent.

These figures show less agreement with the sightings from *Discovery II* but this check is less satisfctory than the first. In the first place the catches were biased in those days by the gunners' preference for Blue whales because they were so much more valuable than Fins.

The ratios held good only during the thirties but after the war they underwent sweeping changes. The proportions of Blues and Humpbacks were progressively reduced, reaching vanishing point by the early sixties. There was a great increase in the proportion of Fin whales, then latterly a decline of Fins and an increase in the proportions of Sei and Sperm. Nevertheless the figures for the thirties form a useful point from which to assess subsequent changes since they really represent the numbers and ratios of the Antarctic population at the outset of pelagic whaling. They present a picture of the whale population of the Antarctic almost in a state of nature, before exploitation had begun to make a serious impact.

In order to use the same sighting observations from *Discovery II* in forming a numerical estimate of the total population (stock size) of each of the three species the ship's track was taken to represent a sample viewing strip of Antarctic sea. Only those parts of the track were used where the ship's course was straight, with no zig-zags or turns, and they formed a series of viewing strips about twenty miles wide, taking ten miles as the limit of visibility for a man in the masthead look-out. All tracks made in darkness or poor visibility were left out of account. It was assumed, after certain corrections had been made, that the numbers of whales sighted within the strips, which in all totalled a distance of 47,000 miles, would bear to the total whale population the same proportion as did the area of the viewing strips to the total area of the ice-free zone of Antarctic sea.

Taken month by month the numbers of whales sighted within the viewing strips increased steadily from very low numbers in the spring to a pronounced maximum in February, and then fell away again to low numbers in the autumn. This, indeed, was what was to be expected from all the other existing evidence about the movements of Antarctic whales. Mackintosh and Brown (1956) believed that their viewing strip samples of the total population, though certainly very small, were nevertheless valid ones. They showed that February was the month during which the whole southern whalebone whale population, with possibly a few exceptions, was assembled in Antarctic waters. The whales seen in the viewing strip twenty miles wide during February, therefore, could be taken as a representative sample of the entire Antarctic population.

In these estimates the species were not distinguished from one another but were just lumped together as 'whales'. On this basis the total southern population of whalebone whales was estimated to lie between 142,500 and 340,000 during the late thirties. A mean between these two figures (241,000) gives a margin of 100,000 in either direction. If we apply to the upper estimate (342,000) the percentages of the three main species we find the population made up of 250,000 Fin whales, roughly 50,000 Blues and 34,000 Humpbacks.

These figures have been fairly widely criticized (Symons, H. W., 1956 and Slijper, E. J., 1962) on the grounds that the samples represented by the viewing strips are too small to be truly representative of the whole of the Antarctic, and also that it is not known exactly how carefully the observations were taken.

Although open to criticism these estimates do perhaps give an idea of the order of magnitude of the Antarctic population of whalebone whales in the late thirties. It may have been something in the order of 40,000 to 50,000 Blue whales, 200,000 to 250,000 Fins and about 20,000 Humpbacks (south of Australia and New Zealand only). The scientific committee of the International Whaling Commission calculated that in the early fifties there remained rather less than 10,000 Blue whales, about 40,000 Fins and, in the seas south of Australia and New Zealand, only about 1,600 Humpbacks.

How Near Extinction?

Very little is known about the utmost limits to which populations can be reduced without actual extermination. When the survival rate of a species is reduced below a certain level recovery becomes impossible and a kind of momentum carries the race out of existence, along with the giant reptiles, the mammoth and the dodo. It is not known what this lowest survival rate is but it probably differs widely among species and might depend on the ability of the animal to defend itself, on the dominance or presence of natural enemies or on resistance to disease. The nature of the breeding cycle, the birth rate and the fertility are also important factors.

On the whole whales seem to be resistant to disease and to be healthy animals. One sees no sign of epidemic disease, which cannot be said of many fish, and their parasites do not seem to get out of control. The only diseases one notices rather frequently on the plan are bone tumours, ankylosis (coalescence) of vertebrae and old healed fractures. Perhaps anything more serious would kill the whales off and not be visible anyhow. Sometimes we found, as have many others, curious spherical or oval limy concretions within the muscle tissue, occasionally in large numbers and as big as cricket balls. They are called 'husks' by the whalers but their cause is quite unknown. It has been suggested that they may be the resting or encysted stage of some internal parasite, but if so the parasite itself has never been found and the 'husks' seem to have no effect on the whale.

The slow birth rate of whalebone whales—one, rarely two, young every two years—certainly does not make for quick recovery from over exploitation. Two animals of opposite sex would obviously be the smallest population which could hope to survive but, where whales are concerned, the enormous expense of modern whaling expeditions tends to act in their favour since whaling is likely to cease to be a paying proposition before the whale population has been reduced to near extinction. Yet the more profitable species, like the Blue, might disappear while a skeleton industry struggled on, keeping itself going on the less profitable species. Blues and Humpbacks could have been exterminated while the industry subsisted on Fins and then, having finished these off, struggled on to exterminate the Sei. After that there would be only the Sperm whale left and it might be on these that the industry would finally peter out, as did the American Sperm whaling in the nineteenth century.

Every species of animal and plant now living will one day become extinct, some sooner, some later, even man himself. But there are reasons for thinking that the great whales, even if mankind left them alone or brought them back from the edge of doom, would be among the earliest to go, reckoning time by geological standards, in millions of years.

In the first place their gigantic size may be taken as one of the signs of approaching departure. During the history of evolution many creatures have reached vast size shortly before quitting the stage. The giant reptiles of the Tertiary epoch are the best known example and the mammoths are another. The latter disappeared comparatively recently, only about a million years ago. Gigantic sharks, probably over a hundred feet long, inhabited the deep oceans of the Cretaceous period but disappeared about a hundred million years ago. All these were the descendants of much smaller and more efficient forebears. The whalebone whales were at their prime in the Upper Eocene period some 30 to 40 million years ago and were then much smaller and more compact, about the same size as our modern highly efficient porpoises and dolphins.

Another weakness of the whalebone whales is their high degree of specialization, which is a dangerous condition for any race. Every year they are obliged to make a long, exhausting migration from what one must assume is their ancestral home in tropical waters to feeding grounds thousands of miles away in polar seas. They do this in order to feed for six months exclusively on a single species of abundant shrimp-like crustacean, the krill. For this purpose they have developed an exceedingly specialized filter method of feeding which is now so minutely adjusted to their restricted diet that it could not be used for feeding on anything else. But the krill is also fed upon by seals, penguins, many other birds, dolphins, fish and squids. Competition for it is therefore intense but the competitors, except the whale, have unspecialized methods of feeding which would enable them to survive on other diets. What would happen if by some accident of nature, by no means inconceivable, the krill should become scarce? This might come about owing to an alteration of polar climate causing a change of sea temperature or some other oceanic change. This, again, is by no means inconceivable for our northern cod fishery owes its existence to a change, fortunately favourable, in Arctic waters which took place in 1931. There might, too, be a sudden increase in one or more of the whales' krill-feeding competitors. What, then, would happen to the whalebone whales which, alone among the krill feeders, are unable to change to any other diet?

Another disadvantage which the whalebone whales suffer from is that they have very little defence against their natural enemy the Killer whale. In the far south the necessity to breathe air is also a disadvantage among ice, especially for Piked whales.

No such dangers and disadvantages seem to threaten the smaller toothed whales, porpoises and dolphins, which are small and compact. They feed on squid and fish, the supply of which is not likely to fail, unless man's activities cause a shortage, and they are unspecialized in their feeding habits. Sperm whales, however, besides their great and ill-omened bulk, have the disadvantage of being specialized in their feeding apparatus for they have no teeth in the upper jaw and the lower ones seem to be of little use for any purpose except seizing.

In the past man has exterminated his fellow creatures largely through thoughtlessness or ignorance. The dodo was exterminated in Mauritius by the dogs thoughtlessly introduced by the first settlers. The Greenland Right whale was brought to the verge of extinction because it never occurred to anyone that it did not exist in inexhaustible numbers. But if the great whales of the Antarctic disappear they will surely be the first victims of man's sheer greed and rapacity, wiped out by him in the full knowledge of what was happening, with all the results of modern scientific research on the table and the remedies at hand, waiting only for a few signatures. This being the case there seems no reason why the big game animals of Africa, the fisheries of the continental shelf, the giant tortoise of Aldabra and the Atlantic salmon should not all go the same way, so that our planet will become a desert before our eyes while we are trying to reach the others.

Appendix

Scientific Names

Order: Cetacea
Sub-order: Mystacoceti—Whalebone whales
Fam: Balaenopteridae—Rorquals

Blue whale, Sibbald's Rorqual	*Balaenoptera musculus*
Pygmy Blue whale	*Balaenoptera musculus brevicauda*
Fin whale, Finback, Common Rorqual	*Balaenoptera physalus*
Sei whale, Rudolphi's Rorqual	*Balaenoptera borealis*
Piked whale, Lesser Rorqual, Minke whale	*Balaenoptera acutorostrata*
Bryde's whale	*Balaenoptera brydei*
Humpback whale	*Megaptera novaeangliae*

Fam: Balaenidae—Right whales

Greenland Right whale, Bowhead	*Balaena mysticetus*
Biscay Right whale, Black Right whale, Southern Right whale	*Balaena glacialis*
Pygmy Right whale	*Neobalaena marginata*

Fam: Eschrichtiidae—Grey whales

California Grey whale	*Eschrichtius glaucus*

Sub-order: Odontoceti—Toothed whales
Fam: Physeteridae—Sperm whales

Sperm whale, Cachalot	*Physeter catodon*
Pygmy Sperm whale	*Kogia breviceps*

Fam: Ziphiidae—Bottle-nosed or Beaked whales

Bottle-nosed whale	*Hyperoodon rostratus planifrons*

Fam: Delphinidae—Dolphins and Porpoises
Sub-fam: Delphinapterinae—Neck vertebrae not fused

Narwhal	*Monodon monoceros*
Beluga, White whale	*Delphinapterus leucas*

Sub-fam: Delphininae—At least two neck vertebrae fused

Killer whale, Grampus	*Orcinus orca*
False Killer whale	*Pseudorca crassidens*
Pilot whale, Blackfish, Caa'ing whale	*Globicephala melaena*
Common Dolphin	*Delphinus delphis*
Commerson's Dolphin	*Lagenorhynchus commersoni*
Bottle-nosed Dolphin, Common porpoise (U.S.A.)	*Tursiops truncatus*
Common Porpoise (U.K.)	*Phocaena phocaena*

List of References

Ash, C. E., 1955. *Norsk Hvalfangsttid.*, 44 Årg. (1): 20–26.

Bannister, J. L. and Gambell, R., 1965. *Norsk Hvalfangsttid.*, 54 Årg. (3): 45–60.

Bargmann, H., 1937. *Discovery Reports*, 14: 325–50.

—, 1945. *Discovery Reports*, 23: 103–76.

Beale, T., 1839. *The Natural History of the Sperm Whale*, Van Voorst, London.

Bennett, F. D., 1840. *Narrative of a Whaling Voyage round the Globe from 1833–36*, Bentley, London.

Brandt, K., 1940. *Fats and Oil Studies, No. 7*, Food and Research Inst., Stanford Univ., Calif., U.S.A.

Brown, S. G., 1957. *Marine Observer*, 27: 157–65.

—, 1962. *Discovery Reports*, 33: 1–54.

Budker, P., 1958. *Whales and Whaling*, Harrap, London.

Bullen, F., 1898. *The Cruise of the Cachalot*, Reprinted 1961, John Murray, London.

Caldwell, David K., Melba C. Caldwell and Dale W. Rice, 1965. *Whales, Porpoises and Dolphins, No. 30*, Univ. Calif. Press: 677–717.

Chittleborough, K. G., 1953. *Aust. Journ. Mar. Freshwat. Res.*, 4 (2): 219–226.

—, 1960. *Norsk Hvalfantsttid.*, 49 Årg. (3): 120–4.

Clarke, R., 1954. *Discovery Reports*, 26: 281–354.

—, 1955. *Norsk Hvalfangsttid.*, 44 Årg. (10): 589–93.

—, 1956. *Discovery Reports*, 28: 237–98.

Comber, L. C., 1968. *Biology in the Modern World*, Thames and Hudson, London.

Dana, R. H., 1834. *Two Years Before the Mast*, Nelson, London.

Dawbin, W. H., 1960. *Norsk Hvalfangsttid.*, 49 Årg. (2): 61–75, and (9): 401–9.

—, 1965. *Whales, Porpoises and Dolphins, No. 9*, Univ. Calif. Press: 145–170.

Dawbin, W. H. and R. A. Falla, 1953. *Proc. 7th Pacific Sci. Congr.*, 4: 373–82.

Dudok, van Heel, 1962. *Netherlands Journ. Sea Res.*, 1 (4): 407–507.

— 1965. *Whales, Porpoises and Dolphins, No. 27*, Univ Calif. Press: 597–606.

Foxton, P., 1956. *Discovery Reports*, 28: 191–236.

Fraser, F. C., 1936. *Discovery Reports*, 14: 1–192.

—, 1937. J. R. Norman and F. C. Fraser; *Giant Fishes, Whales and Dolphins*, Putnam, London (New Ed. 1948).

Fraser, F. C. and P. E. Purves, 1954. *Bull. Brit. Mus. (Nat. Hist.), Zoology 2* (5): 101–113.

—, 1960. *Bull. Brit. Mus. (Nat. Hist.), Zoology 7* (1): 1–140.

—, 1955. *Nature, London*, 176: 1221–2.

Gambell, R., 1967. *Symposia of the Zool. Soc., London*, No. 19.

Gambell, R. and Grzegorzewska, C., 1967. *Norsk Hvalfangsttid.*, 56 Årg. 117–121.

General H.Q. Far East Command, 1948. *Norsk Hvalfangsttid.*, 37 Årg. (12): 500–504.

Gunther, E. R., 1949. *Discovery Reports*, 25: 113–42.

de Haan, Reysenbach, 1957. *Hearing in Whales*, Acta Oto-Laryng. Suppl. 134.

Hardy, A. C., 1956. *The Open Sea*, Collins, London.

—, 1967. *Great Waters*, Collins, London.

Harmer, S. F., 1923. *Proc. Zool. Soc.*, 55: 1085–9.

—, 1928. *History of Whaling*, Proc. Linn Soc., London, Session 140: 51–95.

—, 1931. *Southern Whaling*, Proc. Linn. Soc., London, Session 142: 85–163.

Hart, T. J., 1935. *Discovery Reports*, 10: 247–82.

Hawes, C. Boardman, 1924. *Whaling*, Heinemann, London.

Hinton, M. A. C., 1925. *Report on the Papers Left by the late Major Barrett-Hamilton*, Crown Agents, London: 57–209.

Hunter, John, 1787. *Phil. Trans. Roy. Soc.*, London, 77: p. 371.

International Whaling Commission, 1965. *15th Report of the Commission Appendix III and V*, London.

—, 1969. *19th Report of the Commission*, London.

International Whaling Statistics, 1932, 3, Oslo.

—, 1960, Oslo.

Kramer, M. O., 1960. *New Scientist*, 7 (181), 1118–20.

Kükenthal, W., 1908. *Anat. Anz., Bd. 33*, Berlin.

Lahille, F., 1908. *Anal. Mus. Nacion.*, Ser. 3 (9), Buenos Aires.

Laurie, A. H., 1933. *Discovery Reports*, 7: 363–406.

Lund, J., 1950. *Norsk Hvalfangsttid.*, 39 Årg. (2): 53–60, and (7): 298–305.

—, 1951. *Norsk Hvalfangsttid.*, 40 Årg. (8): 384–6.

Mackintosh, N. A., 1937. *Discovery Reports*, 16: 365–412.

—, 1942. *Discovery Reports*, 22: 197–300.

—, 1965. *The Stocks of Whales*, Fishing News (Books), London.

Mackintosh, N. A., and S. G. Brown, 1956. *Norsk Hvalfangsttid.*, 45 Årg. (9): 469–80.

Mackintosh, N. A. and J. F. G. Wheeler, 1929. *Discovery Reports*, 1: 257–540.

Marr, J. W. S., 1962. *Discovery Reports*, 32: 33–484.

Matthews, L. H., 1931. *South Georgia*, John Wright, Bristol.

—, 1937. *Discovery Reports*, 17: 7–92.

—, 1938. *Discovery Reports*, 1: 93–163 and 183–290.

Melville, Herman, 1951. *Moby Dick or The White Whale*, Dent (Everyman Edn. 1907), London.

Moulton, J. M., 1960. *Biol. Bull.*, 119, Wood's Hole, Mass., U.S.A.

Nishiwaki, M. and K. Hayashi, 1950. *Sci. Rep. Whales. Res. Inst., Tokyo*, 3: 132–90.

Norris, K. S., J. H. Prescott, P. V. Asa-Dorian and P. Perkins, 1961. *Biol. Bull.*, 120 (2), Wood's Hole, Mass, U.S.A.

Ohsumi, S., 1962. *Norsk Hvalfangsttid.*, 41 Årg. (5): 192–8.

—, 1964. *Sci. Rep. Whales Res. Inst., Tokyo*, 18, 49–58.

Olsen, Ø, 1913. *Proc. Zool. Soc.*, 1913, 1073–1090.

Ommanney, F. D., 1933. *Discovery Reports*, 7: 239–52.

Perkins, Paul J., Marie P. Fish and William H. Mowbray, 1966. *Norsk Hvalfangsttid.*, 55 Årg. (10), 199–200.

Pike, G. C., 1951. *Journ. Fish. Res. Board of Canada* (8), p. 275.

Purves, P. E., 1955. *Discovery Reports*, 27: 293–302.

—, 1963. *Nature, London*, 197: 334–7.

Purves, P. E. and M. D. Mountford, 1959. *Bull. Brit. Mus. (Nat. Hist.)*, 5 (6): 123–61.

Racovitza, E. G., 1903. *Cetacés*, Resultats du Voyage S.Y. *Belgica* en 1896–9: 1–142.

Rayner, G. W., 1940. *Discovery Reports*, 19: 245–84.

Rice, Dale W., 1961. *Norsk Hvalfangsttid.*, 50 Årg. (6): 219–25.

—, 1963. *Norsk Hvalfangsttid.*, 52 Årg. (7): 182–87.

Risting, Sigurd, 1928. *Rapp. Cons. Internat. Explor. Mer*, 50: 1–122.

Roe, H. S. J., 1967. *Discovery Reports*, 35: 1–30.

Ruud, J. T., 1940. *Hvalråd. Skr.*, 23: 1–24.

—, 1945. *Hvalråd. Skr.*, 29: 1–69.

Sanderson, I., 1958. *Follow the Whale*, Cassell, London.

Scammon, C. M., 1874. *The Marine Mammals of the North Western Coast of North America*, San Francisco and New York.

Scholander, P. F., 1940. *Hvalråd. Skr.*, 22: 1–131.

Scoresby, William, Jnr., 1820. *An Account of the Arctic Regions*, Edinburgh.

Shaw, Evelyn, 1960. *Physiol. Zool.*, 33 (2).

Slijper, E. J., 1936. *Die Cetaceen*, Nijhoff, The Hague.

—, 1962. *Whales*, Hutchinson, London.

Sweeny, H., 1963. *Oils and Fats from Far Away*, The Times (Suppl. on Margarine Industry, May 22nd, 1963).

Symons, H. W., 1956. *Norsk Hvalfangsttid.*, 45 Årg. (11): 611–13.

Thompson, D'Arcy W., 1942. *On Growth and Form*, C.U.P., London.

Townsend, C. W., 1935. *Zoologica*, New York. 19 (1): 1–50.

True, F. W., 1904. *Smithsonian Contr. Knowl.*, 33 (1414): 1–332.

Wheeler, J. F. G., 1930. *Discovery Reports*, 2: 403–34.

Zemsky, V. A. and V. A. Boronin, 1964. *Norsk Hvalfangsttid.*, 53 Årg. (11): 306–11.

Zenkovic, B. A., 1962. *Norsk Hvalfangsttid.*, 51 Årg. (5): 198–200.

Index

Abdomen, of Rorquals, on the plan, 112-114.

Acids, saturated and unsaturated, 55; fatty, 56.

Aerial observations, Humpback whales, 235-6; Sperm whales, 224; Sei whale, 245.

Age, of whalebone whales, Blue whales at puberty, 122; Fin whales at puberty, 163; at physical maturity, 122, 163, 173; Humpback whales at puberty and physical maturity, 238; Sei whales at puberty and physical maturity, 246; Sperm whales at puberty and physical maturity, 231; whalebone whales, individuals of approx. known age, 169, 173; clues to age of whalebone whales, 162-5, 171-3; scars in ovaries, 163; baleen, 163-4; ear plug, 164-5; results of whale marking, 171-3; Sperm whales, sections of teeth, 217.

Albatross, Wandering, 180, 183, 199; Sooty, 183.

Albino whales, 217.

Alcohol, consumption among whalers, 174-175; aboard factory ship, 175.

Ambergris, 65-8; physical properties, 66.

Ancestors, of Cetacea, 28-30.

Ancients, beliefs about whales, 23, 52.

Angola, W. Africa, Sei whales at, 246.

Antarctic, British Territories, 9, 13.
    South American Sector, 13.
    Whaling in, 11-22; Rorquals in, 34-42; Humpback whales in, 40-42, 232, 233-238; Sperm whales in, 46, 217; Sei whales in, 38, 244-6.
    Whaling areas, 187.
    Bottom Current, 203.
    Circle, 182.
    Convergence, 180-182.
    Region, northern boundary of, 182; entering, 182.

Antarctic, fl.f., 9, 15; whaling ship (Swedish Antarctic Exped.), 98.

Architeuthis sp., giant squid, 229.

Arctic Regions, 30; Rorquals in, 35, 42; Greenland Right whales in, 31-2; Whaling in (Dutch and English), 70-9; Whaling in (Norwegian), 96-7.

Asdic, for tracking whales, 19; definition of, 249; beam, used by whales for echolocation, 249-250, 252-4.

Asymmetry, Sperm whale's skull, 220-1; of organs in Mammals, 221; theories of origin, 221.

Auditory apparatus, in mammals generally, 151-2; in bats, 150-1; in man, 151; in whales, 151-5.

'Aunts', Sperm whales, 230; Humpback whales, 236; other mammals, 231.

Australia, 'Bay' whaling, 79-80; Humpback whales and whaling, 233-6; Western, 233.

Azores, Sperm whaling at, 222, 243; Sperm whales at, 225, 229, 230; squids, 229.

Backbone, 132; physical maturity, 131-2.

Back fin, as stabilizer, 25; of Rorquals, 35-41.

Balaenidae, fam., 31; descriptions, 31-4.

Balaenopteridae, fam., 31, 34; descriptions, 34-42.

Baleen, feeding, 30-31; plates, in various species, 31, 32, 33, 36, 38, 39, 40-41, 43, 108-110; disposal of, 109-110; commercial uses, 61-2; as a clue to age, 163-4.

Baleen (whalebone) whales, 30, 31, 31-44.

Barrel/s, unit of measurement of whale oil, 57.

Basques, whaling, 70-73; nos. of whales taken, 73; flensers in foreign ships, 73, 75, 78.

Bay of Whales, *Discovery II* at, 39; Piked whales at, 39.

'Bay' whaling, 79-80.

Beaked whales, fam., 31, description, 47.

Beluga, see White whale.

'Bends', the, see Caisson sickness.

Bergen, Norway, method of whaling near, 243.

Biological work, 10, 175; at whaling station, 100-132; on board factory ship, 189-192.

Birth/s, frequency of, 122; of Rorquals, 129; season of, Blue and Fin whales, 128; Humpback whales, 238; Sei whales, 246; Sperm whales, 230.

Biscay Right whale, fam., 31; description, 33; recognition at sea, 140; swimming speed, 142.
    Basque whaling based on, 70-73; disappearance of, 32, 73; hunted by American Indians, 80-81; off New England, 82; early Antarctic whaling, 236; off New Zealand, 242.

Blackfish, see Pilot whale.

Black Right whale, see Biscay Right whale.

Blood, quantity of, 110; circulation and distribution, 149-50; transport in whale's body, 162.

Blowhole/s, 28; Sperm whale, 45, 220, 225.

Blubber, insulating layer, 24; oil from, 56; stripping in American whaling ships, 91; at South Georgia, 105-7; blubber boys, 107, 191.

Blue whale/s, fam., 31, 134; description, 35–6; recognition at sea, 140; swimming speed, 142; diving, 146–7; baleen, 36; testis, 113; diatom film on, 117–18; ovum, 122; spermatozoa, 130; spout, 139; in northern hemisphere, 158; greatest length measurements, 158; weight of body, 159–60.

Migrations, 169–71; nos. marked, 168–9; relation to ice edge, 36, 184; greatest concentration in Antarctic waters, 187; Proportion in Antarctic catches, 11, 19; proportion at South Georgia, 11; Antarctic catches, 16; South Georgia catches, 19.

Food in northern hemisphere, 198; food in southern hemisphere, 119.

Declared protected, 258; species ratio, 259–61; forecasts of catches and sustainable yield, 258; est. Antarctic population (1930's), 262; (1950's), 262; Pygmy Blue whale, 36.

Unit, 18, 57, 243.

Boilers, extraction of oil in, 56; arrangement of on station, 102; Kvaerner, 56; steam cleaning of, 193; position in factory ship, 176.

Bottle-nosed dolphin/s, 51; swimming on their sides, 37; birth, 128–9; echolocation, 157, 252; 'aunts', 230.

Bouvet Island, Fin whales marked at, 171; ice-edge, 185.

Breaching, of Humpback whales, 42; of Sperm whales, 227.

Breathing, 28, 147; panting, 147.

Breeding, Rorquals, 122 et seq.; Sperm whales, 230; Humpback whales, 237–8; Sei whales, 246.

Brit, food of Greenland Right whales, 33; of Sei whales, 198, 245.

British Antarctic Territories, 9, 13.

Arctic whaling, 73–9.

Government, 16; duty on foreign oil (1788), 83.

Museum (N.H.), research on whale's ear, 151; foetus measurements at, 129; See also Natural History Museum, South Kensington.

Sperm whaling, 84.

Whalers, disappearance from Antarctic, 19–22.

Bronchii, of Rorquals, 111.

Bryde's whale, fam., 31; description, 40.

Bull/s, Blue and Fin whales, length, 158–9; Sperm whales, length, 46, 216; lone (Sperm whales), 216, 222–3; Humpback whales, 235–6, 241.

Bulla, tympanic, 110, 154.

Bullen, Frank, 84, 95, 223.

Caa'ing the whale, 50, 248.

Cachalot/s, see Sperm whale/s.

Caisson sickness, the 'Bends', 149.

18

Calanus, Copepod food of Greenland Right whales, 33, 198–9.

Calf/ves, of Blue and Fin whales, size and weight, 126; length at birth and weaning, tongue, mother's devotion, 126–9; of Sperm whales, 230–233; of Humpback whales, 236, 238; of Sei whales, 246.

Carcass/es, use of, 13, 15 et seq, 56; of Rorqual on plan, 104–14; of Rorquals, sinking, 94–6; flagging and pumping, 96; towing, 96.

'Case', the, Sperm whales, 60, 91, 218.

Catch/es, Antarctic, 11, 16; South Georgia, 11, 12; Deception Island, 12; Pelagic whaling, 99; Blue and Fin whales, 16, 19, 258; Humpback whales, Antarctic, 237, 239–41; Sei whales, 243–4, 258; Sperm whales, 215; of Basque whalers, 73; Greenland Right whales, 77; of Dutch and English Arctic whalers, 77; of American Sperm whalers, 84–5; Humpback whales off N.Z., 239–41; of fl.f. *Salvestria*, 1939–40, 196; early Antarctic whaling, 236; forecasts of, 258–9; per unit of effort (catcher's day's work), 257; statistics, 256.

Cerumen, ear wax, 153.

Cetacea, as mammals, 23–7; Order, 27–8; relationships, 27; Sub-orders, Families, Sub-families, 31.

Chase, of whale, 87–91, 136–146.

Chief Engineer, of *Salvestria*, 178–9; of whale catcher, 138.

Circulation of Antarctic surface water, 185; vertical, in the Antarctic, 203.

Clarke, Dr. Robert, 67, 90, 222, 225, 228, 230, 231.

'Clumsy cleat', 87.

Cold Deep or Antarctic Bottom current, 203, 208–9. See also Current/s.

Collecting boats, 18, 146.

Common dolphin/s, 51.

Compania Argentina de Pesca, 98, 100.

Concretions, resembling ambergris in Blue whale, 67–8; in muscle tissue, 263.

Cook, H. F. 238–9.

Cook Strait, N.Z., Right, whales in, 241; whaling in, 241–3; Humpback whales in, 241.

Copulation, 124–5; of Humpback whales, 238; of krill, 206.

Corpus luteum, 125; of pregnancy, 125.

Cow/s, Blue and Fin whales, length, 158–9; Blue and Fin whales, breeding, parturition, nursing etc., 122 et seq.; Sperm whales, 216, 222, 223, 224, 230; Humpback whales, 235–6, 237–8; Sei whales, 246.

Cross River dolphins, 54.

Current/s, Antarctic Bottom or Cold Deep, 203, 208–9; krill eggs in, 208; krill larvae in, 208; more research needed in, 209; plankton in, 205.

Current /s (*cont.*)
Warm Deep, 203; krill larvae in, 208; nets in, 208.
Weddell Sea, 185, 203; krill in, 208–9; krill larvae in, 208.

Death struggle, Sperm whale, 90; Fin whale, 144.
Deception Island, 12, 98.
Delphinapterinae, Sub-fam., 31, 53; descriptions, 53–4.
Delphinidae, fam., 31, 48; descriptions, 48–54.
Delphininae, sub-fam., 31, 53; descriptions, 48–53.
Dentine, in Sperm whales, 45; in Narwhal's tusk, 53.
Dependencies, Falkland Islands, see Falkland Islands, Dependencies of.
Dermis, 26–7.
Derwent River Inlet, Tasmania, Right whales at, 80.
Development ascent, of krill larvae, 208.
Diaphragm, 23; of whales, 111; during dive, 149.
Diatom film, on Blue and Fin whales, 117–18.
Diatom/s, 118, 182–3.
Discovery, barque, 9, 10, 85; Henry Hudson, 73.
'Discovery' Committee, 9, 14, 166, 175, 189.
'Discovery' Investigations, 14, 17, 68, 69, 99, 199.
Discovery II, Royal Research Ship, 9–11, 34, 39, 101, 168, 201, 209, 215, 259–62.
'Discovery' Staff, 17, 167.
Disc/s, intervertebral, 131–2, 217.
Disease/s, among whales, 262–3.
Dive, diving, of Rorquals, 146–150; depth reached, 147; duration, 146; of seals, 147; of Sperm whales, 225–6.
Dolphin/s, fam., 31, 48; description, 51–2; in Greek legends, 52; noises made by, 155–7; swimming speed, 26; swimming on their sides, 37; in tanks, 26; fresh water, 54; vegetarian, 31, 54.
Dolphin fish, Dorado, 48.
Drag, of motion through liquid, 26.
Drift, East Wind, 185; krill in, 205, 207–9. West Wind, 185.
Durban, Natal, 211–15; whaling stations at, 212–15; catch of whales at, 215; Sperm whales at, 215–16; work on plan, 213–14; Blue and Fin whales at, 215; Humpback whales at, 215; Sei whales at, 245.

Ear, 151–5; external aperture, 151; of mammals, 152; drum, 152; human (hearing), 152; of whalebone and toothed whales, 153; wax plug, 153–4; as a clue to age, 164–5, 172–3; locating krill, 202–3.

Echo-location, in bats, 156; in whales, 156–157, 249, 252–4; in Sperm whales, 229, 249; in Bottle-nosed dolphin, 252; errors in, 252–4.
Eel, fresh water, larvae of, 206–7.
Egg/s, see also Ovum/ova; of Rorqual, 122; shedding of, whales and mammals generally, 123–5; scars in ovary, 125, 163; of krill, 206, 207–8; of fish, 208.
Elephant Island, 194–5.
Engine/s, of whale catchers, 133.
Eschrichtiidae, fam., 31; description, 42–44.
Euphausia superba, 199; see also Krill.
Exploitation, of populations, 255–6.
Extinction, how near? 262–5.
Eye/s, 24; of Rorquals, 24, 35; of Sperm whales, 45.
Eyesight, in whales, 151, 202.

Factory ship/s, advantage of, 12; conversion from merchant ships, 12–13; new factory ships, pre-war, 14, 15; post-war, 18–19; increase of, in Antarctic, 14 et seq.; at South Georgia, 12, 14, 15; at Deception Island, 12; catches of, 15, 16, 19, 99; Russian, Japanese and Dutch, in Antarctic, 19; Norwegian, 12, 15, 17, 19; British, 15, 19; British, 1939–40, 174; Norwegian, 1943, 17; war losses, 17, 195; voyage on board, 174 et seq.; at work, 188 et seq.
Falkland Islands, Dependencies of, 9, 13; Government of, 9, 10; incorporation, 13; issue of whaling licences, 13; whaling regulations, 13; first factory ship at, 98.
False Killer whale/s, 50; records of strandings, 251.
Feeding, of whalebone whales, 30–1, 38, 119–20, 198–9; grounds, 185, 233–4; of Right whales, 33; of Sei whales, 38, 245; of Sperm whales, 46, 228–30; of Humpback whales, 235; of toothed whales generally, 44; of Bottle-nosed whales, 47; of Killer whales, 49–50; of dolphins and porpoises, 51; of river dolphins, 54.
Fertilization, of ovum, 122–3; of Rorquals, 124; of krill eggs, 206.
Fighting, of Sperm whales, 227–8.
Fin whale/s, fam., 31, 34; description, 36–7; recognition at sea, 140–1; swimming speed, 141; diving, 146; asymmetry, 36; diatom film, 117; spout, 139; swimming on its side ('bolstering'), 37; schooling, 37.
Proportion in Antarctic catches, 11, 19; proportion in South Georgia catches, 11; northern hemisphere, 158; largest length measurements, 159; numbers marked, 168–9; migrations as shown by marking, 170–1; evidence of age, 171–173; distribution in relation to pack ice, 37, 118, 184; greatest concentration in

Antarctic waters, 187; number in *Salvestria* catch, 1939–40, 196; food in northern hemisphere, 198; forecast of Antarctic catches, and sustainable yield, 257–8; estimates of species ratio, 260–1; estimates of total Antarctic population (stock size), 1930's and 1950's, 262.

'Fish Royal', 23.

Fish shape, of whales and other animals, 23–4.

Flagging, of carcasses, 145–6, 91.

Flenser/s, 75, 101, 103, 105–7.

Flensing, 91, 103–7.

Flipper, see Forelimb/s.

Flukes, tail, use in propulsion, 25–6; fairing of, 15; out of the water, Humpback whales, 42, 141, 236; out of the water, Sperm whales, 225; cutting off at sea, 145; shape of, Sperm whale, 225.

Flurry, of Sperm whale, 89–90; of Fin whale, 144.

Foetus/es, of Rorqual, 126–8; development of baleen, 128; sizes of, 126–8; multiple, 126; wt. of body from wt. of foetus, 159; smallest Rorqual foetus, 215.

'Follow-my-leader' (Social facilitation), in Sperm whales, 226; Pilot whales, 247; in stranded whales, 247 et seq.

Forelimbs, as flippers, 24; as stabilizers, 25; Humpback whales, 41.

Fore-runner/s, 88, 135.

Fraser, Dr. F. C., 151, 154, 251.

Frequency, of sound vibrations perceived by the ear, 151; of sounds emitted by whales, 155–6; in asdic, 250; modulation of, 250; of waves used by whales for echo-location, 254.

Fulmar petrels, 193, 183.

Galapagos Islands, American whalers at, 83.

Glycerine, from whale oil, 58–9.

Graham Land, peninsula of, 185.

Grampus, see Killer whale.

Gravid female/s, krill, 206.

Greenland Right whale/s, Greenland whale/s, fam., 31, 42; description, 42–4; swimming speed, 32; spout, 140; diving, 146–7; food and feeding, 33, 198–9; protected, 32; baleen plates, 109. Basque whalers, 73; Dutch and English whaling for, 74–9; meat, 64, 77; near extinction, 32, 265. whaling, 73–79.

Grenade, explosive, 134, 228.

Grey head/s, Sperm whales, 217, 228.

Grey whale/s, fam., 31, 42; description, 42–44; behaviour when attacked by Killer whales, 227.

Grooves, ventral, absence in Right whales, 32; of Rorquals, 34; Blue whales, 41; Humpback whales, 41; Sei whales, 38;

Piked whales, 39; Sperm whales, absence in, 46.

Grytviken, *Gryt Vik* (Norw.), 10; Japanese at, 19; establishment of whaling station, 98; Pot Bay, 98; description of, 100–102; work on plan at, 102 et seq.; church and other buildings at, 102–3.

Guard, Captain John, 241.

Gunner/s, 134–6, 138, 139, 142, 143, 145, 179, 184; Number One or Senior, 178, 179.

Gunther, E. R., 146, 200.

Hairs, vestigial, 24, 41.

Hardy, Sir Alister, 145, 166, 202, 209.

Harem bands, Sperm whales, 222–3.

Harmer, Sir Sydney F., 16, 166, 250.

Harpoon, Basque, 71; derivation of word, 70; bone-headed, 80; in American Sperm whaling, 88; in Dutch whaling, 88; electric, 144; harpoon line/s, 71, 88, 89, 134–6, 144, 180; as a measure of depth of dive, 147; American made harpoons in Barentz Sea, 166; harpoon gun, 94–6, 133–4, 242; explosive head, 134, 242.

Harpooner, Basque, 71; Dutch, 78; in American Sperm whale beats, 86–8; at Azores, 222; New Zealand, 239.

Head, of Rorqual, removal of, 110; of Right whale, 32; of Rorqual, 35; of Blue whale, 36; of Sei whale, 38; of Sperm whale, 45, 218–21.

Hearing, in whales, 152–3; human beings and other mammals, 152; in porpoise, 252; directional, 152, 252.

Heart, of Rorqual, 111, 113; of Cetacea, 23; of giants, 162.

Heat, exchange in whales and other mammals, 160–1.

'Heat' period, in mammals generally, 123–4; in Rorquals, 124; in the male, 130.

Helicopters, for spotting whales, 18, 235.

Herd/s, whalebone whales, 12; Sperm whales, 223.

Herring whale/s, 198.

High explosive, from whale oil, 59.

'Horsepieces', blubber, 91, 107.

Humpback whale/s, fam., 31, 34; description, 40–42; recognition at sea, spout, tail flukes, 140–1; swimming speed, 142; swimming, 42, 142, 236; numbers marked, 168; migrations, 233–6; protected, 237, 259; natural history, 233–8; northern hemisphere, 233; southern hemisphere, 233–8; Antarctic feeding areas, 233–4; breeding grounds, 233–6; breeding, 237–8; mating, 237–8; copulation, 238; puberty and physical maturity, 238; aerial observations, 235–6; excess of males in tropics, 241. Early South Georgia whaling, 236; limitation of catches, 237; New Zealand whaling, 238–43; species ratio, 260–61;

Humpback whale/s, (*cont.*)
forecasts of Antarctic catches and sustainable yield, 259; estimate of total Antarctic population (stock size), 1930's and 1950's, 262.

Indian Ocean, American Sperm whalers in, 84; Sperm whale feeding grounds in, 225; krill in, 209.
Indians, American, whaling off New England, 80–81.
'*Inspektor*', (Norw.), 177, 179.
Intercommunication, in whales, 155–7.
International Bureau of Whaling Statistics, 256.
Whaling Commission, 18, 19, 173, 216, 237, 257; scientific committee appointed by, 257; Report to 14th Annual Meeting, 257; Report to 19th Annual Meeting, 217.
Whaling Conference, 188, 237.
Whaling Convention, 16, 17, 188.
Whaling *Statistics*, 257.
Iwashi Kujaira (Jap.), Sardine or Sei whale, 38.

Japan/ese, whalers and whaling regulations, 16; not on International Whaling Commission, 18; return to Antarctic, 19; factory ships, 19; whaling for Grey whales, 43; consumption of whale meat, 62–3; whaling, history and methods, 92–4.
Jaws, upper and lower, Greenland Right whale, 32; Biscay Right whale, 33; Rorquals, 35; Humpback whale, 41; Sperm whale, 45; Killer whale, 49; Removal of lower, on plan (Rorqual), 108; jawbones of skull in whalebone and Sperm whales, 218; Sperm whales, deformed lower jaw, 217.
'Junkpiece', 60, 91, 218.

Killer whale/s, fam., 31, 48; description, 48–50; feeding, 31, 49; aggressive behaviour, 50.
Knolhval (Norw.), Humpback whale, 41.
Koku Kujaira (Jap.), Devil fish, Grey whale, 42.
Krill, 119, 198–210; in stomachs, 119; area of greatest abundance, 205, 208–9; sizes of, 121–2, 205–6; North Atlantic, 198; basic or staple whale food, 198–9, 200; swarming of, 199–201; summer distribution, 208–9; breeding, 206–7; difference of sexes, 206; gravid females, 206; copulation, 206; spermatozoa, 206; larval development, 206–8; signs of spawning, 207; 'spent' females, 207; eggs, 206, 207–8; developmental ascent, 208; circulation in Antarctic waters, 205–9; eastward stream, 209; rate of grazing by whales, 210; surplus in polar waters, 210; human food, 210.

Laboratory, marine, at South Georgia, 10; materials, aboard factory ship, 174; improvised, aboard factory ship, 193–4.
Lactation, 130; see also Nursing.
Lactic acid, in muscle contraction, 148.
Lake dolphin/s, fam., 31; description, 54.
Lamina/e, in ear plug, 164–5, 171–3.
Laminar flow, 26; see also Flow.
Lampreys, cause of skin scars? 116–17.
Lance/s, 71, 89; 'lance warp', 89.
Laurie, Alec H., 11, 159–60, 211.
'Lay' system, New England, 81; American Sperm whalers, 84–5; in Antarctic factory ships, 190.
Leith Harbour, South Georgia, 183–4.
Leptocephalus, eel larvae, 206–7.
Lemmers, 103, 107, 191.
Lemming, 103, 107 et seq.
Lesser Rorqual, see Piked whale.
Lobster krill, 199, 245.
Look-out, in Basque whaling, 71; on Nantucket Island, 81; masthead, in American Sperm whalers, 87; Japanese whaling, 93; masthead, in modern whale catcher, 133, 139; Cook Strait, N.Z., 243; masthead, *Discovery II*, 259.
Lung/s, of Rorqual, 111; during diving, 148; emission of sounds? 156.

Mackintosh, Dr. N. A., 10, 17, 255.
Dr. N. A. and Wheeler, J. F. G., first scientific account of Rorquals, 69–70.
Mammalia, mammals, mammalian characteristics of whales, 23–4; primitive ancestral, 28–9; cervical vertebrae of, 52–3, 110; diaphragm, 111; stomach, 120–2; ovaries, 122; oviducts, 123; reproduction and sexual season, 123–5; egg production, 123–4; follicles, 125; embryo, 126; male sexual activity, 130; small and large, size problems in, 160–2.
Mammary gland/s, 24; Rorqual, 105, 130.
Margarine, manufacture of, 58–9.
Marineland, Fla., 51, 122, 128, 129.
Marking, of whales, 165–173; of fish, 165; bearing on migration, 169–171; bearing on age, 171–173; nos. marked, 168–9; Humpback whales, marking of, 171.
Marr, Dr. J. W. S., 200, 202, 207, 208.
Mating, duration of season (Rorquals), 124; months of season in southern and northern hemisphere, 124; frequency of (Rorquals), 129; Sperm whales, 230; Humpback whales, 237; Sei whales, 246.
Maturity, sexual, Rorquals, 114; age at (Blue and Fin whales), 122, 131, 163; Sperm whales, 231; Humpback whales, 238; Sei whales, 246.
physical, Rorquals, 114; age at (Blue and Fin whales), 131–2, 163, 173; Sperm whales, 231; Humpback whales, 238; Sei whales, 246.

Matthews, Dr. L. H., 217, 223, 230, 246.
Migration/s, of whalebone whales, 10, 165; shown by marking (Blue and Fin whales), 170–71; of Sperm whales, 224; of Humpback whales, 171, 233–6; of Sei whales, 245–6.
Milk, of Rorqual, 130.
Minke whale/s, see Piked whale/s.
Moby Dick, 217; by Herman Melville, 33.
Morsa, whale catcher, 136–146, 147, 155.
Mortality, natural, rate of, 255–6; fishing or catching, rate of, 256.
Mucous secretion, in wind pipe, 141; in ear, 154; in intestine, 66.
Muscovy Company, The, 74–6; failure of, 76.
Myohaemoglobin, 148; in Sperm whales, 222.

Nantucket Island, early whaling, 81–2; beginning of Sperm whaling, 82; during War of Independence, 83; decline as a whaling port, 83.
Narwhal/s, fam., and sub-fam., 31, 53; description, 53; whaling for, 94.
National Institute of Oceanography, 168; Whale Research Unit of, 172, 217.
Natural History Museum, South Kensington, 17, 34, 175; see also British Museum (N.H.).
Neck vertebrae, 23, 34, 52–3; at physical maturity, 132.
Netherlands Institute of Sea Research, 249.
Nets, whaling by means of, Japan, 93; New Zealand, 243; Russian, 239; Bergen, Norway, 243; North Carolina, 51.
New Bedford, Mass., founding of, 82–3; chief American whaling port, 82.
New England, early whaling, 82–4.
Newfoundland Banks, Basque whalers at, 63.
New Zealand, 'Bay' whaling, 79–80; Right whales, 80, 241; American whalers at, 80; Humpback whales and whaling, 233–5.
Noises, emitted by whales, 54, 155–7; hydrodynamic, 212–3.
Noordse Compagnie (Dutch), 75–6.
Nordkaper (Dutch), see Biscay Right whale/s.
North East Passage, 73–4.
North Pacific, whaling, 22; Sperm whales in, 46, 225.
North West Passage, 73.
Norwegian, crews and seamen, 15, 137–8; factory ships, 14, 15, 19; Government, 97; Whaling Union (*Norsk Hvalfangstforbund*), 18; scientists, 70, 166; whalers in Antarctic, 14, 15, 19, 97–9, 102–3; in Japan, 94, 97; whaling in northern waters, 96–7; whaling stations, 12–13; characteristics, 191; at Durban.
Nostril/s, 24, 28, 143, see also Blowhole/s.

Nursing period, 128; Blue and Fin whales, 129; Sperm whales, 230; Humpback whales, 237; Sei whales, 246.

Odour/s, on plan, 113; of whale oil, 55, 59; at Durham, 212.
Oils and fats, post-war shortage, 17; vegetable and fish, in manufacture of margarine, 59.
Organ/s, internal, of Rorqual, 110–13, 118–31; auditory, see Ear; Reproductive, 122–131.
Ovary/ies, rabbit, human, 122; Rorqual, 122–5.
Oviduct/s, 123.
Ovum/a, Rorqual, 122; mammals generally, 122–5.
Oxygen, storage in whales, 148.

Pacific Ocean, modern whaling in, 22, 46; American Sperm whalers, 84; Sperm whaling grounds in, 46, 225.
Pack ice, 184–5; melting of, 185, 204; nets under, 209; edge of 183, 187; whaling fleet at, 184; Blue whales in relation to, 27, 36, 118; Fin whales in relation to, 37, 118; plankton in relation to, 204–5; variations in position, 185.
Parasite/s, internal, of Rorquals, 112; external, of Rorquals, 116; Right whales, 33; Humpback whales, 42; Grey whales, 43; Sperm whales, 227.
Parturition, Rorquals, 128–9; Sperm whales, 230; Humpback whales, 238; Sei whales, 246.
'Peggies', 178–9, 188, 193.
Penella, copepod parasite, 116, 166.
Penguins, on ice floes, 188.
Penis, of Rorquals, 62, 103, 105.
Perry, Commodore, U.S.N., 92.
Petrel/s, silver grey fulmar, 139, 183; Antarctic, 187.
Physeteridae, fam., 31, 44; description, 44–6.
Pierce's darting gun, 95.
Piked whale/s, Lesser Rorqual, Minke whale, fam., 31, 34; description, 39–40.
Pilot whale/s, Caa'ing whale/s, Blackfish, fam., 31, 48; description, 50; at sea, 183; hunting and stranding in Faroes, 247–8; reports of strandings, 251.
Plan, 102–104; objectives of work on, 115; on factory ship, 176, 189 et seq.
Plankton, animal, 204–5; phosphorescence, 202; circulation of in Antarctic waters, 205.
plant, 182–3, 204.
Plant/s, unicellular, 117–18.
Platanistidae, fam., 31, 54; description, 54.
Plates, whalebone, 30, 108–10; as a clue to age, 163–4; see also Baleen.
Pollack whale/s, see Sei whale/s.
Population dynamics, 255–6.

Populations, Blue and Fin whales, 257; Humpback and Sei whales, 258–262.

Porpoise/s, fam., 31, 48; sub-fam., 31, 53; difference between dolphin and, 48; common porpoise (U.K.), 51; common porpoise (U.S.A.), 51; hunting in N. Europe, 70; directional hearing, 252.

Portuguese, whalers in American ships, 86, 222; W. Africa (Gaben) whaling stn., 215.

Pots, blubber, Basque, 73; in American whale ships, 85, 91; sealers', at Grytviken, 98.

Pregnancy, *corpus luteum* of, 125; percentage in cow Blue and Fin whales at South Georgia, 129–30, 165; season of (Blue and Fin whales), 128–9; duration of (Blue and Fin whales), 129; signs of, 125; frequency of, 129; duration of (Sperm whales); season of (Sperm whales), 230; season and duration of (Humpback whales), 237; season and duration of (Sei whales), 246.

Pressure, atmospheric, 148–9; hydrostatic, when diving, 149; internal regulation of, 150; equalization of, in ear, 154–5. boilers, for whale oil, 56.

Prion, whale bird, 138, 183.

Purves, Dr. P. E., 151, 154.

Pygmy Blue whale/s, 36.
    Right whale/s, 34.
    Sperm whale/s, 46.

Queen Charlotte Sound, N.Z., 241.

Quota/s, seasonal, of Blue whale units, 18.

Radar, 249.

Radio buoys, on whale carcasses, 18, 146.

Rawalpindi, H.M.S., Armed Merchant Cruiser, 195.

Regulations, whaling, 13, 16, 17, 189–90.

Research, fisheries, 10, 18, 70, 165; whaling, 10–11, 70, 115; fund for, 14; on krill, 207; need for, 209.

Resting period, Blue and Fin whales, 129; Sperm whales, 230; Sei whales, 246.

Ribs, of Rorqual, removal of, 111.

Right whale/s, see Greenland Right whale and Biscay Right whale.

River dolphin/s, fam., 31, 54; description, 54.

Rorqual/s, fam., 31, 34; descriptions of, 35–42; in northern hemisphere, 35, 42, 158; meat of, 63; first account of, 69; 'wrong' whales, problem of capture, 31, 94–6; general description of dismemberment on plan, 100–114; swimming and diving, 146–7; swimming speed, 141–2; length and weight, 158–160; breeding, 122–131; feeding, 119, 198; baleen, 109; spout, 139–141.
    Lesser, see Piked whale/s.
    Rudolphi's, see Sei whale/s.

Sibbald's, see Blue whale/s.

Ross Sea, 99, 185, 187.

Russian whalers, arrival in Antarctic, 19; factory ships, 19; in North Pacific, 22; in Kamchatka, 243.

Saldanha Bay, Cape Province, 10, 40, 171, 211; Sei whales at, 245.

Salvesen, C. A. & Co., 174, 183.

Salvestria, fl.f., 175 et seq.; catch and oil production, 1939–40, 196; sinking, 197.

Sardine whale/s, see Sei whale/s.

Scammon, Capt., C. M., 41, 44.

Scars, on skin of Rorquals, 116–17; in ovaries, 125; as a clue to age, on skin, 162–3; in ovaries, 163.

School/s/ing, Blue whales, 36; Fin whales, 37; Sperm whales, 222–3; Humpback whales, 41, 235–6.

'Schoolmasters', among Sperm whales, 222.

Scoresby, William, junr., Capt., 69, 146.

Scurvy, among British whalers, 64; avoidance by Dutch whalers, 64, 77–8.

Seamen, Norwegian in factory ships, 15, 175, 177; Shetland in factory ships, 177, 191; in American whalers, 86.

Sea sickness, 136, 137, 138.

Seal/s, diving, 147; swallowing stones, 228.

Sealers, South Georgia, 98; N.Z., 241.

Sealskin, bladders as floats, 93, 80–1.

Season, sexual, 123–4; Rorquals, 124; Blue and Fin female, 128; male, 130; Sperm whales, 230; Humpback whales, 237–8; Sei whales, 243–4.

Sei whale/s, fam., 31, 34; description, 37–9; natural history, 243–6; food and feeding, 238–245; migrations, 245–6; breeding, 246; puberty, 246.
    Antarctic catches, 19, 243; post-war catches, 244; appearance at South Georgia, 238, 244; northern hemisphere, 238–44; stock size, 258; estimate of Antarctic population, 258; forecasts of Antarctic catches, 258; sustainable yield, 258.

Seje (Norw.), coalfish, see Sei whale/s.

Sex/es, of Rorquals, notes on sex ratios, 115; length differences (Blue and Fin whales), 158–9; Sperm whales, 46, 216; segregation in Sperm whales, 22–3; in Humpback whales, 236; Sei whales, 244; krill, 206.

Shackleton, Sir Ernest, grave of, 10; naming of Bay of Whales, 39; boat journey from Elephant Island to South Georgia, 194.

Shallop/s, Basque, 70–1; Dutch, 78; American, 86.

Shetlanders, 179, 191.

Shoaling, fishes and krill, 201.

Sibbald, Sir Robert, 35.

Sibbald's Rorqual, see Blue whale/s.

Skin, of whales 27; 107; of dolphins, folds in, 26; ridges on, 27; commercial uses of, 62.

Skull, of whales, flattening, 24; of Greenland Right whale, 32; of Biscay Right whale, 34; of Pygmy Right whale, 34; removal from carcass (Rorqual), 110; telescoping, 218; Sperm whale, 45; asymmetry, 220–21.

Sleep, of whales and other animals, 226.

Sletbag Slettibaka (Icel.), 72, see Greenland Right whale/s.

Slick, 143.

Smeerenburg, Spitsbergen, 76.

Smell, sense of, in whales, 151.

Social facilitation (Follow-my-leader), 226.

Sonar, 249.

Sounding, deep diving, 89, 146, et seq.

South Africa, coast of, 10–11; Bryde's whale, 40; feeding of Rorquals, 119; whale marks, 170–71; Durban, 211–15; Humpback whales, 233–4.

South America, coast of, 10; American Sperm whalers, 83; whales marked off Brazil, 171; S. American sector of Antarctic, 13.

South Atlantic Ocean, 50, 182, 158, 58, 203, 233.

South Georgia, 10–17, 19–20, 58, 63–4, 98–9, 100 et seq., 119, 124, 137–8, 158, 163, 175, 180, 183–4, 187, 189–90, 194, 196; krill at, 199–200, 206–7; whale marking, 166, 169, 171; sperm whales at, 216; Sei whales at, 38, 244.

South Orkney Islands, 195; whales asleep near? 226.

South Shetland Islands, 12–13, 98; melting of pack ice, 204.

Southern Right whale/s, see Biscay Right whale/s.

Species ratio/s (Blue, Fin and Humpback whales), 259–262.

Sperm oil, 60; yield per whale, 60; demand in eighteenth century, 82–4; first American factory for, 82.

Sperm whale/s, Cachalot, fam., 31, 44; description, 44–6; natural history, 222–231; length and weight, 216; internal structures, 217–22; blowhole, nasal passage, larynx, 218–19; skull, 218–19; feeding, 228–30; breeding, 230; Noises emitted by, 156–7; Echo-location, 229–253; recognition at sea, swimming speed, 225; diving, sleeping, 225–6; social facilitation, gambolling, aggressive behaviour, fighting, 226–8; 'harem bands', schoolmasters, cows, 222–3; schooling, herds, 'gams', migrations, 223–4; American whaling, chase and death of, 87–91; American whaling, nineteenth century, 84–92; decline of, 91–2; whaling grounds, 84, 224–5; strandings, 251.

Catches, Antarctic, 215 (Fig. 1b); Durban, 215; *Salvestria* 1939–40, 196; South Georgia, 216.

Spermaceti, 46, 60, 91; yield per Sperm whale, 60.

Spermatophore/s, of krill, 206.

Spermatozoa, Blue whale, 113, 130; krill, 206.

Spes et Fides, whale catcher, 95–6.

Spitsbergen, discovery of, 74; whaling at, 75–6; French claim to, 77.

Spotting whales at sea, Rorquals, 139–41; Sperm whales, 225; Right whales, 140.

Spout, 28, 139–41; Sperm whales, 225.

Squid/s, food of Sperm whales, 225.

Station Whaling, South Georgia, 10, 11–13; Deception Island, 12; Durban, 212–215; Gabon (Portuguese West Africa), 215; Saldanha Bay, Cape Province, 40; Northern Europe and Atlantic, 96–7; Vancouver Island, 16; New Zealand, 238–243.

Steersman, Basque, 71; Dutch, 78; American, 86–8; Azores, 222.

Stock size/s, pre-war, 257 et seq.; total Antarctic population, counts of, 261–2.

Stomach, of Rorqual, 118–22; other mammals, 120–21; Sperm whale, contents, 228.

Submarine cable/s, Sperm whales entangled in, 226.

Sub-orders, of Cetacea, 31 et seq.

Sulphur-bottom whale/s, 117.

Survival rate, of species, 262.

Sustainable yield, 256, 257–9.

Swedish Antarctic Expedition, 98.

Swimming, whales and other animals, 25–7; whales at surface, whalebone whales, 141–2; Fin whales, dolphins swimming on their sides, 'boltering', 37; Humpback whales, 236; Sperm whales, 225–6; krill, 199–201.

Tape worms, in Rorquals, 112; at Durban, 214.

Tasmania, 'Bay' whaling, 79–80.

Tax, on whale oil, 14; duty on foreign oil (eighteenth century), 83.

Teeth, rudiments in Rorqual foetus, 128; Sperm whale, 45, 230; as a clue to age, 217, 229; Bottle-nosed and Beaked whales, 47; Dolphins and porpoises, 48; Killer whales, 49; Narwhal, 53; Beluga, 53.

Terra Nova, Scott's Expedition, 34, 50.

Testes, Rorqual, 112–13; activity of, 130.

Thoracic cavity, of Rorquals, 111; vascular networks in, 149–50.

Thorax, dismemberment of (Rorqual), 110–111; in diving, 149.

Tongue, Rorqual, 107–8; of Rorqual calf, 129; Sperm whale, 230.

Trachea, windpipe, of Rorqual, 11; Sperm whale, 220.

'Ugly' whales (Sperm), 89.
Ungulates, whales in relation to, 27–8; even-toed, 27–8, 111, 123, 125.
Unicorn, legend of, 53.
U.S.A., whaling in North Pacific, 22; fossil whales in, 29; commercial use of whale oil, 59; early whaling, 80 et seq.; Sperm whaling, 84–92; records of strandings, 251; common porpoise, 51; marketing of whale meat in, 63.

Vitamins, in whale tissues, 59–60.
Volume/weight ratio in animals, 160–1.

War, American Independence, 82–3; of 1812, effect on American whaling, 84; American Civil, 92; World War I, 14, 236; World War II, outbreak, 17; effect on Antarctic whaling, 17.
Warm Deep current, 203–5, 209–10.
Weaning, 129; baleen plates at, 128; Sperm whales, 230.
Weddell Sea, 97, 195, 207–8.
   Current, 185; melting of ice in, 185; krill in, 185, 205; krill eggs and larvae in, 207–8.
Weight of body, Blue whales, 159–60; Sperm whale, 216.
Weight of ovaries (Blue whale), 122.
Weight of testes (Blue whale), 113.
'Whale', derivation of word, 27.
Whale/s, sub-orders, families, sub-families of Cetacea, 31; description of important species, 31–54; fish or mammal? 24–5; recognition at sea (whalebone whales), 140–141; Sperm whales, 225; Humpback whales, 236; body form, structure, movement, 23–27; ancestry (fossils), 28–30; produce of, 55–68; diving and breathing, 147–9; feeding, 30–31, 38, 119–20, 198–9, 228–30, 245, see also Feeding; breeding, 122–31, 230, 237, 246, also see Breeding; migrations, 169–171, 224, 233–6, 245–6; noises made by, 155–7; echo-location, 249; evidence of age, 162–5; estimates of species ratios, 259–61; birth rate, 263; estimates of total Antarctic populations, 261–2; specialization, 264; defence against enemies, 264; possible extinction, 262–5.
Whalebone, see Baleen.
Whale catcher/s, nos. per station, South Georgia, 12; nos. per factory, ice edge, 19; early Norwegian whaling, 97; modern, 133; a trip on board, 136–146; *Salvestria*, 185.
   hunting, 87–91, 136–146, 241–3; as a

sport, 135; cruelty of, 144.
lice, 33, 43.
mark/s, marking, 165–173; cruises, 166–167, 169, 260; nos. of whales marked and recovered, 168–9; marking and migrations, 169–71, 233; marking and age, 171–73; marking and species ratio, 260.
meat, 62–4, 23, 94.
oil, impregnation of whales' tissues, 28; 'train', 54–6; boiling aboard ship, 73, 91; mineral, supplanting whale oil, 56, 92; total Antarctic production, 56, 92; standard unit of production (Blue whale unit), 18, 57, 188, 243; grades of oil, 55–6; variations in yield, 57; yield per whale, 57; yield per body wt., 57–8; method of extraction, 56–7; commercial uses, 59–60; storage, 56–7; refinement, 58; hydrogenation, 59; hardening, 59; vitamin content, 59–60; price, 60; Sperm oil, 60; yield per Sperm whale, 60; price, eighteenth century, 82.
Whaling, Antarctic, peak years and nos. of men employed, 11; companies' profits, 11; shore based, 12; pelagic (floating factories), 12–16, 97–9; Norwegian, 12–16; British, 15; control, pre-war, 16–17; control, post-war, 17–18; South Georgia, 11–16, 98–9; South Shetland, 12–13; ice edge, 14, 185–7; Arctic, 70–9, 96–9; South Africa, 214–15; Australia, New Zealand, 233–45; History, 69–99.
   areas, Antarctic, 187.
   fleet, distribution of, 185–6.
   grounds, Antarctic, 186–8; Sperm whales, 224–5.
   clothes, 101.
   Inspector/s, 16–17, 174 et seq.
   licence/s, 13.
   Greenland, 74–79.
   Sperm, see Sperm whaling, American.
   station/s, see Stations, whaling.
White whale, Beluga, fam., and sub-fam., 31; description, 53–4; whaling for, 44; noises made by, 54, 155.
William Scoresby, Royal Research Ship, whale marking cruises, 166–7, 260.
Womb, mammals generally, 124–5; Rorqual, 123–4.
'Wonder networks', 149–150, 154.

Yankee whalers, hunting Grey whales, 44; Sperm whaling, 90–2; 'Bay' whaling, 80; Indian Ocean, 83; New Zealand, 80; whaling ships, 85; decline of, 91.
Yellow body (*corpus luteum*), 125; of pregnancy, 125; as a clue to age, 125, 162.

Ziphiidae, fam., 31, 47; description, 47.